Introduction to
Information
Behaviour

Every purchase of a Facet book helps to fund
CILIP's advocacy, awareness and accreditation programmes
for information professionals.

Introduction to Information Behaviour

NIGEL FORD

facet publishing

© Nigel Ford 2015
Published by Facet Publishing
7 Ridgmount Street, London WC1E 7AE
www.facetpublishing.co.uk

Facet Publishing is wholly owned by CILIP: the Chartered Institute of
Library and Information Professionals.

British Library Cataloguing in Publication Data
A catalogue record for this book is available from the British Library.

ISBN 978-1-85604-850-7

First published 2015

Text printed on FSC accredited material.

Typeset from author's files in 10/13 pt Palatino Linotype and
Frutiger by Facet Publishing Production.
Printed and made in Great Britain by CPI Group (UK) Ltd,
Croydon, CR0 4YY.

Contents

List of figures and tables ix

1   Introduction 1
    References 3

PART 1 BASIC CONCEPTS 5
2   What is information behaviour and why do we need to know about it? 7
    Introduction 7
    Defining 'data', 'information' and 'behaviour' 10
    Defining 'information behaviour' 13
    Information behaviour and cognate areas..25
    Summary 27
    References..28

3   Changing conceptions of information needs 29
    Introduction 29
    Information needs...30
    Information-related needs 41
    Summary 44
    References..45

PART 2 WHAT DO WE KNOW OF INFORMATION BEHAVIOUR? 47
4   Information seeking and acquisition are key components of information
    behaviour 49
    Introduction 49
    Basic information-seeking processes and activities 49
    Information-seeking strategies 54
    Serendipity..64

Case study: serendipity 66
Summary 70
References..73

5   **Information behaviour can be collaborative**...**77**
Introduction 77
Definitions..78
Characteristics of collaborative information behaviour.............................81
Case study: collaborative information behaviour 90
Summary 94
References..95

6   **Factors influencing information behaviour** **99**
Introduction 99
'Internal' factors 101
External influences 119
The relationship between 'internal' and 'external' factors 125
Summary...131
References 132

7   **Models and theories in information behaviour research**....................**141**
Introduction 141
Models of information behaviour 142
Theories of information behaviour..147
Summary...163
References 165

**PART 3 DISCOVERING AND USING KNOWLEDGE OF INFORMATION
            BEHAVIOUR** **169**
8   **Research approaches** **171**
Introduction...171
Different types of research – and different types of knowledge 172
Research paradigms..176
Research methodologies and methods...180
Assessing quality in research 180
The 'darkness to light' ratio 184
Research and practice 186
Summary...192
References 193

9   **Research methodologies in action**..**195**
Introduction...195
Hypothesis testing: a deductive quantitative study 195
Situational Analysis: an inductive qualitative study................................198

Mixed-methods research: a mixed-methods study 204
Comparing approaches 208
Summary 214
References 215

10 Using knowledge of information behaviour to design information systems ..217
Introduction 217
Cole's 'enabling' information retrieval system interface 220
The PATHS project 223
Supporting serendipitous knowledge discovery: the IF-SKD model 229
Summary 232
References 233

11 Conclusion 237
References 243

Appendix: defining 'information' and 'information behaviour' 245
References 247

Index 249

List of figures and tables

Figures

2.1 Components of information behaviour 17
2.2 Information behaviour defined 23
3.1 Information needs, information-related needs and information behaviour 43
4.1 Wilson's combined model blending those of Ellis and Kuhlthau 53
6.1 Factors that can influence information behaviour 100
6.2 Wilson's general model of information behaviour 102
6.3 Mansourian's model of bounded rationality and satisficing 126
6.4 Wilson's revision of his 1981 'general model of information-seeking behaviour' 128
6.5 Wilson's 'revised general model of information behaviour' 129
7.1 Wilson's model of information seeking incorporating Ellis' model 143
7.2 Wilson's 'revised general model of information behaviour' 144
7.3 Godbold's model of information behaviour 145
7.4 Mansourian's model of information invisibility 145
7.5 Robson and Robinson's (2013) information-seeking and communication model 148
7.6 Wilson's (2006) diagrammatic representation of Activity Theory components
      and processes 152
9.1 Social worlds/arenas map from the study by Sen and Spring 203
9.2 Positional map from the study by Sen and Spring 203
10.1 Interactions between cognitive style and interface support features in the
      PATHS system 228

Tables

4.1 Broad and narrow information-seeking strategies 57
5.1 Links between stages and affective elements in Kuhlthau's Information Search
      Process model 84
6.1 Savolainen's 'mastery of life' styles 112

7.1   Ellis' (1989) model of information seeking..143
7.2   Types of activity in Robson and Robinson's (2013) information-seeking and
       communication model 149

1

Introduction

This book is about an activity that pervades every aspect of our lives. Constantly as we traverse the landscape of people, things and places making up our lives – and even as we dream – we are constantly processing information.

Information is the raw material of knowledge: used effectively it can lead to wisdom. It is the intellectual equivalent of our food. And just as our eating habits and nutritional intake can be good or bad, with concomitant good and bad effects on our physical health, so can the quality of information we acquire, and the effectiveness with which we process it, affect the quality and effectiveness of our intellectual health.

We are constantly bombarded with information – and misinformation. The ability to seek out quality information and to subject it to careful critical scrutiny is more important than ever. More than ever we live in an information-rich environment, with online access to vast stores and the ability of all of us easily to contribute to these stores. But whilst we may all be incredibly information-rich, this does not equate to being knowledge-rich.

The intensity and scope of research into information behaviour has expanded considerably since the 1960s when research interest in how people go about finding information began to take off (Greifeneder, 2014; Wilson, 2010). Since then the use of qualitative to complement quantitative research approaches has grown, as has the scope of the research field more holistically to embrace not only the seeking of information but also its evaluation and use – as well as other kinds of information-related activity such as information avoidance.

The contexts in which information behaviour occurs – and the types of information included in research studies – have also grown in scope to include information behaviour relating to social media, everyday and leisure information use to complement more traditional contexts such as academic, health and commerce and more formal types of recorded information. Parts 1 and 2 of this book attempt to map out major themes relating to what information behaviour is and what we know about it.

However, despite the volume and range of research studies into this complex phenomenon, and the substantial progress made over the years in our understanding of it, much remains to be learned. In particular, we need to develop robust understanding based on a strong combination of quantitative and qualitative studies. These, it is hoped, will help us to develop better information systems capable of minimizing the contribution of computers (enabling them to support us by doing what they are better at) and maximizing human capability by increasing our understanding of our own information needs and processes (so that we can optimally exploit machine and human capabilities in interaction).

Part 3 of the book addresses how best we can develop new understanding via a range of approaches to research, and explores the issue of the relationship between theory and practice. Information behaviour research may help improve the awareness of information users, information providers and information system developers of how we can maximize the quality and effectiveness of the way information is presented, sought, discovered, evaluated and used.

To do this effectively, we will need a symbiosis of theory and practice. This book is based on academic research, which reflects the background of its author. But it also attempts to forge links with practice in terms of drawing out practice-based implications in relation to its key themes, and includes a discussion on the relationship between theory and practice in Chapter 8.

This book is intended as a primer for students and practitioners interested in information behaviour. It aims to provide a gentle introduction to key concepts, issues and themes along with descriptions of key research studies that are illustrative of these. It is therefore intended to complement more comprehensive and detailed treatises of the field such as, notably, Case's (2012) excellent *Looking for Information*.

The study of information behaviour has expanded rapidly in recent years, as have conceptions of what it embraces and how it might best be investigated. Models and theories abound, focusing on different components and aspects of information behaviour and illustrating different approaches to its study. This book attempts to provide a clear path through this complex maze by (a) establishing a firm conceptual base by clearly defining the components and processes making up information behaviour and (b) being highly selective in the models and theories introduced, in order more clearly to focus on what in the view of the author are generic key concepts and ideas essential for a deep understanding of the field.

The book is structured to move from the basics to the more complex, and employs the pedagogical device of **'Think!'** boxes which invite the reader to think about concepts as they are introduced in order to consolidate their understanding of them before moving on to consider more complex issues. These **'Think!'** boxes are offered as a means of encouraging the reader actively to engage with an issue before reading what the author has to say about it. This is intended to have one of two possible effects:

- If you already have a view about the issue, this will enable you briefly to review your thoughts prior to reading those of the author so that you can readily compare to see if you agree or disagree; or
- if you do not already have a view on the issue, this will highlight what it is about the issue, in the author's view, that is problematic, or at least not as straightforward as may first appear, causing it to require further thought to resolve or clarify.

Each chapter concludes with a round-up of what has been covered, highlighting where appropriate implications for professional information practice. The reader is also referred to more detailed treatments of the themes and issues discussed in the chapter.

References

Case, D. (2012) *Looking for Information: a survey of research on information seeking, needs and behaviour*, 3rd edn, Bingley, Emerald.

Greifeneder, E. (2014) Trends in Information Behaviour Research. In *Proceedings of ISIC, the Information Behaviour Conference, Leeds, 2–5 September, 2014: Part 1*, (paper isic13), http://InformationR.net/ir/19-4/isic/isic13.html.

Wilson, T. D. (2010) Fifty Years of Information Behavior Research, *Bulletin of the American Society for Information Science and Technology*, **36** (3), www.asis.org/Bulletin/Feb-10/FebMar10_WIlson.pdf.

PART 1
Basic concepts

2

What is information behaviour and why do we need to know about it?

Introduction

Human information behaviour is all about how we need, find, process, and use information. But we do this all the time. So why do we need to study and research it?

Well, it's a bit like studying nutrition and the human body. The more we understand how the body works, what nutrients it needs and the different effects of different foods (for better or for worse) the more we can teach and advise people about healthy diets, train up elite sportsmen and women, and identify, treat and prevent disorders. Information is nutrition for the mind. It is the fuel of learning, and the basis of our knowledge. Like food, we need a constant supply. And information has its fast food, gourmet and high-performance diet equivalents.

To take one example, research into the information behaviour of people affected by HIV/AIDS has generated insights that are directly useful to those who provide information on both prevention of and living with the disease. Such information must be accurate, reliable, authoritative, up to date and easily available. But research suggests that other factors are also highly influential in determining whether people successfully find and engage with information they need. Accurate, reliable, authoritative and up-to-date information may be readily available. Yet some HIV/AIDS sufferers may ignore or avoid – even hide or destroy – information which possesses these desirable qualities. Information behaviour research suggests that it is one thing to make HIV/AIDS information readily available in, say, a city's public library, but quite another thing for a person who fears or has experienced stigma and discrimination relating to the disease to risk being seen accessing and reading it in such a public location. Also, information may not necessarily be timely in terms of a person's readiness to accept it. What might objectively be accurate, reliable and authoritative information may be ignored, not understood or rejected by some HIV/AIDS sufferers who, for a time after learning of their diagnosis, may simply be unreceptive due to being in a state of shock, anxiety or even denial. The more that information providers (in this case, medical and social workers, support organizations and information professionals) are aware of such difficulties and complexities, the greater is their chance of being able effectively to bring people into contact with the information they need.

More generally, greater knowledge of information behaviour can help us enhance access to and use of information to the benefit of individuals, organizations and communities. Understanding of information behaviour can add value to:

- the effectiveness of our role as information professionals in advising and helping people find and evaluate the information they need
- the design of information systems to enable effective exploration, navigation and retrieval of information
- the way information is organized and managed by individuals and organizations in order to provide effective access by those who need it
- training and education designed to help people develop the ability to find, evaluate and use information in relation to their needs
- the way information is communicated by authors and information providers.

But before going on to discuss information behaviour in more detail, it is necessary to introduce a caveat. Many models of information needs, and of information seeking to satisfy them, that are generated by researchers (many of which will be found in this book) are geared to explaining relatively complex cases. The reader may legitimately question whether finding information is really so problematic and complicated – particularly in the modern era of fast and apparently efficient search engines.

If I want to find information on how to write web pages or publish a blog, it is a quick and simple task to tap a few keywords into Google and be presented with a wide range of sites brimming with useful information. If I want to find the times of trains from Sheffield to London, a quick search for 'train times Sheffield to London' will take me direct to an appropriate source of information. This hardly seems complex or problematic. So why have information behaviour, and its constituent elements of information needs and information seeking, been the focus of strenuous research efforts over many decades, and the subject of a plethora of theoretical models?

Of course, some searches for information are more difficult than others. Trying to find the best medical advice relating to a set of symptoms you are experiencing may pose rather more problems than finding the time of the next train to London. Also, the level of complexity of information needs, and the information-seeking behaviour required to satisfy them, depend on their granularity. A low granularity need might be to answer a very specific question, or solve a narrow and specific problem.

But our need for information may operate at a much higher level of granularity – not geared to solving a narrow problem but, say, to learn how to be a good parent, to complete a PhD research project, to practise as an evidence-based professional in our work, or to be a good citizen. These different levels of information need can co-exist. Large-scale, long-term and possibly ill-defined information needs can encompass and be served by more specific, less problematic, ones.

The models of information behaviour discussed in this book presume relatively complex information needs. With this important caveat, let us now explore basic definitions and the components of information behaviour in more detail.

Note also that the examples early in the book relate mainly to the individual person, as opposed to groups and communities. However, it is important to realize that:

- information behaviour may be observed not only at individual level, but also as people work in interaction with others at the levels of groups, organizations and communities
- information-based interactions take place not only between people but also between people and non-human artefacts and forces
- information behaviour can be a distributed activity – i.e., it may be more than the sum of the activities of the individuals making up a group or community.

The following sections define a number of key terms, including data, information, knowledge and information behaviour. Although drawing where appropriate on existing definitions, the author is careful to present in detail those definitions he has adopted for use consistently throughout this book.

These terms may at first sight seem obvious – surely we already know what they mean, and even if we are not so sure, definitions abound in the literature. However, many existing definitions in the literature display variations between them. Many – particularly definitions of 'information behaviour' –

are arguably not sufficiently extensive to provide clear answers to a number of probing questions relating to where the boundaries of these terms – and of the field of information behaviour – are drawn. Answers to such questions are needed in the case of a field of study which has rapidly developed to embrace a wide range of foci, perspectives and methodologies.

Insufficiently elaborated definitions risk under- or over-specifying the field. We need to avoid restricting information behaviour to its relatively narrow library-based origins and to embrace its increasingly expansive coverage. At the same time, we must avoid under-specifying information behaviour in a way which makes it excessively inclusive and fails to differentiate it clearly from related fields in which the processing and use of information is central – such as psychology, education and communication.

For the reader interested in investigating the potential ambiguity and uncertainty in these key terms – which have prompted the author to spend time elaborating terms in some detail below – they are elaborated in Appendix 1, which should be read before proceeding.

Defining 'data', 'information' and 'behaviour'

The first thing we need to do in order to understand information behaviour is to define what we mean by 'information' and 'behaviour'. At first sight, these terms seem clear enough. A train timetable, a book, or a news broadcast clearly contains *information*. Reading a book or looking for information is clearly *behaviour*. So what's the problem?

THINK!

Consider the following three questions:

1. Meteorologists interpret cloud formations to forecast the weather. So are clouds an information source? And if so, is weather forecasting information behaviour?
2. Are the words two people use as they chat to one another information? If so, is talking to someone information behaviour?
3. And if I *think about* a piece of information someone has given me, but I do or say nothing, is this 'behaviour'?

Think about your answers for a couple of minutes before reading on . . .

It all depends, of course, on how you define 'information', 'behaviour', and 'information behaviour'. We need to establish definitions before we can decide on answers to the questions above, and before we can proceed to discuss these concepts in depth. Definitions used throughout this book are as follows:

- **Behaviour** is defined broadly as some response to a stimulus. It includes thoughts as well as actions. Thus perceiving that one has a problem requiring information is as much behaviour as doing something about it (e.g., information seeking).
- **Information** is the subject of many complex definitions in the literature (see, for example, Case (2012) and Floridi (2010)). However, within the context of this book it is simply defined (Kitchin, 2014) as a meaningful pattern of stimuli which can be converted into knowledge (see below).

Many definitions in the literature distinguish information from data. Data has been defined as:

> . . . the raw material produced by abstracting the world into categories, measures and other representational forms – numbers, characters, symbols, images, sounds, electromagnetic waves, bits – that constitute the building blocks from which information and knowledge are created
>
> Kitchin, 2014, 1

Information is data rendered meaningful (Floridi, 2010) via analysis and structuring. Using these definitions, phenomena such as cloud formations represent data – i.e. potential information insofar as they are stimuli with potential for being interpreted in terms of meaningful patterns.

Learning is defined here as the process whereby information is converted into knowledge (Ford, 2008). *Knowledge* is what a person knows. It is internal to a person, whereas information is external. When processed by a person and integrated into his or her existing knowledge, information becomes part of that knowledge. When people communicate parts of their knowledge, they do so by converting them into information and putting it 'out there' in the form of, for example, speech, text or movement, which in turn can be interpreted by other people and become part of their knowledge. 'Knowledge' includes beliefs as well as factual and procedural knowledge. However, moods and feelings – though they may affect and be affected by knowledge – are not included in this definition of knowledge.

The definition of knowledge used in this book situates knowledge within a human brain. So how does this square with the notion of *distributed* knowledge, as conceived within social constructivist perspectives, in which meanings and knowledge are negotiated and shared within a community (as opposed to being objectively and accurately knowable)? It is often said that communities can possess knowledge which is more than simply the sum of individual knowledge – the knowledge possessed by the individual members of those communities. Particularly with computer assistance, it is increasingly easy for communities to leverage 'the wisdom of the crowd', using collective knowledge to which individuals contribute but which no one individual possesses. Recommender systems are an everyday example.

THINK!
Can a community *really* possess knowledge which is more than the sum of the knowledge of the individual members of that community?
If so, where does this knowledge reside? And how is it generated?

Collective, shared, or distributed 'knowledge' can only, strictly speaking, refer to the *overlap* in the knowledge of the individuals making up the particular group or community being referred to. Let us consider a simple example. A group of people can meet to discuss an issue. By speaking, each member puts forward information that may be processed and considered by other members of the group. The discussion may lead to shared new knowledge – insights into the issue being discussed, or realization of new ways to solve some problem, generated by the collective thought processes of the group. But the 'collective' or 'distributed' knowledge that can be said to have emerged from the meeting does not hang mysteriously in a cloud over the group in the room. It can only exist as the overlap in the knowledge possessed by each individual in the group.

The case of a recommender system is somewhat different, since knowledge appears to be generated which is not simply the overlap in the knowledge of the contributors to the system. However, such systems process data to generate new information – not new knowledge. Humans can input data to such a system, which in turn can generate information which no individual contributor has the knowledge to generate. But what is often referred to as collective or distributed knowledge is in fact information generated by such a system. Like any other information, this information may be processed by individual members of the community and ingested, becoming part of their knowledge. In other words, I argue that there is no knowledge that exists 'between' rather than within humans.

THINK!
Having read my definition of 'information', what is 'data'? Does it differ from information, and if so, how?

'Data' is defined here as stimuli not (yet) integrated into a meaningful pattern. Thus, for example, a series of apparently unrelated and meaningless numbers would remain data until integrated by the perception that they represent train times. It should be noted that the classification of a particular stimulus as data or information is relative, and depends on a person's perception of a meaningful pattern in the data. Thus one person's data might be another's information, and vice versa. To take the 'clouds' example given earlier, clouds may or may not be data. They *are* data to someone who can interpret them meaningfully – such as a meteorologist. They are *not* data to someone who sees no pattern or meaning in them.

But what about the use of 'data' in concepts such as databases and data analysis? In both these cases the data referred to is hardly devoid of meaning. Qualitative data analysis is often applied to interview data, which can be rich in meaning before it is ever analysed by a researcher. Also, data residing in a structured database is by definition organized in meaningful fields or categories.

Well, information that is meaningful at one level can be considered data in the context of a higher-level meaning. For example, a paragraph of text may be meaningful in its own right. However, if it is only part of a larger text, it represents *data* for a reader who is trying to perceive a higher order meaning (the message of the text taken as a whole). The same applies to qualitative data – for example, interview recordings or transcripts. Individual interviews are meaningful in their own right at one level, but in the context of higher order themes or theories that the researcher is trying to perceive in the interviews, they are data.

Defining 'information behaviour'

Having defined information and behaviour, we are in a better position to consider in detail what is meant by 'information behaviour'. Pettigrew, Fidel and Bruce (2001) define it as:

> the study of how people need, seek, give and use information in different
> contexts, including the workplace and everyday living
>
> Pettigrew, Fidel and Bruce, 2001, 44

Ingwersen and Järvelin (2005, 259) include the generation and management of information in their definition of information behaviour as 'generation, acquisition, management, use and communication of information, and information seeking'.

Wilson, who originally coined the term, has provided a more detailed definition of human information behaviour as:

> the totality of human behavior in relation to sources and channels of information, including both active and passive information seeking, and information use. Thus, it includes face-to-face communication with others, as well as the passive reception of information as in, for example, watching TV advertisements, without any intention to act on the information given.
>
> Wilson, 2000, 49

Wilson's 1996 model (Wilson and Walsh, 1996) differentiates between information searching, information seeking and information behaviour. In this nested model, information behaviour is a concept that embraces (but is not limited to) information-seeking behaviour. Information-seeking behaviour, in turn, embraces but is not limited to information-searching behaviour.

- **Information searching** entails using a particular search tool (for example, a search engine or database).
- **Information seeking** is a broader concept, embracing strategies a person devises in order to find information, which may include – but is not limited to – searching. It may include the selection and use of a variety of search tools, and the use of other strategies such as browsing and monitoring.
- **Information behaviour** is even more general, embracing information seeking but also including information behaviours other than information seeking.

THINK!

If information behaviour is not limited to information seeking, what else might it include? Think about this for a few moments before reading on . . .

Recall from the introduction to this chapter the description of some HIV/AIDS sufferers who may ignore or avoid – even hide or destroy – information through fear or anxiety about their illness. These actions certainly do not entail seeking information. But they are examples of information behaviour. Serendipity, or encountering information accidentally, is another example of information behaviour that does not entail seeking information. By definition, serendipity is unplanned and unintentional, unlike information seeking. *Using* information is yet another example of information behaviour that is not information seeking.

The definitions given by Wilson and by Pettigrew et al. are excellent, widely accepted definitions. However, some further elaboration may be useful. This is because it is important to know how the field of information behaviour has developed and expanded from an early emphasis on individuals seeking information from formal library-based information sources, and to appreciate that it is constantly evolving.

Much early research in the field we now know as information behaviour concentrated on which types of information sources particular groups of people, such as scientists, made use of in their work, and on how people searched for information in libraries and databases. But over the years, the field has developed (a) to embrace more complex and wide-ranging views of the interactions between people, organizations and information, and (b) to differentiate more clearly the different elements that constitute information behaviour. Important lines of development have included the following:

- The focus of information behaviour research is no longer restricted to individuals, but also includes groups, organizations and communities.
- An increasing focus of information behaviour research is on the evaluation and use of information – its application and impact in the real world.
- The range of types of information embraced by information behaviour studies has expanded beyond more traditional recorded textual or audiovisual sources to embrace, for example, tweets and data from flight control instruments.
- Increasing attention has been paid to the context in which interactions between people and information takes place, and to studying such interactions within people's natural environments such as home or work.
- Research attention is also increasingly being paid to the information behaviour of particular groups of people – for example those with specific health needs or marginalized groups such as refugees.
- The assumed starting point for information behaviour has moved beyond information needs to include more fundamental needs (e.g. some problem to be solved, or some mental or physical state to be achieved or maintained). Thus, ignoring and avoiding information, whilst hardly representing behaviour associated with an information *need*, are examples of information behaviour. In this book I differentiate between *information needs* and *information-related needs*. Information-related needs are needs that have implications for the way in which we interact with information, whether seeking or avoiding it. Information-related needs are more general than, but include, information needs.

- Linked to the previous point, an increasing focus has been placed on aspects of information behaviour not confined to the active seeking and use of information, to include, for example, encountering information serendipitously, and avoiding as well as searching for information.

With such an expansion in conceptions of what information behaviour research covers, it is all the more important precisely to define the boundaries of the field, and to negotiate its relationship with other established fields which may appear to overlap. The danger is of under-specifying the field, risking overlap and confusion with other well established areas of research and knowledge. Information behaviour may both contribute to and draw from – but is distinct from – other fields such as psychology, sociology, communication, management and education. For this reason, we need a firm definition.

We exist in a constant stream of visual, auditory and tactile stimuli providing us with constant data and information. Whenever we act or think, we make use of knowledge which has been generated by processing information and integrating it into our knowledge structures.

However, based on the definitions we have so far, applying anything we have learned from our parents, peers or teachers (all information sources) could be information behaviour. Indeed, it is difficult to think of an activity which is *not* some form of information behaviour in that it entails thoughts or actions based on knowledge derived from processing information.

It is difficult to tweak the individual definitions of information and behaviour in such a way that simply combining them results in a satisfactory definition of information behaviour. In this sense, its definition is more than just the intersection of the definitions of its constituent terms. The reader interested in exploring this issue in slightly more depth in terms of considering the potential ambiguities inherent in adopting a simple intersection of the terms is referred to Appendix 1.

Information behaviour, whether viewed through individual or social perspectives, entails a number of component elements. They are outlined in Figure 2.1, which shows the author's conception of information behaviour.

Let us now explore each of these elements in more detail.

Information-related needs, information behaviour and its effects

Information *behaviour* is not the same thing as the *need* to which it relates, and the *effects* it has. This is why these are separated in Figure 2.1. A need is not in itself a behaviour — although *perceiving* and *expressing* a need *are* behaviours.

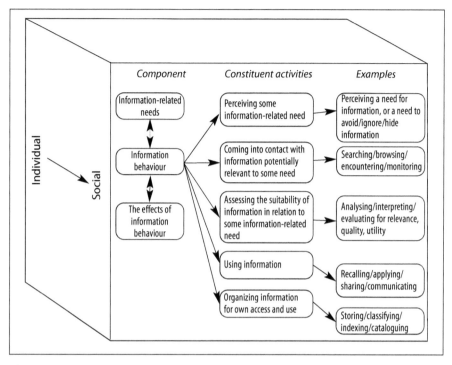

Figure 2.1 Components of information behaviour

And although the effect of engaging in information behaviour may be further behaviour (for example, deciding to take a particular course of action) the effect of a particular behaviour cannot at the same time *be* that behaviour. Nevertheless, the needs that drive information behaviour, and the effects that behaviour has, are important elements in its study.

Each of the components of information behaviour shown in Figure 2.1 will be introduced below. Note that the names given to each of the components are generic, in the sense that each includes both positive and negative instances. In other words, 'perceiving some information-related need' relates to whether or not a person perceives an information-related need – i.e. it includes both perceiving and failing to perceive. Failing to perceive some need is just as much information behaviour, and may be just as interesting to researchers and practitioners as perceiving it. Similarly, 'coming into contact with' and 'using' information embrace both coming into contact and failing to come into contact, and both using and failing to use. The same is true for all the headings and sub-headings. Thus information behaviour can include hiding, avoiding, ignoring and destroying information as well as seeking and using it.

Perceiving some information-related need

Perceiving an information-related need is a key component of information behaviour, representing its motivational component. But the need itself is not a constituent process of that behaviour.

Note that, as previously mentioned, an information need is not the same as (but is one type of) an information-related need. An information need is a need to acquire information to solve some problem or address some gap in our knowledge. However, information-related needs are needs which have implications for the way we interact with information. As previously noted, sometimes people feel the need to avoid or ignore information – for example, if they fear being upset by it. Such a need *relates to* information but is not a *need for* information.

It is also important to note that perceiving an information-related or information need does not necessarily precede coming into contact with information. Awareness of a previously unconscious need may sometimes be stimulated by encountering information serendipitously, or thinking about information related to some other need. Thus an information-related or information need is not the sole starting point for studying information behaviour.

A need becomes an information-related need at the point where implications for information are perceived. If you are at home and feeling hungry, your hunger may be satisfied by a quick trip to the fridge. But if you are in an unfamiliar city, you may need information about nearby restaurants. As soon as you begin thinking about the type of information you need (information about local restaurants with good reviews), and maybe information you do not need (information about fast food outlets) you are engaging in information behaviour.

Coming into contact with information potentially relevant to some need, with a focus on the characteristics of the information, or the way in which it was discovered

Note that this heading is longer than that shown in Figure 2.1. I have added 'with a focus on the characteristics of the information, or the way in which it was discovered'. This will be explained below.

'Coming into contact' with information is a broader concept than 'seeking' information. Coming into contact with information that is potentially relevant to some need may result from intentional information seeking (whether focused searching or more general browsing and monitoring), or from encountering information serendipitously.

The inclusion of 'potentially relevant to some need' in the heading for this section reflects the fact that unless a person encountering information perceives it as potentially relevant to some need (not necessarily at the time, but possible some time later) the encounter may simply not register with the person. If a person comes into contact with information of which they are completely unaware and which totally bypasses them, this does not constitute information behaviour on their part. It would, however, if the relevance of the encounter were realized at some later point. This qualification rules out coming across information that is totally irrelevant to a person, and which thus may not even be noticed or remembered. Only when it is perceived as potentially interesting/useful can it be regarded as an 'information encounter' as opposed to constant everyday reality in which all our senses are constantly bombarded with data and information.

However, further qualification is needed if we are to be able accurately to classify examples of 'coming into contact with information' as instances of information behaviour. Take, for example, the case of a person coming across a new algorithm for solving a particular computing problem:

> I came across Quinlan's ID3 algorithm, which is much better than the other algorithms I was exploring for solving my particular problem. The reason the algorithm is so much better is that . . .

I argue that this would only constitute information behaviour to the extent that substantial reference is made to the characteristics (the nature or type) of the information source where the algorithm was found, or the circumstances of coming across it (e.g. searching, browsing, encountering) as in, for example:

> I came across Quinlan's ID3 algorithm when I searched using Google Scholar. Google Scholar proved more effective in this case than Google . . .

THINK!

Imagine the case where Person A encounters a piece of information but does not notice it. Someone else (Person B) thinks that this information is potentially relevant to Person A. Can Person A's encounter be considered a case of information behaviour?

The key question in deciding this is whether the information is or is not 'potentially relevant' to Person A. If Person A was a patient suffering from a particular condition, and Person B was a doctor recognizing that the information encountered could in fact have been useful to Person A, then studying the reasons for and the result of Person A failing to notice the information – provided that there is a focus on the characteristics of the information, or the way in which it was discovered – would constitute information behaviour research. Recall that these definitions are generic – so focusing on the way in which information failed to be discovered would also render this information behaviour research. Thus information can be potentially relevant to a person without that person necessarily recognizing this.

Assessing the suitability of information in relation to some information-related need

A key component of information behaviour is judging the suitability of information with which a person comes into contact in relation to some need. 'Suitability' is used broadly here to include intelligibility, relevance, trustworthiness and usefulness in relation to some need. The information may be suitable in terms of helping to satisfy, partly satisfy, focus, refine, stimulate, or even discard a need. Note that assessing the suitability of information does not, in the definitions used in this book, include engaging in its basic decoding (e.g. reading and comprehending the message that it gives). Otherwise, information behaviour research would embrace studies of the way in which children learn to read, listen and speak. Considering the extent to which information is or is not easily intelligible, however, is included.

Using information – or knowledge with a focus on the characteristics of the information from which it was derived

Note again that the heading above is more extensive than that in Figure 2.1. This is explained below. *Using* information includes recalling, applying, sharing and/or communicating it. Note, however, that there is a difference between 'using information' and 'using knowledge'.

THINK!

Recalling the previous discussion of the difference between information and knowledge, can you think of an example of using *information* as opposed to *knowledge* (i.e. a person using information which is not part of his or her knowledge)?

Strictly speaking, whether it is *information*, or *knowledge* derived from that information, that is being used by a person on a particular occasion depends on the extent to which the information has been processed by that person such that it has become part of his or her knowledge. If information is used (for example shared or disseminated) verbatim, with minimal intellectual ingestion by the person passing it on – i.e. without it being processed to become part of that person's knowledge – then the person can be said to be using information. But if what is being applied or passed on is knowledge derived from the information (i.e. if it has been processed and integrated into the person's knowledge structure) then the person can be said to be using or sharing knowledge (derived from information). It is difficult to see how a person could *apply* information (as opposed to knowledge), in that 'apply' (as opposed merely to passing it on) implies understanding on the part of the person doing the applying – in which case it is *knowledge* (derived from information) that is being applied.

If we were to include 'using knowledge' in our definition of information behaviour then any instance of thought, or conscious action which makes use of any knowledge, would be included. And surely just 'thinking' (a use of our knowledge) does not of itself constitute 'information use'?

But if we specify 'using information (and not knowledge)', this rules out activities in which the person has understood the information they are using (since it will have become part of their knowledge). This would rule out a study of the comparative effectiveness of a cookery book and a YouTube video (different types of information source) on how to make bread. The key measure of effectiveness would be the extent to which a sample of people was able to apply the information (which implies they have incorporated it into their knowledge) and go on successfully to bake a loaf. But surely this would be a good example of an 'information behaviour' study? It seems neither viable nor desirable to rule out of the domain of information behaviour research any case where the information being studied is successfully understood!

THINK!

It seems as though we can only either *under*-specify information behaviour (by including any sort of thought!), or *over*-specify it (by excluding making use of any information that has been understood!).

Can you think of a solution to this problem in relation to 'using information' or 'using knowledge'? Spend a few moments thinking about this before proceeding.

The solution I have adopted here is to elaborate the definition to become:

'Using information – or knowledge with a focus on the characteristics of the information from which it was derived.'

This does two things:

1 It enables the *inclusion* within 'information behaviour' of behaviour which does not necessarily entail the person engaging with the content and integrating it into his or her knowledge. Thus, avoiding, ignoring, hiding or destroying an information source can be considered to be types of information behaviour.

2 At the same time, it *excludes* examples simply of the application of a person's knowledge – for example, how a person uses his or her knowledge to solve a mathematics problem, or what is the best way to remember road signs in order to pass one's driving test – without reference to the information from which the knowledge was derived.

Organizing information for one's own access and use

Information may be organized and managed in many ways – both formal and informal. Libraries typically use classification and indexing schemes to enable subject access to information sources, and cataloguing rules to enable access by authors and titles. Organizing and managing information is clearly behaviour, and this behaviour is clearly applied to information.

THINK!

So are librarianship and information management included within (i.e. are just aspects of) information behaviour? And if not, what is the essential difference between them and information behaviour?

Take a few moments to think about this before reading on . . .

Some qualification is required if we are to avoid subsuming under 'information behaviour' the distinct fields of cataloguing, indexing and classification, and indeed most of librarianship and information management.

For this reason I have added 'for one's own access and use' to the heading for this section. This excludes as information behaviour the organization of information services for clients – for example, the cataloguing materials in an academic library. At the same time, it would include the organization of information by particular individuals or groups for their own access and use.

For example, a study of cataloguing in an academic library could be a study of information behaviour if the researcher's focus is on the information behaviour of the academic community in which the library exists and of which it forms a part (in which case, the focus would be on the community's 'own' access and use). Similarly, a study of how a particular group of people organize the information they need and use would constitute information behaviour research.

And finally . . . a definition of 'information behaviour'
So far in this chapter I have:

- defined **information** and **behaviour**
- considered a number of definitions of **information behaviour**
- explored the **components** of information behaviour, and
- identified the **complications** that we must take into account if we are to differentiate information behaviour from closely related but distinct concepts.

We are now in a position to define information behaviour more rigorously. Figure 2.2 shows the formal definition used throughout this book.

Information behaviour is engaging in any or all of the following activities:

- perceiving some information-related need;
- coming into contact with information potentially relevant to some need;
- assessing the suitability of information in relation to some information-related need;
- using information or knowledge

with reference to/a focus on the characteristics of the information in terms of:

- its nature (e.g. accuracy, trustworthiness, style, approach, level);
- its medium (e.g. text, audio);
- its source (e.g. from whom or where it emanates); and/or
- the mode or circumstances of its discovery (e.g. searching, encountering).

- organizing information for one's own use.

Figure 2.2 Information behaviour defined

THINK!

Let's now test this definition. Consider the following research questions. All of them entail studying people's processing or use of information (i.e. behaviour applied to information). But to what extent would you consider each as clearly falling within the scope of 'information behaviour'?

1. How do people learn to read?
2. What does a driver need to know in order to pass the driving test?
3. What are the causes of dyslexia?
4. How justified are claims that Mary Shelley's novel *Frankenstein* is a Romantic Feminist reading of Milton's *Paradise Lost*?
5. Which of two TV adverts is more effective?
6. What is the best way to teach management?
7. How do meteorologists interpret cloud formations to predict the weather?

8. What is the most accurate mathematical formula for engineers to use in predicting stress on a bridge caused by a cross-wind?
9. What are the most effective forms of political spin?

All of these examples entail *behaviour* (thoughts or actions) relating to *information*. But do they fall within the scope of *information behaviour*? To what extent are they the province of education, psychology, literary criticism, sports science, marketing, management, engineering and politics? Can we really – and would it be desirable to try to – appropriate them to the field of information behaviour? Take a few minutes now to think about each example, in terms of whether you think it does or does not fall within the scope of information behaviour – and why. Once you have decided, read on.

Here are my own answers, based on the discussion and resultant definition of information behaviour above.

1   **How do people learn to read?** The closest activity in the definition of information behaviour is 'assessing the suitability of information', but reading is basic decoding (as opposed, for example, to assessing the degree of its intelligibility) and does not qualify as information behaviour.

2   **What does a driver need to know in order to pass the driving test?** This could be reformulated as 'What are the information needs of drivers intending to take their driving test?' Such a study of information needs would not *per se* qualify as a study of information behaviour. Recall that an information need is the cause of information behaviour but not information behaviour itself. No behaviour is specified as the focus of the study (e.g. how different people may perceive their information needs differently). No reference is made to the nature of the information or the circumstances of acquiring it.

3   **What are the causes of dyslexia?** As in (1), basic decoding (reading) does not qualify as information behaviour according to the definition used here.

4   **How justified are claims that Mary Shelley's novel *Frankenstein* is a Romantic Feminist reading of Milton's *Paradise Lost*?** This study does not entail any of the activities listed. It involves analysing information (*Frankenstein* and *Paradise Lost*) in order to address an information-related need (to assess how justified the claims are) but it does not focus on the characteristics of the information in any of the senses listed.

5   **Which of two TV adverts is more effective?** If this study explored consumers' assessment and subsequent use of the information in relation

to a need (for the product), and if it focused on the role of characteristics of the information (e.g. the adverts' different styles or approaches) then it would qualify as an information behaviour study.

6 **What is the best way to teach management?** As in (5), if this related to the role of characteristics of information (e.g. different types or channels) and if it also focused on 'assessing the suitability of information in relation to some information-related need' (to learn about management) then it would qualify as an information behaviour study.

7 **How do meteorologists interpret cloud formations to predict the weather?** This entails the use of information, and if the study focused on the characteristics of the information (cloud formations), for example assessing the suitability of this type of information compared with other types of information, then it would qualify as an information behaviour study.

8 **What is the most accurate mathematical formula for engineers to use in predicting stress on a bridge caused by a cross-wind?** Although the implied activity entails assessing the relative suitability of two pieces of information in relation to an information need, there is no focus on the characteristics of the information in any of the senses listed in the definition.

9 **What are the most effective forms of political spin?** As in (5), if this study focused on the effects of particular characteristics of the information (e.g. different styles or approaches) on consumers' assessments and subsequent acceptance or rejection of the political message, then it would qualify as an information behaviour study.

Information behaviour and cognate areas

Information behaviour is related to – but distinct from – information literacy, information management, knowledge management and information retrieval. Let us briefly explore how these concepts relate to information behaviour, and how they are different.

Johnston and Webber (2003) define information literacy as:

> the adoption of appropriate information behaviour to identify, through whatever channel or medium, information well fitted to information needs, leading to wise and ethical use of information in society
>
> Johnston and Webber, 2003

'Literacy' is a value-laden (as opposed to value-free) concept, in that it is generally accepted that to be literate is better than to be illiterate. Information behaviour, on the other hand, can include undesirable as well as desirable behaviour. As noted by Johnson and Webber, information literacy is associated with information behaviour that is *effective* in terms of achieving a desirable goal ('wise and ethical use of information').

Information and knowledge management also require understanding of the information behaviour of the groups, organizations and communities on which they focus. Managing information and knowledge (including the design, development, deployment and evaluation of information systems and strategies) clearly represents information behaviour on the part of the group, organization or community whose information or knowledge is being managed. However, the activities of the individuals engaged in such management do not represent the information behaviour of those individuals (unless their management activities are focused on their own information-related needs). Thus, a study of how an individual, group, organization or community organizes and manages its own information and knowledge (as opposed to managing information for others) does fall within the province of information behaviour research. A study of, for example, cataloguing practices in an academic library would not qualify as a piece of information behaviour research according to the definition used in this book unless the study was focusing on the information behaviour of the academic community served by the library.

'Information retrieval' is a term often used in two ways. Firstly, it can refer to the process of finding information from a retrieval system. Secondly, it is often used to refer to the processes of designing systems that enable people to retrieve information. Thus the field includes both information behavioural and technical aspects. Examples of the latter are system design, testing and evaluation. Studies of these activities would not qualify as information behaviour research. Examples of the former are studies of the way in which people use and interact with a retrieval system in terms, for example, of the needs they bring to it and the strategies they use. Such studies would be included in the definition of information behaviour used here. In this case, information retrieval would be equivalent to information searching (insofar as retrieving relevant information is the goal of information searching). Information searching is considered here to be a subset of information seeking. Information searching (in keeping with information retrieval) is generally used to imply the use of some search tool. Information seeking includes, but is not limited to, searching using a specific tool.

A study of a person (or team) designing an information retrieval system, however, would not constitute a study of that person's (or team's) information behaviour – unless the system was designed to support the information-related needs of the person or team, as opposed to other users the system was designed to support.

Summary

A satisfactory definition of 'information behaviour' cannot be generated simply by combining the definitions of 'information' and 'behaviour'. This chapter has attempted to clarify all three concepts.

At one level, this does not really matter. No information professional is going to withdraw from helping a client because the information-related problem they are facing does not fit an academic definition of 'information behaviour' such as the one presented here. No researcher interested in the way people solve information-related problems is going to abort a line of inquiry because it takes him or her outside such a definition. After all, a research project does not need a label to proceed – any given project may bring aspects from multiple fields of study. There is nothing to say that an information behaviour investigation cannot draw from and include aspects of psychology, communication studies or management.

However, at another level, a precise working definition is useful insofar as it enables the reader of this book to share with the author a clear understanding of precisely what are the scope and boundaries of what is being discussed. It also enables the author to be consistent in his use of terminology and concepts relating to 'information', 'behaviour' and 'information behaviour' throughout this book, and coherent decisions to be made as to what is included and excluded. The definition adopted is arguably sufficiently broad to reflect the new and broader directions in which researchers and practitioners are taking us in this field, and at the same time sufficiently narrow to avoid unprincipled and unreasonable claims of the field to cover almost any form of human thought and behaviour.

It is important inadvertently to adopt an Alice in Wonderland approach to word definition:

> 'When I use a word,' Humpty Dumpty said in rather a scornful tone, 'it means just what I choose it to mean – neither more nor less.'
>
> Carroll, 2013

If we are studying information behaviour in depth, we must be clear about its nature. This relates to exactly what it consists of (what are its constituent elements and how they interact), how it relates to, and how it is distinct from closely related concepts such as information *needs* and the *effects* of information behaviour, and closely related fields of practice and research such as information and knowledge management and information retrieval.

The definitions explained above are offered as working definitions that provide a consistent base for the introduction of themes and issues in the rest of this book. They are not claimed to be universally accepted, or to address the depth and complexity of some discussions, particularly of the nature of data and information. For more in-depth discussion of basic concepts and terminology, the reader is referred to Chapter 3 of Case (2012) and to Fisher and Julien (2009).

Having addressed these basic issues, the book now turns in the next chapter to the driver and motivating force behind information behaviour – information-related needs.

References

Carroll L. (2013) *Alice Through the Looking-Glass* (Google eBook), London, Fantastica.

Case, D. (2012) *Looking for Information: a survey of research on information seeking, needs and behaviour*, 3rd edn, Bingley, Emerald.

Fisher, K. E. and Julien, H. (2009) Information Behaviour, *Annual Review of Information Science and Technology*, **43**, 1–73.

Floridi, L. (2010) *Information: a very short guide*, Oxford, Oxford University Press.

Ford, N. (2008) *Web-based Learning Through Educational Informatics: information science meets educational computing*, Hershey, PA, Information Science Publishing.

Ingwersen, P. and Järvelin, K. (2005) *The Turn: integration of information seeking and retrieval in context*, Dordrecht, Springer.

Johnston, B. and Webber, S. (2003) Information Literacy in Higher Education: a review and case study, *Studies in Higher Education*, **28** (3), 335–52.

Kitchin, R. (2014) *The Data Revolution: big data, open data, data infrastructures and their consequences*, London, Sage.

Pettigrew, K. E., Fidel, R. and Bruce, H. (2001) Conceptual Frameworks in Information Behavior, *Annual Review of Information Science and Technology*, **35** (1), 43–78.

Wilson, T. D. (2000) Human Information Behavior, *Informing Science*, **3** (2), 49–55.

Wilson, T. D. and Walsh, C. (1996) *Information Behaviour: an interdisciplinary perspective*, Sheffield, University of Sheffield, Department of Information Studies.

3

Changing conceptions of information needs

Introduction

Much research into information behaviour has focused on seeking information to satisfy some 'information need'. The typical scenario is one in which a person becomes aware that they need to know something to help solve a problem or learn about some topic of interest, and this leads them to engage in information behaviour in order to acquire relevant information. Although (as will be explored in the Summary at the end of the chapter) there are starting points and drivers of information behaviour other than 'information needs', they have nevertheless formed the focus of a considerable body of research over many years which has provided useful insights into information behaviour.

In much early research into 'user studies', information needs were *inferred* from the types of information sources particular groups of people made use of. Later researchers became much more interested in the psychology of information needs – particularly in the intellectual (cognitive) processes underlying them. Even more recently, there has been a bourgeoning interest in sociological aspects of information behaviour, which brings a different and complementary perspective to what constitutes information needs. There has also been increasing interest in information behaviour that is not geared to satisfying a need for information, but rather to avoiding information. As will be discussed in the Summary, such needs are still related to information but not in the sense of needing or seeking it.

Information needs

Early theorists

An early writer on information needs was Taylor. His seminal work (Taylor, 1962; 1968) is particularly interesting in that he distinguished between four different levels of information needs and their articulation. These continue to inform current research, including that of Cole (2012), whose recent work on information needs will be introduced in the next section, 'Information-related needs'. Taylor differentiated between four levels of need:

1 A person's actual (underlying) information need (independent of whether s/he is aware of it).
2 The person's general idea of what it is that s/he needs to know (which may be relatively vague).
3. A rationale and precise description of the question requiring an answer.
4. A formal query made to an information system (such as a search engine), in the language the person thinks is required by the system. This represents a compromised form of the question. It is compromised in that it has to take account of the limitations of the information system (the language and syntax perceived by the searcher to be required by it).

According to Taylor, people may vary in the precision of – and the extent to which they are aware of – their information needs. He also stresses the fact that a translation must be made between a person's description of the question to be answered (level 3), and what they actually type into an information system in an attempt to acquire information that will help answer the question (level 4).

THINK!

As a librarian or information manager, would you need to interact with a person coming to you for help in finding information who is at level 2 differently from a person at level 3? And if so, in what way?

It is not uncommon for a person who is experiencing an information need at level 2 to feel the need to give the appearance of being closer to stage 3 than they really are. Some people may feel that expressing vagueness and uncertainty in an interaction with an information professional is not desirable, and they may express their need with more certainty than they actually have. The information professional can play an important role here in gently teasing out (if appropriate) their level 1 need as far as they are able, and helping them move from there via level 2 to level 3. This may involve doing some (level 4) information seeking and using the feedback from this to inform the iterative revisiting of levels 1, 2 and 3. Another approach is to accept the client's level 3 description, and to assist in searching at level 4, using the client's reactions to what is found to try to discover what the person's level 1 need is, and iteratively to help him or her to move again through 2 and 3 to 4.

Taylor distinguished between the way in which a person describes his/her information need to an information system or librarian, and the need itself. You may think that these are more or less the same thing. However, describing a gap or anomaly, and describing what is needed to fill the gap or resolve the anomaly, can be very different.

One of the first information science researchers to explore these differences from a psychological point of view was Belkin. Like Taylor, he focused on the potential disconnect between a person's actual information need and the formal query required by an information system to respond to it.

Belkin developed what he called the Anomalous State of Knowledge (ASK) model. This model proposes that a need for information is experienced as an anomaly in one's state of knowledge. Information is required in order to resolve this anomaly. A key point made by Belkin is that it is difficult for a person to know precisely what information is required to resolve the anomaly s/he is experiencing. It is much easier to describe the anomaly itself. Belkin, Oddy and Brooks (1982, 62) noted that 'in general, the user is unable to specify precisely what is needed to resolve that anomaly'.

This highlights the question of how an information seeker can specify a request to an information retrieval system describing what it is s/he does not know. Thus, even when a person is clearly aware of the nature of the anomaly needing resolution, the process of describing it in terms of what information is required is far from unproblematic. Bear in mind, too, that we cannot necessarily assume at a given point that a person yet has a clear awareness of the anomaly. Recall that Taylor drew attention to the fact that at his level 2 information need people are not necessarily fully aware of their need. We will also be seeing in the case of Cole's model (see 'More recent work' below) that becoming fully aware of all aspects of one's information need may be an iterative process which can change during, and as a result of, ongoing searching for information.

There is a further potential difficulty in that even when the person has a clear idea of the information they need to find, there may be a linguistic problem that needs to be overcome in that s/he must use words to describe the information that is needed in such a way that an information system can find it. Belkin, Oddy and Brooks (1982) drew attention to the limitations of information retrieval systems, most of which work by attempting to match

(a) words used by the system to index information sources to (b) words typed into the system by the searcher.

However, viewed from a wider perspective, this matching process is only one component in the overall process of connecting people with the information they need. Ford (2012) lists a number of these components, including some that have been discussed above, noting that disconnects may occur at and/or between any of them:

 1 What the person does not know that s/he needs to know (the knowledge gap).
It can be difficult to know what it is that you don't know.

2 The information that will satisfy the knowledge need (the information need).
It can be difficult to translate what you know you don't know (and need to know) into words describing the information that will enable you to find out.

3 The search tool(s) most appropriate to finding the needed information.
There are many different search tools, some of which may be more, or less appropriate for finding the type of information the person requires.

4 The words the person types into the search tool (the query – the expression by the searcher of his/her information need).
The same concepts and ideas can be expressed in many different ways. Although search tools are becoming more intelligent and less reliant on verbatim matches between query words and index terms, they are still limited in this respect.

5 The search facilities provided by the search tool.
Within a particular search tool, the success of a search may depend on which of a range of search facilities the person is familiar with and uses.

6 The words used by the search tool to describe information sources (index terms).
See (4) above. These words may not match the words the person uses to describe the information s/he needs.

7 The words used by the author to express his/her message (the author's expression of his/her message).
The same message can be expressed in many different linguistic ways.

8 What the author of an information source wishes to communicate (the author's message).

Viewed from this perspective, satisfying a complex information need entails an iterative process which starts with the information seeker's best guess (a tentative hypothesis) at what it is they need to know. In the light of information retrieved, the tentative hypothesis may be refined, and over time if successful the information seeker will gradually 'home in' on a resolution to the anomaly, or a solution to the problem. During these stages, it may become apparent that to solve the initial overall problem, sub-problems may need to be solved. Also, during this process, it may be that the very nature of the problem is perceived differently.

More recent work

Perhaps the most elaborated treatment of information needs to date comes from Charles Cole. Cole (2012) has built on the work of Taylor and Belkin, as well as a range of other theoretical work, including Bruner's model of the perceptual cycle, Minsky's frame theory and Donald's evolutionary psychology to formulate a theory of information needs.

   Cole uses Taylor's model to differentiate between (a) the view of information needs which he claims is characteristic of computer scientists involved in designing information systems, and (b) the view of information needs as typically conceptualized within library and information science. Computer scientists often embrace, as their default view of an information need, Taylor's last level – the query a person types into an information system. Library and information scientists, on the other hand, tend to embrace a more complex and holistic view of information needs to include those levels characterized by uncertainty and lack of precision on the part of the person needing information, reflected in Taylor's first two levels.

   In Cole's model, searching consists of three phases: Pre-focus, Focus and Post-focus. In the Pre-focus stage the person's picture of the topic s/he is investigating is constantly shifting and evolving. During this phase, the person is likely to engage in an exploratory information-seeking strategy of the type described by Bates as 'berrypicking' (see under 'Information-seeking strategies' in Chapter 4). S/he will explore aspects of his or her information need, as distinct from the whole information need, which will not be fully realized until the Focus phase. At this stage, the person's query to the information system will reflect a compromised information need (Taylor's level 4), and will not be connected to the deeper levels of need (Taylor's levels 1–3). In the Focus stage, the person achieves a clearer idea of the topic, and is able to progress to more focused searching in the next phase – the Post-focus phase. At this stage, the person's query will be connected to Taylor's deeper (1–3) levels.

   Cole argues that it is only in the Post-focus stage – when the person is in a position to generate a formal query that can be presented to an information system – that s/he experiences an information need in the way typically conceived in computer science. Information science is concerned with all stages.

Other researchers have taken a broader focus on information needs, and indeed information behaviour. Annemarie Lloyd, for example, has explored the information-related needs of people as they seek to integrate into new social and work environments. Although people in this situation may have multiple specific problems to solve and tasks to accomplish that require information – all representing information needs as discussed so far in this chapter – their ultimate 'information need' is broader and represents the need to learn about, become familiar with and adept at navigating new 'information landscapes'. Lloyd's work relates to information literacy, but recall that this may be defined essentially as the deployment of appropriate and effective information behaviour. Research on the development and application of information literacy can therefore illuminate information behaviour more generally.

Lloyd has studied information-related aspects of how people entering communities familiarize themselves with a new environment, and learn how to navigate within, and ultimately become an integral member of, the community. The subjects of her studies have included firefighters entering the profession, and refugees entering a new country. But the concepts developed are applicable more generally to situations in which people are engaging with a community, and moving from inexperience and novice status to becoming experienced expert members of that community, whether it be academic, health-related, work-based or social.

A number of concepts underpin Lloyd's work. Much of our work and social life involves engaging in communities, in which groups of people work together in pursuit of particular goals. Each community is characterized by an 'information landscape' consisting of knowledge, information, and mediators (people who can bring others into contact with the information they may need). An individual may be engaged with multiple communities, and communities may inter-connect with, or may be nested within, others. Lloyd describes information landscapes thus:

> Landscapes are characterized by different topographies, climates, and complex ecologies. They can therefore be interpreted in many different ways depending on what is already known about them and what can be learnt from them. The structure and organization of the landscape affords a range of opportunities for people to engage with the sources of information that give the landscape its unique shape and character. Affordances relate to the opportunities offered by the landscape to engage with it (Gibson, 1979).

In a workplace landscape, affordances relate to a range of opportunities, activities, symbols, artefacts and practices that the workplace as a space, and the people who work in that space, provide to facilitate learning and knowing. In the library landscape affordances may relate to practices such as orientation sessions that enable the clients to engage with information about the library, with the bibliographic layout of the library and the range of services available to them. They may take the form of learning about the landscape of digital environments. Through affordances, people, as they engage with the landscape, perceive the artefacts and symbols that characterize the landscape and the meaning that is attributed to them.

Lloyd, 2006, 572

Information is needed to solve particular problems and achieve particular goals. However, the individual needs also to learn about the information landscapes of the communities with which s/he needs to interact and of which s/he may need to become an integral active member. S/he needs to learn what are accepted ways of knowing.

A community will often work to shared assumptions about what is accepted knowledge and wisdom within the community, what are acceptable sources of information, and what information is particularly important in particular circumstances. What to an experienced member of a community may be a normal expectation may be a 'hidden agenda' for the newcomer.

Lloyd describes this arena of study as information *practice* rather than information *behaviour* – a distinction made by Savolainen (2008). He argued that information *behaviour* has become primarily associated with a cognitive view of information activity which tends to focus on behaviour triggered by an individual's needs and goals. Information *practices*, however, reflects a social constructivist viewpoint emphasizing more the influences on information activities of social and cultural factors. He defines information practice as:

a set of socially and culturally established ways to identify, seek, use and share the information available in various sources

Savolainen, 2008, 2

According to Lloyd et al.:

practice is understood to be constituted through a web of social, material, and corporeal activities that afford opportunities for engagement with information and knowledge that are specific to the particular setting. Practice thus enables the accomplishment of projects or ends (for example getting a job, getting an education, or as in the case of this study, becoming settled in a new community).

Lloyd et al., 2013, 126

Another influential researcher, Brenda Dervin, has in her Sense-Making theory used the metaphor of bridging a gap to describe the process of satisfying an information need. However, her focus is broader than individual information needs of the type studied by Taylor, Belkin, Cole, and others – and her conception of information needs is ultimately broader than that of Lloyd. Rather than exploring information needs as a particular question to be asked or a specific problem to be solved, or of integrating into a particular community, Dervin focuses on our fundamental need to make sense of our life situation (which will of course include specific instances of problem solving and question answering).

She argues that as we travel through life (across time and space), we experience discontinuities, of which we constantly strive to make sense, and this need drives information behaviour. We constantly make, unmake and remake sense of what we are experiencing. Dervin uses the metaphor of gaps and bridges. A person experiences a problematic situation as a gap, and attempts to find solutions to bridge the gap so that s/he can continue their journey after crossing the bridge. This process pervades experience. Savolainen (1993) summarizes Dervin's proposition as follows:

> The philosophical foundations of the sense-making theory rest on Richard F. Carter's assumption of a *discontinuity* condition presenting a mandate for humans to take steps to construct sense in constantly changing life situations. Discontinuity is seen as a fundamental aspect of reality. Discontinuities are assumed to be found in all existence, for example, between reality and human sensors, between the mind and tongue, between message created and channel, between human at time one and human at time two, and between human and institution (Dervin, 1991, p. 62).

'Making sense' is not restricted to acquiring knowledge. It includes a wider range of thoughts and feelings that reflect a person's interpretation of a situation, including intuitions, opinions, hunches, effective responses, evaluations, and questions.

Building on Dervin's description of sensemaking, Klein, Moon and Hoffman define it as:

> a motivated, continuous effort to understand connections (which can be among

people, places and events) in order to anticipate their trajectories and act effectively

Klein, Moon and Hoffman, 2006, 71

Kolko notes how according to Klein, Moon and Hoffman (2006) sense-making is applicable not only at the level of the individual person, but also at organizational level. He describes it as:

> . . . a way of understanding connections between people, places and events that are occurring now or have occurred in the past, in order to anticipate future trajectories and act accordingly. Their work positions sensemaking as an internal and reflective activity, where one is actively trying to solve a specific and contained problem, but also as an external and communal activity, where a group of people are trying to solve multiple problems in pursuit of larger, organizational goals . . . Their view of the process is one shared of many organizational theorists . . . where, in a large organization, various people may hold different pieces of data, and different levels of awareness of events, that are all critical to the success of a given project.
>
> Kolko, 2010

Much information behaviour research has focused on work situations. In 1995 Savolainen published a model of information-seeking behaviour which related specifically to 'everyday life'. The model is based on the concept of 'mastery of life' – a more general and diffuse concept than specific problems to be solved, or knowledge gaps to be filled. In this, his theory is more akin to Dervin's idea of the need to 'make sense' of things than to more prescribed and formal conceptions of 'information needs'.

As we have just seen, Dervin argues that people are constantly working to make sense of discontinuities. Savolainen also stresses our need to maintain some sort of coherence and consistency in our lives. He draws on the concept of 'the order of things' which results from the choices we constantly make in our lives in order to maintain a relatively coherent and consistent framework of values and practices. 'Mastery of life' relates to keeping things in meaningful order. This does not imply that people do not deliberately allow disorder and tension into their lives. Indeed, such things may stimulate new ideas or relieve boredom. Rather, over time people tend towards choices consistent with their preferred order of things. Our cultural and class environments may have an effect on our choices insofar as there may be generally accepted norms and values inherent in them.

Savolainen's framework is based in part on the concept of 'habitus' developed by Pierre Bourdieu (1984). As Savolainen notes:

> Habitus is a relatively stable system of dispositions by which individuals integrate their experiences and evaluate the importance of different choices. . . . habitus manifests the incorporation of norms and social expectations within an individual; thus, habitus is more than an aggregation of 'purely' personal dispositions. As a socially and culturally intermediated system of classification, habitus renders a general direction to choices made in everyday life by indicating which choices are natural or desirable in relation to one's social class or cultural group. As a system of socially and culturally determined dispositions habitus forms the base on which one's way of life is organized.
>
> Savolainen, 1995, 263

Information behaviour fits into this framework, since information is needed to enable choices to be made as one exercises mastery of life in order to keep things in order.

THINK!

To what extent should librarians (academic or public) be involved in helping people integrate into new communities and/or 'master life'? Should their concerns stop at helping people solve specific information needs?

An interesting approach has been taken to conceptualizing information needs by Shenton (2007). He adapted a framework devised by two psychologists as a model of self-awareness known as the Johari Window (after their names: Joseph Luft and Harrington Ingham). This simple model (Luft and Ingham, 1955) differentiates between four aspects of individuals that are known both to themselves and/to others:

1   The 'public self', consisting of those aspects of which both the individual and others are aware.
2   The 'blind self', relating to aspects of the individual known to others but not to the individual.
3   The 'private self', meaning aspects known only to the individual and not to others.
4   The 'unknown area', referring to aspects unknown to both the wider public and the individual him or herself.

This framework has been used in a range of scenarios including self-help, education and business. However, applications within the library and information area have not to date included the information needs domain, which Shenton directly addresses. Shenton's modified the original framework specifically to apply to information needs. The new framework consists of the following categories:

1 'Misguided information needs' – misunderstood by the individual, whether (i) known to the information professional or (ii) not known to the information professional.
2 'Expressed needs' – known to the individual and known by the information professional.
3 'Unexpressed needs' – known to the individual but unknown to the information professional.
4 'Independently met needs' – known to the individual but not known to the information professional.
5 'Inferred needs' – known to the information professional but not known to the individual.
6 'Dormant or delitescent needs' – known to neither the individual nor the information professional.

One of the main changes to the original framework is the inclusion of an additional category 'misunderstood by the individual' and the replacement of 'others' with 'the information professional'.

   Categories 3 and 4 are broad, and include both (i) information needs that fall within the first three levels of Taylor's classification (described earlier in this chapter) before they reach the state whereby they can be rationally expressed, and (ii) expressed information needs that fall within Taylor's fourth level – but expressed not to an information professional but independently to a search engine or some other person known to the individual. In relation to category 3, Shenton notes that:

> It is, of course, entirely possible for the individual to develop a clear personal grasp of the information that is needed but be entirely lacking in the vocabulary or subject knowledge necessary for the private understanding to be translated into an explicit statement upon which the information professional can act. In these circumstances, the need may well remain undisclosed in any form to the practitioner. Even if the need can be meaningfully articulated, it may be that the individual undertakes no information-seeking action at all . . .
>
> Shenton, 2007, 489

Shenton's framework has an information-professional focus in that it distinguishes between information needs expressed to such a professional and those expressed by the searcher independently to a search system and/or to a person other than an information professional.

Whilst category 3 consists of information needs known by the individual and expressed to an information professional, category 5 concerns needs that are unknown to the individual but which the information professional infers from his or her knowledge and/or research – as opposed to knowledge obtained directly from the information seeker.

Category 6 needs are those which exist but of which neither the individual nor the information professional is aware. Recall that Taylor's first level relates to an individual's actual (underlying) information need whether or not s/he is aware of it.

Shenton's additional category 1 relates to misconceptions on the part of the information seeker whereby 'the acquisition of material deemed necessary by the individual will not actually help to resolve the wider problem in the manner anticipated' (Shenton, 2007, 491). It may sometimes be the case (category 1 (i)) that an information professional is able to develop a more effective conception of the individual's real information need, and interaction between the professional and the information seeker may result in a successful outcome.

THINK!

Can you think of an example (either hypothetically or from your own experience) of an information need being better known by a librarian than an information seeker consulting him or her?

Librarians and information professionals working in any area will build up knowledge and expertise relating to the nature of, and difficulties and complexities associated with, the information needs of their clients. One example of this would be that of an experienced academic librarian working with first-year undergraduate students. As Shenton notes:

> Students beginning a university course may, at its outset especially, know considerably less about the information needs that face them than does an information practitioner who has, over a period of some years, served previous students undertaking the same course.
>
> Shenton, 2007, 490

Shenton concludes that the framework can be helpful in highlighting stumbling blocks impeding people in their quest to solve their problems and address their needs. Noting Walter's (1994) comments that young children's limited world experience causes them to lack the ability to articulate many important information needs, Shenton (2007) notes that:

> Conceptualising young people's information needs from the Johari Window viewpoint shows that, in terms of this naivety, significant stumbling blocks emerge in two different panes. The onerous task of representing the need in the appropriate language even before it is articulated to another party may be considered [a category 3] problem, and a youngster's ignorance of many of his or her key information needs, thereby perhaps leading to the information professional relying rather too heavily on inferring needs from existing source material, forms a problem within [category 5] .
>
> Shenton, 2007, 493

He acknowledges that with the pervasiveness of modern electronic information systems, people are increasingly carrying out their own searches for information without any mediation by an information professional. There is a danger, he argues, of people missing out on the usefulness of being able to crystallize their information needs in interaction with an information professional, and not defining their needs 'sufficiently precisely to be able to recognise and then work with appropriate material even if they find it' (Shenton, 2007, 494).

Information-related needs

As noted in Chapter 2, there has been increasing recognition that focusing on some 'information need' is not the only, and not necessarily always the best, starting point for thinking about information behaviour. This is especially so if we are focusing on aspects of information behaviour that do not entail seeking information – such as avoiding it. Nor is it, according to Wilson (2006), necessarily the best place to start in thinking about information-seeking behaviour. Wilson argues that there is a basic confusion

> in the association of the two words 'information' and 'need'. This association imbues the resulting concept with connotations of a basic 'need' qualitatively similar to other basic 'human needs'.
>
> Wilson, 2006, 663

He notes that research into human needs more generally has tended to classify them into three interrelated types: physiological needs, cognitive needs and affective needs. Physiological needs include our basic requirement for food and shelter and other bodily needs. Cognitive needs relate to our drive to engage in intellectual activity such as planning and problem-solving. Affective needs are emotional needs such as achievement, reassurance, freedom from anxiety and comfort.

Information seeking is not a need in itself, but rather takes place in order to satisfy a more fundamental need. Wilson went on to suggest that it may be advisable to replace 'information needs' with the concept 'information seeking towards the satisfaction of needs'. But why should a slight shift in terminology matter?

Well, if we think of information seeking as all about 'satisfying information needs', then arguably we are privileging a focus on cognitive aspects of information behaviour, since information is a cognitive construct. This is no bad thing if we are interested primarily in studying information seeking to satisfy cognitive needs. But by equating information seeking with the satisfaction of cognitive needs, we may be inadvertently casting a shade over the importance of information seeking to satisfy affective and physiological needs. This may have the effect that, rather than being thought of as possible needs in their own right, affective and physiological aspects may be considered as essentially contextual factors possibly affecting information seeking to satisfy cognitive needs. Information seeking to satisfy affective and physiological needs is a different phenomenon worthy of research in its own right. Although the process of information seeking is essentially a cognitive activity, the use to which information discovered as a result of it is put may be relevant to satisfying affective or physiological needs.

Also, if we associate information behaviour too exclusively with information seeking and acquisition, we risk shifting focus away from other important aspects, such as fear of information and information avoidance. For this reason, I have used the term 'information-related needs' to address both potential problems.

Figure 3.1 is a diagrammatic representation of the relationships between information needs and information-related needs, and between these and different types of information behaviour including, but not limited to, information seeking and acquisition.

The phrase 'information-related needs' is conceptually compatible with Wilson's recommended reformulation of information needs as 'information seeking to satisfy needs' and encourages a perspective on information behaviour which does not privilege information seeking and acquisition aspects. As noted in Chapter 2, an information need is a need to acquire information to solve some problem or address some gap in our knowledge. Information-related needs, on

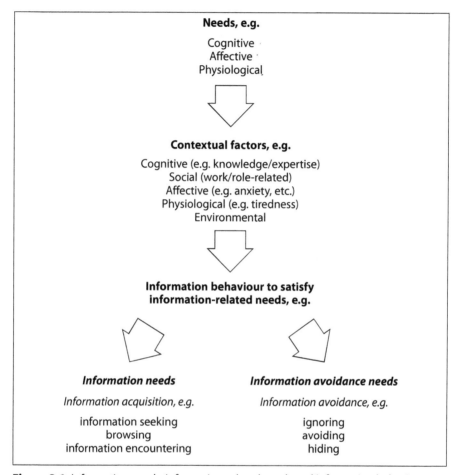

Figure 3.1 Information needs, information-related needs and information behaviour

the other hand, are defined as needs that have implications for the way in which we interact with information, whether seeking or avoiding it. They are more general than, but include, information needs.

An example of information-related needs entailing anxiety about health issues leading to a desire to ignore and avoid information perceived as likely to cause emotional distress, and fear of stigma leading to an avoidance of information seeking, is provided in the work of Namuleme (2013). She conducted an ethnographic study of 40 people infected with or affected by HIV/AIDS. Her investigation revealed some of the subtleties and complexities of information behaviour influenced by affective as well as cognitive and physiological needs. In particular, she found evidence not only of information seeking and sharing, but also of covert information seeking, information behaviour driven by panic and emotion, and information behaviour geared to avoiding, hiding and destroying information.

Summary

This chapter has presented a number of different analyses of information needs. A distinction was drawn between information needs and information-related needs. Information-related needs include but are not limited to information needs, and do not necessarily entail the seeking of information. For example, a person may perceive a need to ignore or avoid information if they fear or are anxious about its implications for them. Such aspects of information behaviour, particularly in health-related contexts, are receiving increasing research interest.

Information needs have long formed a principal focus of research efforts, and researchers have identified a number of aspects which are important to know about if one is dealing with clients as an information professional. There has been increasing awareness that information seeking can be driven by an information need of which a person is not fully aware, and which they are not able effectively to articulate. There has also been increasing interest in forms of information behaviour driven by needs which do not imply seeking and engaging with information, but rather ignoring or avoiding it.

There are arguably a number of implications for information professionals:

- Even assuming that they are perfectly well aware of exactly what information they need, some people may sometimes not be able to articulate this need well enough to use a search tool effectively. Help from an experienced information professional can be useful in translating a client's expression of their information need into an effective system-friendly query – and if necessary iteratively reformulating the query over time as a search progresses.
- People may not always be aware of the precise nature of the real (deep) need underlying their feeling that they need information. Again, an experienced information professional can be helpful in teasing out this deeper need.
- The latter point may also relate to information-related needs such as a desire to avoid information. Clearly, there is a basic problem here in that a person wishing to avoid information is hardly likely to present to an information professional with an expressed desire to seek information.

But there may be other channels, opportunities and encounters with people where this disconnect may be apparent to an information professional. An example is drawn from Namuleme's (2013) research described above. Some people affected by HIV/AIDS feared that being seen to seek or engage with information about the disease and its treatment could reveal their HIV-positive status, resulting in their suffering undesirable social, mental and sometimes physical effects of stigma. If information professionals and others involved in supporting people affected by HIV/AIDS are aware of such difficulties they are able to organize more private access to needed information than simply making provision in public libraries and other locations that, from the perspective of an HIV/AIDS sufferer, are highly visible and exposed.

- The research described above suggests that it may sometimes be useful for information professionals to attempt consciously to take a more holistic view of a client's needs than one restricted to the expressed query presented to them, and to be aware of the possibility of unexpressed aspects of a client's needs. Exploring the potential utility of a framework such as that provided by Johari may be useful in this respect.
- At the same time, in considering how to tease out and explore deeper and possibly latent needs, information professionals must be aware of potential difficulties, not least of ethical problems that may be associated with such activities to the extent that they may entail highly sensitive issues.

To explore further the concept of information needs, the reader is referred to Chapter 4 of Case (2012) and to Cole (2012).

References

Belkin, N. J., Oddy, R. N. and Brooks, H. M. (1982) ASK for Information Retrieval: part I. Background and theory, *Journal of Documentation*, **38** (2), 61–71.

Bourdieu, P. (1984) *Distinction: a social critique of the judgement of taste*, London, Routledge.

Case, D. (2012) *Looking for Information: a survey of research on information seeking, needs and behaviour*, 3rd edn, Bingley, Emerald.

Cole, C. (2012) *Information Need: a theory connecting information search to knowledge formation*, Medford NJ, Information Today.

Dervin, B. (1991) Comparative Theory Reconceptualized: from entities and states to processes and dynamics, *Communication Theory*, **1** (1), 59–69.

Ford, N. (2012) *The Essential Guide to Using the Web for Research*, London, Sage.

Gibson, J. J. (1979) The Theory of Affordances. In Shaw, R. and Bransford, J. (eds), *Perceiving, Acting, Knowing*, Hillsdale, NJ, Lawrence Erlbaum.

Klein, G., Moon, B. and Hoffman, R. (2006) Making Sense of Sensemaking 1: alternative perspectives, *Intelligent Systems*, **21** (4), 71.

Kolko, J. (2010) *Sensemaking and Framing: a theoretical reflection on perspective in design synthesis*, Austin, TX, Austin Center for Design, www.designresearchsociety.org/docs-procs/DRS2010/PDF/067.pdf.

Lloyd, A. (2006) Information Literacy Landscapes: an emerging picture, *Journal of Documentation*, **62** (5), 570–83.

Lloyd, A., Kennan, M. A., Thompson, K. M. and Qayyum, A. (2013) Connecting with New Information Landscapes: information literacy practices of refugees, *Journal of Documentation*, **69** (1), 121–44.

Luft, J. and Ingham, H. (1955) The Johari Window: a graphic model of interpersonal awareness, *Proceedings of the Western Training Laboratory in Group Development*, Los Angeles, CA, UCLA (University of California at Los Angeles).

Namuleme, R. K. (2013) *Information and HIV/AIDS: an ethnographic study of information behaviour*, PhD thesis, University of Sheffield.

Savolainen, R. (1993) The Sense-making Theory: reviewing the interests of a user-centered approach to information seeking and use, *Information Processing & Management*, **29** (1), 13–28.

Savolainen, R. (1995) Everyday Life Information Seeking: approaching information seeking in the context of 'way of life', *Library & Information Science Research*, **17** (3), 259–94.

Savolainen, R. (2008) *Everyday Information Practice: a social phenomenological perspective*, Lanham, MD, Scarecrow Press.

Shenton, A. K. (2007) Viewing Information Needs Through a Johari Window, *Reference Services Review*, **35** (3), 487–96.

Taylor, R. S. (1962) The Process of Asking Questions, *American Documentation*, **13** (4), 391–6.

Taylor, R. S. (1968) Question-negotiation and Information Seeking in Libraries, *College and Research Libraries*, **29**, 178–94.

Walter, V. A. (1994) The Information Needs of Children. In Godden, I. P. (ed.), *Advances in Librarianship*, Vol. 18, Academic Press, London, 111–29.

Wilson, T. D. (2006) On User Studies and Information Needs, *Journal of Documentation*, **62** (6), 658–70.

PART 2

What do we know of information behaviour?

4

Information seeking and acquisition are key components of information behaviour

Introduction

Information seeking is only one component in the broader concept of information behaviour, which (as we have seen in Chapter 3) includes behaviours such as information avoidance – the converse of information seeking – as well as information evaluation and use. However, it has formed the basis for much work in information behaviour over many years, and it continues to be a major element of study. Indeed, in her review of trends in information behaviour research between 2012 and 2014, Greifeneder (2014) concludes that 'information seeking is still the major topic of interest'. The following sections introduce some of the major milestones in our understanding of information seeking.

People may seek information in many different ways, using very different strategies, and the choice of strategy made by people and groups may be influenced by many factors. These can relate to their psychological make-up, the nature of their goals, their attitudes and their perceptions, and the context within which they are operating. The present chapter focuses on describing the nature of these strategies. Factors affecting the adoption of particular strategies will be discussed in Chapter 6.

Strategies 4+6

Basic information-seeking processes and activities

A number of writers have proposed simple models of the information-seeking process entailing a cycle of actions, including identification of an information need, formulation of a query to a search tool and inspection of the search results – in the light of which the query may be reformulated, looping into a fresh query. Sutcliffe and Ennis' (1998) model, for example, consists of four main activities:

- problem identification
- articulation of information need
- query formulation
- results evaluation.

Marchionini and White (2007) expand these basic activities to include:

- **Recognition of a need for information** (cognitive)
  This is an intellectual (cognitive) stage in which a need is perceived.
- **Acceptance of the challenge to take action to fulfil the need**
  This stage is motivational in that it entails an affective (emotional) commitment to do something about the perceived need.
- **Problem formulation**
  This stage entails figuring out the nature of the need (what it comprises, and what are its boundaries), thinking about the kind of information that will be required to satisfy the need, and identifying potential sources of information.
- **Expression of the information need using a search system.**
- **Examination of the results of the search**
  In the case of all but the simplest of queries, typically the results initially retrieved will not completely satisfy the information need. This may lead to a number of iterations whereby the user re-expresses his/her need, or reformulates the problem.
- **Deciding when to stop the search**
- **Using the resultant information**
  Models such as these map out the basic processes involved in seeking information using a search system (such as a search engine). Most modern models recognize the iterative nature of the information-seeking process, especially in relation to expressing one's need, examining search results and re-expressing the need, or reformulating the need, in the light of feedback on its ongoing success or failure. Information discovered during a search can change the searcher's knowledge of the topic area and may result in a reformulation of his or her original need.

A model which has become well established, and tested in environments other than that in which it was created (a study of academic researchers) is that of Ellis (Ellis, 1989; Ellis, Cox and Hall, 1993; Ellis and Haugan, 1997). Ellis identified different components of the information-seeking behaviour of academics. His focus was on cognitive aspects of the information-seeking behaviour of individuals in formal, systematic information-seeking contexts

(as opposed, for example, to everyday information seeking by the general
public). The categories of activity identified by Ellis are as follows:

Ellis

- **Starting**
  Identifying information sources that are potentially starting points for
  seeking information.
- **Chaining**
  Following up leads from sources identified in information sources
  consulted. Backward chaining entails following up references cited in an
  information source you are consulting. Forward chaining involves
  finding citations *to* an information source you are consulting in new
  information sources.
- **Browsing**
  Scanning documents in the hope of finding useful information. This may
  entail flipping through a journal, scanning indexes or tables of contents,
  scanning library shelves, etc.
- **Differentiating**
  Selecting those sources, from all those of which you have become aware,
  that seem potentially most useful. Criteria for selection may include not
  only relevance, but approach and quality as judged, for example, from
  reviews or the opinions of colleagues.
- **Monitoring**
  Keeping watch on sources identified as likely to contain relevant
  information relating to an identified area of interest. Core journals may
  be scanned regularly for new articles, or a particular database search
  may be repeated regularly in order to become aware of new information.
- **Extracting**
  Working through information sources already identified as potentially
  containing useful information in order to identify useful information
  actually contained within them.
- **Verifying**
  Checking the accuracy of information.
- **Ending**
  Conducting a final search for information at the end of the project.

Apart from starting and ending, these activities are not necessarily sequential
stages, and may be deployed iteratively and in different orders.

This model has been studied extensively by others as well as Ellis, and has
been found to be a valid model of this type of information seeking. That is,
the model has been used successfully to describe information behaviour in a

range of contexts, including the information-seeking behaviour of physicists and chemists, industrial engineers and scientists, and humanities scholars. The model is descriptive rather than explanatory. That is, it tells us *what* people do but does not seek to explain *why* they do it.

Kuhlthau (2004) also produced a model of information seeking in her Information Search Process model, which entails the activities shown below. Unlike Ellis' model, that of Kuhlthau represents the activities as *sequential* stages. Kuhlthau's stages are: ~~sequential~~

- **Task initiation**
  Preparing to select a specific topic.
- **Topic selection**
  Choosing a topic on which to focus.
- **Pre-focus exploration**
  General familiarization with the topic prior to more detailed and focused study.
- **Focus formulation**
  Selecting a particular aspect of the topic which will form the precise focus of the study.
- **Information collection**
  Seeking information relevant to the topic.
- **Presentation**
  After deciding that no further information should be sought, using the retrieved information, e.g. to explain it to others and/or put it to some use.

Also unlike Ellis' model, it embraces affective (emotional) as well as cognitive (intellectual) processes. Affective aspects are discussed in Chapters 5 and 6. Wilson (1999) later compared the models of Ellis and Kuhlthau, attempting to map elements of Ellis' model onto Kuhlthau's sequential stages, producing a model integrating the two, as shown in Figure 4.1.

Some of the processes involved in information seeking may be conducted in very different ways – using different modes, sequences and strategies of activity – and a number of models have been developed which reflect this.

THINK!

How else might you obtain the information you need? The models described above seem logical. But think of your own information-seeking experience. Have there been times when you have obtained useful or interesting information – but not through searching for it as described above? Take a moment to think about this before reading on . . .

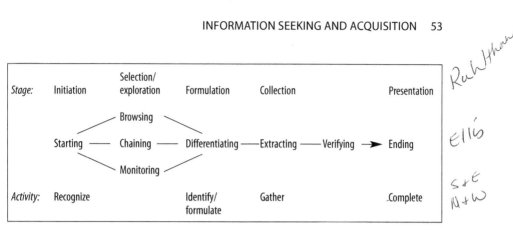

Figure 4.1 Wilson's combined model blending those of Ellis and Kuhlthau

Not all models of acquiring information entail using a search system as such
– for example, information may be sought by browsing rather than searching
(you are still seeking information when you are browsing). The processes and
activities entailed in information seeking can be conducted in different modes
– from passive to active and from directed to relatively undirected. In a review
of information-seeking research Wilson (1997), for example, identified a
number of different modes of seeking and acquiring information, which
consisted of:

- **Passive attention**
  This mode of acquiring information does not entail actively searching for
  it. People may often come across information relevant to some need
  when casually reading, watching the television or listening to the radio.
  The information need is not uppermost in their mind at the time, and
  was not the reason for choosing to attend to the information source.
- **Passive search**
  Wilson acknowledges that this mode seems to be a contradiction in
  terms, but notes that it 'signifies those occasions when one type of search
  (or other behaviour) results in the acquisition of information that
  happens to be relevant to the individual' (Wilson, 1997, 562). Thus, a
  search for information in relation to one information need might
  unexpectedly throw up information relevant to another.
- **Active search**
  This is the mode of information seeking in which the seeker sets out
  specifically to search for information on his or her topic of interest.
- **Ongoing search**
  Wilson uses this term to refer to occasional searching to update or
  expand knowledge previously acquired by other methods on a topic.

Information-seeking strategies

Adopting a relatively passive or active mode implies a strategic decision on the part of the information seeker. Adopting a *strategy* implies making a *choice* from alternative ways of going about a task. Thus an information seeker may choose, for example, a browsing or a search strategy at different times or for different information-seeking tasks. A number of different information-seeking strategies identified in the research literature are presented below.

Browsing and monitoring

We have already mentioned browsing and monitoring as components in the models of Ellis, Kuhlthau and Wilson described above. However, we focus in on these activities in more detail here, since there is increasing interest in information-seeking strategies other than those which entail active focused searching.

Marchionini's (1995) description of different types of browsing includes activities that range from the relatively active and directed to the more passive and unfocused. He differentiated three types of browsing, based on (a) the specificity of the information targeted and (b) the extent to which the person makes use of systematic tactics:

- **Directed browsing** entails scanning one or more information sources in a systematic way, looking for specific information. This might include, for example, scanning a number of journal papers looking for a specific piece of information.
- **Semi-directed browsing** is halfway between directed and undirected, and refers to a situation in which the person is actively searching, but not in an intensive systematic and focused way. An example is entering a general word into a search engine and browsing through what is retrieved to see if there is anything interesting.
- **Undirected browsing** refers to a situation in which the person is not focusing on any specific information need – for example, when flipping through a magazine.

Bates (2002) separates out the two dimensions of activity/passivity and directedness/undirectedness, which in fact can operate independently of each other. She uses these dimensions to differentiate between monitoring and browsing. Monitoring entails relatively directed but passive activity. Browsing is relatively undirected but more active.

In the case of monitoring, we have a topic or question in the background of our mind, and maintain alertness to coming across anything relevant. We do not engage in active effort to find anything. In the case of browsing, we actively engage in scanning one or more information sources in the hope of finding something of interest. The difference is that we do not have the same degree of focus or specificity relating to what we hope to find. Bates makes the point that monitoring (like active searching) is a strategy for finding information that we know we need. Browsing is a strategy for finding information that we do not know we need.

Many models, including those described so far in this chapter, have been based on the information seeking of *individuals*, in many cases working on individual research or coursework in academic environments. However, a number of researchers have focused more on information seeking within *organizations.* Choo, Detler and Turnbull (1999), for example, based on work by Weick and Daft (1983), Daft and Weick (1984) and Marchionini (1995), distinguish between different types of information seeking used by organizations. These types of information seeking relate both to Wilson's active search and to his more passive information-seeking categories. They are:

- **Undirected viewing**
  Associated with scanning a wide range of information sources in what the authors describe as a 'sweeping' information-seeking strategy, linked to browsing and serendipitous discovery. This is geared to trying to identify early signs of change.
- **Conditioned viewing**
  Relates to more focused inspection of particular topics and/or particular information sources, in what is described as a 'discriminating' strategy linked to building understanding about the topic. This is geared to evaluating the potential significance of the information or developments identified.
- **Informal search**
  Entails seeking information in a relatively casual (not particularly rigorous or exhaustive) way in a 'satisficing' strategy (geared to finding information that is 'good enough') linked to elaborating on the topic of interest, in order to assess whether the organization needs to act/respond.
- **Formal search**
  Involves a more planned, focused and systematic 'optimizing' information-seeking strategy relating to a particular issue. The intention is to gather the best available (rather than just 'good enough') information that will be useful to the organization in addressing the issue.

The studies described above all focus on the component activities entailed in information behaviour. Some of these represent types of activity – whether sequential *stages* (e.g. Kuhlthau's initiation, selection, exploration, collection and presentation) or activities which are not necessarily sequential (e.g. Ellis' browsing, chaining and monitoring, which Wilson groups as taking place within Kuhlthau's selection and exploration stages). Others represent *modes* of information behaviour – e.g. Wilson's passive and active seeking, and Choo, Detlor and Turnbull's formal and informal. In the following section we will explore another strategic approach to information seeking which relates to the relative breadth of focus.

Broad and narrow strategies

Ford (2002) has mapped four broad types of information-seeking strategy onto key components of learning proposed by Gordon Pask. Based on extensive research over many years, Pask (1976a, 1976b and 1988) formed a theory of human information processing in which he claimed that all learning (whether formal or informal) consists of two basic components: descriptions and procedures.

A 'description' (in Pask's technical sense) is a conceptual overview of a topic to be learned. He used an architectural analogy to characterize descriptions as the overall functional and aesthetic design of a building – what the building should enable and facilitate, what it should look like, and how it fits into its surroundings. Procedures, on the other hand, relate to the mechanics of how components of the building actually work – for example, the wiring and plumbing systems.

The building example is an analogy for all learning. Whether conceptualizing and solving a problem, or preparing and writing an essay, description-building and procedure-building are necessary to achieve full understanding. In terms of, say, an academic essay, the description is the broad conceptual overview of the topic and its main components, and how these fit together to form an overall 'big picture'. Procedures are the more detailed evidence and logical argument that support the overall picture.

Effective learning entails both 'description building' and 'procedure building'. Description building is all about relating ideas to synthesize a conceptual overview. Procedure building is all about analysing the factual and procedural details that support the overview. Both are necessary. The overall picture lacking supporting detail risks incorrect over-generalization. The details without an overall map (big picture) represent 'failing to see the wood for the trees'.

The strategies described by Ford are shown in Table 4.1. These categories relate particularly to complex information seeking in academic contexts, but the general principle of broader and narrower searching to support the acquisition of an overall picture and supporting detail are relevant more widely. Broad and specific search map onto Pask's description and procedure building. Factors which influence the adoption of these different strategies will be explored in Chapter 6.

The point about strategies is that people may approach ostensibly the same task in very different ways. According to Pask, if they are to achieve full learning, they need to use *both* description building and procedure building. But his experiments discovered that different people may deploy them at different times, in different sequences and with different levels of intensity and success.

Ford further investigated these strategies in relation to information seeking, identifying search strategies that emphasize either breadth or depth in terms of the sequence of activity (broad searching before narrower more detailed searching or vice versa). A number of such strategies were identified in a

Table 4.1 Broad and narrow information-seeking strategies		
Broad search	Searching for information to satisfy description building where the person is focusing on relating ideas to synthesize the 'big picture'. Information is sought to establish a good conceptual map of the topic, in which the individual components are inter-linked to form a coherent whole.	
	Broad exploratory searching	Exploring the literature broadly but not too deeply to form an initial (provisional) overview. It entails adopting a wide-ranging focus as you gather a collection of information sources for subsequent more detailed consideration.
	Broad exhaustive searching	Checking that no important information has been missed rather than exploring new territory.
Specific search	More narrowly focused searching compared to broad search, entailing searching for information to enable procedure building – the close examination of details and evidence supporting the overview established during description building.	
	Specific detailed search	Finding information sources enabling a detailed study of the specifics of the topic under investigation which provide sufficient depth for you to build detailed understanding of the topic.
	Highly specific detailed search	Checking that you have not missed any important details, and making sure your claims and arguments are thoroughly supported by evidence and stand up to detailed scrutiny. This entails exercising great control over the search in order to specify what is needed with high levels of precision.

study by Ford and Ford (1993) in which university students were asked to learn about the topic of indexing by searching for information in a specially constructed database. Four types of searcher were identified:

- **Deependers**
  These searchers dived straight into the details of the topic, following a line of inquiry that took them directly (within the first few questions they posed to the database) to the lowest most detailed level in the hierarchy of knowledge about the indexing system they were learning about contained in the database.
- **Midpoolers**
  Midpoolers took almost exclusive interest from the start in a level of detail that avoided extremes of either generality or fine detail.
- **Consolidators**
  These people preferred to work their way down to (as opposed to diving headlong into) greater, detail, then worked back and forth methodically across the levels, placing the detail they obtained within its broader context.
- **Shallowenders**
  People searching in this way placed early emphasis on top level overview material.

The basic distinction between relatively shallow (overview-oriented) and deeper (detail-oriented) searching strategies was mirrored in a later study by Heinström (2002). Unlike the small-scale experimental study by Ford and Ford, Heinström's larger-scale study identified strategies based on a self-report questionnaire. As in Ford and Ford's study, individuals seemed to be typed by the way they tended to go about searching for information, and she labelled them 'fast surfers,' 'broad scanners' and 'deep divers'. Their characteristics were as follows:

- **Fast surfers** These searchers engaged in relatively shallow engagement, in that they adopted a 'least effort' approach, spending relatively little time searching, and not engaging in deep critical evaluation of information.
- **Broad scanners** Broad scanners were active and flexible in their information seeking, using a wide range of information sources. They reported often encountering information serendipitously.
- **Deep divers** These searchers worked hard in an attempt to obtain high-quality reliable information.

THINK!

Thinking of your own information seeking over, say, the past year, do you recognize any of these strategies?

For example, if you are learning about a new topic do you generally like to establish a good overview before getting down to detail? Or do you prefer to get 'stuck in' and let the big picture emerge later?

Do you have a consistent approach – or does it all depend on the nature of what it is you are learning about?

There is evidence that many people display stylistic preferences and strengths in relation to how they go about learning, problem solving and related information seeking. Some people do seem to tend consistently (across different tasks) to prefer an approach whereby they begin by trying to establish a good overview before they get down to finer detail. Others tend to adopt a 'brick by brick' approach, mastering one aspect or sub-topic thoroughly before moving on to the next. Pask did also find evidence of people displaying what he termed 'versatility', seemingly being equally at home with either approach or mixture, as they deemed appropriate to any given task (Pask, 1976a; 1976b; 1988). This would not seem to be related to ability, however. Ford (1985) found evidence that even high-achieving postgraduate Masters students displayed distinct preferences for either a broad overview-first style or narrower details-first style of information processing.

Note that strategies may be purely stylistic, representing different routes to the same result. Thus, one may acquire information to help solve a problem or learn something using a breadth-first approach (starting with 'description building' – seeking to establish a good overview of the topic before going on to flesh out the details) or a depth-first approach (starting with 'procedure building' – generating understanding bit by bit, the overview emerging relatively later on). Using either approach it is possible in the end to achieve the same level of understanding.

However, there is also evidence that such strategies can lead to different levels and types of understanding. This may occur when people engage in either description building or procedure building to the relative exclusion of the other. This results in relatively surface as opposed to deep understanding, which is explored in the next section.

Deep and shallow approaches

Description building without sufficient complementary procedure building results in inaccurate over-generalization – generating an invalid overview which does not stand up to detailed scrutiny. Procedure building without sufficient description building results in 'not being able to see the wood for the trees' – generating understanding of fragmented details but failing to see the 'big picture'.

A number of information behaviour strategies have been identified which relate to relatively deep and surface levels of understanding, for example those reported by the CIBER research group at University College London (University College London, 2008).The CIBER researchers report the results of an extensive literature review, coupled with the analysis of user log files from e-journal databases, e-book collections and research gateways, including British Library and Jisc websites used by people of varying ages. In relation to the way in which scholars search digital libraries, they identified a pattern of information seeking characterized by:

- relatively 'horizontal' or 'skimming' (as opposed to deeper) information seeking, entailing viewing a very small number of pages before exiting. Approximately 60% of people view three pages or fewer, some 65% never returning. The authors refer to this as 'bouncing'.
- 'power browsing' titles, contents pages and abstracts, apparently 'going for quick wins'.
- evaluating the authority of sources quickly by 'dipping and cross-checking across different sites and relying on favoured brands (e.g. Google).'

The report also makes a number of observations about the information seeking of young people of the 'Google generation'. These are people born after 1993. Their conclusions are that young people:

- do not have a good understanding of their information needs
- find it hard to develop effective search strategies, and tend to use simple searches using natural language rather than crafting any more effective search strategy
- make little use of advanced search features, and tend to assume that a search engine understands what it is they are looking for
- prefer to use search tools that require relatively little skill, such as a search engine rather than more scholarly databases and portals
- spend little time evaluating the relevance and trustworthiness of information retrieved, often printing them without examining them in any detail

and that:

- children tend to make simple relevance judgments based on the presence of absence of words that describe exactly their topic, therefore missing potentially relevant information.

Many of these behaviours pre-date the internet, and the report concludes that there is no evidence that young people's information skills have improved or deteriorated over the past 25 years.

The relatively shallow, least effort and 'easy win' search strategies reported in the CIBER Report are reflected in one of a number of information-seeking patterns identified by Mansourian (Mansourian and Ford, 2007). Based on a study of academic researchers, he identified four types of information-seeking strategy, which he classified in two dimensions. The first dimension related to the amount of *effort* expended by the searcher. The second related to the *importance* of information which the person anticipates will be missed by not continuing the search. Mansourian's strategies are as follows:

- **Perfunctory**
  The searcher is not aware of possibly missed information, performs a relatively straightforward search, and trusts that it has provided effective results that do not require further more complex searching.
- **Minimalist**
  The searcher feels that although s/he has probably missed some information, what has been retrieved is sufficient and it is not worth expending the effort to go on searching.
- **Nervous**
  The searcher fears that some important information may have been missed, and for this reason is not sure about when it is safe to stop searching.
- **Extensive**
  The searcher feels that it is highly likely that s/he will miss important information if s/he does not make extensive efforts to search as effectively as s/he can.

Mansourian went on to explore factors that influenced choice of strategy. Since this chapter is focusing on different *forms* of information seeking and searching, the influencing factors that might affect a person in relation to adopting a particular strategy are explored in Chapter 6.

Non-linear information seeking

However, even more active and directed information seeking (as opposed to browsing and coming across information accidentally) is by no means always linear and logical.

Although Taylor (1968, 179) refers to information inquiry as a 'shifting non-linear adaptive mechanism', early models of information seeking often assumed that people search for information in a relatively sequential and systematic way. The search situation was characterized as a question of matching (a) a description (expressed by the person wanting information) of what information was required, with (b) descriptions of documents indexed by the search tool being used. At the simplest level, a search engine would search its index to retrieve any documents containing the keywords used by the searcher to describe the information needed. Although later models took account of the fact that searchers may iteratively modify their search queries in the light of what is retrieved (assuming that they are not completely satisfied with what is found first), the process was still essentially one of progressively 'homing in' on the required information.

An early model of information seeking that countered such a view was Bates' (1989) 'berrypicking'. This model acknowledged the fact that information seeking can be much less planned, ordered and sequential. Information seeking by no means always consists of a relatively static goal and incremental progress towards it. We have seen in Chapter 3 how conceptions of information need can range from the relatively simple and static to a more complex view of needs as evolving over time and having different characteristics at different information-seeking stages.

In her research, Bates found that people could take a more meandering path, picking up information at one point then moving off in another direction depending on what information had been found. Information seeking was an evolving process in which decisions about where to search – and indeed, what to search for – could change as a result of information found at different points in the process. Bates drew an analogy with wandering around picking huckleberries, rather than planning a route and sticking to it until the information required was found.

Non-linear aspects of information seeking formed the focus of a model of information-seeking behaviour developed, on the basis of his doctoral research, by Foster (2004). His 'non-linear model of information seeking behaviour' proposes three core processes (Opening, Orientation, and Consolidation). These processes are affected by various factors relating to *external context* (e.g. the effects of a person's social networking connections in enabling or restricting access to relevant information, time pressures, etc.), *internal context* (e.g. feelings of uncertainty, self-efficacy, etc.), and what Foster terms *cognitive approach* (e.g. mental agility, open-mindedness , 'nomadic' thinking – the ability to approach a topic in diverse ways). Foster concludes that:

> [T]he concepts, represented in the interactivity of the core processes, and the absence of stages in the model, are analogous to an information seeker holding a palette of information behaviour opportunities, with the whole palette available at any given moment. The interactivity and shifts described by the model show information seeking to be non-linear, dynamic, holistic, and flowing.
>
> Foster, 2004, 235

'Easy win' strategies

One of the keys to understanding why information seeking may not always appear to be such a linear and rational process lies in viewing information behaviour within the context of human behaviour more generally, and the way this has evolved as our species has adapted to the environment in which we find ourselves. Cole proposes that:

> Information need is at its deepest level primarily a human adaptive mechanism – at the level of human perception, at the level of society and the world in which the individual operates, and at the level of survival as a species.
>
> Cole, 2012, 78

Evolutionary perspectives focus on information behaviour in terms of its ultimately being a basic adaptive mechanism. Although overlaid with sophisticated logical, rational strategies and mechanisms, basic drives can still be perceived. Arguably, such drives can be useful in explaining and predicting information behaviour.

This perspective is compatible with the view of information behaviour as not exclusively a logical, rational, intellectual response to the need to acquire information. It helps to explain observations that often people seem to take a least-effort approach to finding information, and why people may adopt meandering information-seeking strategies such as berrypicking.

Indeed, 'information foraging' theory is derived from such a perspective. Evolutionary theory suggests that humans have learned to weigh up the amount of energy a particular course of action is likely to take, and the value of the reward it is likely to lead to.

Pirolli and Card (1995) considered that adopting such an evolutionary perspective might be able to illuminate information behaviour. They argued that information-seeking behaviour can be interpreted as essentially an adaptation of human food-gathering behaviour. When hunting for food, early humans calculated the balance between the amount of effort and energy expended and the value of the reward likely to be gained by this expenditure. This is a basic mechanism which can be applied to our information behaviour. We calculate the effort required to find the information we need, and the value that the information would bring to us, and we are careful not to expend more effort than would be justified by the reward. Over time we develop skill and judgement in this process, and it may become subconscious. The goal is optimizing the balance between effort and reward rather than simply maximizing the information we obtain.

Pirolli and Card proposed that when we search for information, we look for the 'scent' of the best information 'patch'. A frequent observation is that when using a search engine, people will focus on the first few hits at the top of the search results page. In this case, the top of the page is associated with the strongest 'scent' (the highest relevance of documents to our need). If we find that this scent is not very strong (there are no highly relevant documents in the first few hits), then rather than ploughing through the second and third pages of hits, we modify our search and try again in the hope that the scent (at the top of the first page) will become stronger. To an extent, this represents an attempt to reduce the effort required to find information.

Indeed, a recurrent theme in research into information seeking is the principle of least effort. Whilst by no means applying generally, this does seem to be a fundamental driving force. The CIBER Report previously described above, in relation to the information-seeking strategies of researchers also makes a number of observations about the information seeking of young people of the 'Google generation' (see p. 60).

Relatively recently, there has been increasing research interest in ways in which people come across information that do not entail the conscious seeking of information. The following section explores this issue in detail.

Serendipity

Serendipity refers to encountering information by accident. Whilst it may seem more likely to be associated with undirected and passive rather than directed and active behaviour, it is independent of these dimensions in that – to the extent that it is accidental – it may occur at any time. Information that we find interesting, or that is relevant to some need that is not currently the focus on our conscious activity, may be encountered when we are actively searching, monitoring or browsing with something else in mind. It may also occur when we are reading for general interest or pleasure, listening to the radio, watching the television or talking with a friend.

THINK!

Have you encountered useful information by chance, without actively looking for it?

If so – is it a very rare occurrence, or has it happened quite a lot? Take a few moments to think about this before reading on . . .

Erdelez (1999) published pioneering work in which she identified four groups of people who differed in terms of the intensity with which they encountered information serendipitously. These differences are based on people's perceptions when asked to recall how frequently this occurs to them.

- **Non-encounterers** reported that they seldom, if ever, encounter information.
- **Occasional encounterers** reported that this does happen from time to time.
- For **encounterers**, the experience happened quite frequently.
- **Super-encounterers** come across unexpected information on a regular basis, and consider it an important route to obtain information. As well as encountering information of personal relevance, they often reported encountering information of use to people with whom they had contact (friends and colleagues).

Erdelez also observed that often people reported a move from relatively negative feelings before an information-encountering event – for example frustration at a lack of progress in finding information for an assignment – to more positive feelings afterwards. She went on to draw out possible implications for information professionals when interacting with people who have consulted them for help in finding information:

> Information encountering may explain why users sometimes do not appear to behave rationally, why they change the focus of their questions during a reference interview and why they sometimes do not follow search directions provided by librarians. In their contacts with users, information service providers should be aware of information encountering and the 'cross-pollination' among users' various problems and interest areas. Information professionals should facilitate or listen for evidence of these different levels and

types of needs that users hold and that users may need answered in parallel with the needs initially presented.

Erdelez, 1999, 28

The notion of serendipity arose spontaneously from a series of interviews in a study by Foster (Foster and Ford, 2003) on the information behaviour of humanities researchers. The interviewees were asked to describe their information-seeking behaviour, and in the accounts there were many references to coming across information by chance. Foster went on to classify these accounts, using two dimensions of difference.

These dimensions related to the extent to which the person (a) unexpectedly came across information that they had been looking for but did not know where or how to find, or (b) unexpectedly came across information that they had not anticipated (i.e. that they did not know that they wanted). Interestingly, the latter category sometimes led them into some unexpected new direction in their research, as opposed to just providing more support for their current direction.

THINK!

If you can think back to an occasion when you came across information serendipitously, to what extent was your encounter *entirely* due to luck? Was there *anything* about the situation – the place, the time, or what you were doing or thinking – that with hindsight made even a small contribution to your encountering the information?

There is an old saying relating to sports: 'The harder I train and prepare, the luckier I seem to get on the field'. Do you think that there is anything you can do to 'make your own luck' – even to a small degree – when it comes to encountering information?

It's good to think about your own views on information encountering now when we have just been discussing it. But make a note of your thoughts relating to this **THINK!** box, because your thoughts will feed into a broader discussion in Chapter 6, which will discuss a wide range of factors that may influence the way in which people go about seeking and acquiring information.

Case study: serendipity

Before moving on to explore collaborative aspects of information behaviour, let us look at a research study which focused on serendipity in the context of the information seeking of interdisciplinary university researchers in the humanities.

In his study, Foster (Foster and Ford, 2003) adopted a qualitative approach, entailing in-depth interviews with a range of researchers. The research was inductive (see Chapter 8 for a discussion of inductive and deductive, qualitative and quantitative research) meaning that concepts emerged from the data rather than being pre-specified by the researcher. Many interesting findings emerged from his study, which formed a basis for Foster's non-linear model of information behaviour described above. The interviewees were asked to describe their information-seeking behaviour, and in the accounts there were many references to coming across information by chance. Foster went on to focus on this aspect of his data, and made a specific analysis specifically to investigate:

- the extent to which interdisciplinary academic researchers experience serendipity
- whether there are different levels and types of 'serendipity'
- the extent to which serendipity is perceived as something that is completely beyond our influence to bring it about
- if it is to some extent possible to bring it about, what strategies might allow us to do this.

The researcher found that in the sample of interdisciplinary researchers studied, coming across information serendipitously was widely experienced. However, the nature of serendipitous encounters differed. Interviewees reported finding information the existence and/or location of which was unexpected. However, there were differences in the impact such serendipitously encountered information had on their research. Information serendipitously encountered may fill some gap that the researchers were trying to fill in their knowledge. However, sometimes the impact of the information on their research was also unexpected, taking their research in some new unanticipated directions. Thus, serendipitously encountering information could strengthen or reinforce the researcher's existing conception or solution of his or her research problem – or take the research in a new direction entailing the reconception or reconfiguration of the problem and/or its solution in some way.

Foster's model of serendipitous information encountering consists of six categories relating to the nature of the encountering and the impact it had on the researchers' work. According to the model, a person may:

1 come across information the need for which they had anticipated, and the probable location where it was likely to be found was also

anticipated. However, this category relates to browsing and searching rather than serendipitous information encountering, to which the other categories do relate.

2   come across information when searching in a place they deem likely to turn up potentially useful information – but be surprised by (did not anticipate) the nature of the information they actually came across and exactly how it would be useful.

3   recognize that they have unexpectedly come across information they knew they needed, but when they were not looking in some likely place.

4   come across information which they find to be of unexpected value. They did not anticipate the information they had come across or the unexpected use to which it might be put. Naturally, they were not aware of any particular location where such unexpected information might turn up.

Foster and Ford included categories relating to the type of usefulness of information encountered in these various ways.

5   Where the nature of what information was needed was known to the person, although the location in which it was likely to be found was not known to them, the nature of its usefulness was as anticipated when it was encountered. In other words, it did not tend to take their ideas in some new unanticipated direction, but illuminated (e.g. strengthened or confirmed) their existing research problem structure and/or solution.

6   However, when they came across new information the nature of which they had not anticipated, this could result in the generation of new ideas and directions in that their research problem structure or solution might be reconfigured or a new direction taken.

Categories 1–4 relate to the process involved in *finding* of information; categories 5 and 6 to the *impact* the information had. Categories 1, 3 and 5 relate to cases where researchers knew the type of information they needed and how it would be useful. Categories 2, 4 and 6 relate to cases where the researchers found information that had unexpected value – taking their research in some new unanticipated direction. An example of where the nature of information needed was known is provided by the following extract from one interview:

> . . . and one of the things that I was interested in was had anybody else done it, so then I started doing a broad search, and starting off with just 'interpreter' and

'sign language' keywords and I was coming up with virtually nothing. . . . Then one day I was just sort of sitting in a waiting room – waiting for a colleague – and I just happened to pick up a fairly old nursing journal and flipped open a page and right there in front of me was a person doing the same job in Scotland that we were planning for Sheffield.

Foster and Ford, 2003, 332

The following illustrates where the value of the information encountered was not anticipated:

. . . one would go through quite a number of channels that one would expect researchers to go through, but I also find that it is the chance factors that are interesting, you hear something on the wireless, and you hear someone say something and it is something that you haven't come across and you recognize it as important, and so you have got another avenue to pursue.

Foster and Ford, 2003, 333

An example of category 2 would be when a researcher is browsing library shelves covering the topic of his research and unexpectedly comes across a previously unknown book on his topic. Another example would be deliberately searching the literature of another discipline which the researcher thinks is likely to throw up some new perspective on his topic:

Well, I think, I am always on the lookout for new avenues, and I think that has always been the way that I work, I don't expect to find things, I am always looking for new viewpoints anyway so I might actually search within an area. For instance I don't normally search the sociology literature, but I might get a sense that I should just have a look in that literature and see what it brings up.

Foster and Ford, 2003, 333

An example of category 3 would be casually listening to the radio and hearing an item describing similar work being done by another researcher of whom one was unaware. If learning about this new work helped the researcher make further progress but did not take his/her research in unanticipated new directions, it would be an example of category 5. If it did result in a reconception or reconfiguration of the research problem, then it would be an example of category 6. Clearly these differences are a matter of degree rather than being clear-cut categories.

The research went on to explore whether the interviewees felt that they could exercise any sort of influence over the extent to which they experienced serendipitous information encounters. A number of them did feel that serendipity as they had experienced it was not always purely random chance. To some extent you can 'make your own luck' by working hard and persisting:

> [T]he historian who goes to the archive and asks to see the papers of the 5th Duke of Richmond and finds in box 27 a previously unknown letter from Gladstone . . . Now is that because he knew that just by searching through what would be an unlikely source, is this just genuine credit for wading through loads of dusty boxes or is it serendipity?
>
> Foster and Ford, 2003, 334

Serendipitous encounters could result from browsing in topic areas next to one's specific focus on nearby library shelves:

> [N]ext to the art journals were the Garden History journals which I hadn't even thought of looking for, and they proved to be very valuable to me, so there is a fortuitous, luck, element, in some of the research that I have found information when I haven't actually been looking for it necessarily, though I have wanted it. ... it isn't simply luck that I found garden history, because libraries are organized logically so that the garden history journals are next to the art history journals and then next to the architecture journals.
>
> Foster and Ford, 2003, 335

In this case, serendipity was facilitated by the classification and shelving scheme of a library which brought together related topics.

Interviewees also thought that certain attitudes and strategies could influence serendipity – in particular, having a mind which is open and receptive to chance encounters with information, and consciously deciding to step back from the narrow focus one is concentrating on deliberately to take a broader view.

Summary

Although representing only one aspect of the broader concept of information behaviour, information seeking for many years took pride of place in research into how humans interact with information, and it still forms a key focus of this research.

In this chapter, a number of different ways in which people may seek information – whether working individually or as a member of a team in a work environment – were explored. A number of basic activities involved in information seeking were identified, some of which logically imply a sequence (e.g. Kuhlthau's *initiation, collection* and *presentation*), others of which do not necessarily imply any particular sequence (e.g. Ellis' *browsing, chaining* and *monitoring*). Also, different modes of information seeking were identified (e.g. Wilson's *passive* and *active* search, and Choo, Detlor and Turnbull's *formal* and *informal* modes. It was also noted that information seeking has an affective as well as a cognitive dimension.

Different people may also exhibit different styles of learning, problem solving and associated information seeking. Styles are a tendency consistently to adopt a particular type of strategy. Strategies that have received considerable research attention are those entailing relatively broad or narrow searching. Sometimes, different strategies are appropriate to different tasks or a different stage in a task.

But styles have been observed whereby people tend to prefer to adopt – and are better at – a relatively broad or narrow strategy. Either can lead to full understanding, entailing both successful 'description building' and successful 'procedure building'. Many people are able to combine these two essential components of understanding using either a breadth-first or depth-first strategy. But there is also evidence that many people are stronger at one to the detriment of the other, leading to characteristic forms of more superficial understanding – in particular over-generalization or fragmentation (failing to see the wood for the trees).

Relatively superficial understanding is by no means necessarily caused by such differences. There is also evidence of 'surface' approaches to learning, problem solving and consequent information seeking in which information may be 'skim-read' and not subjected to deep critical scrutiny. There is nothing wrong *per se* in skim reading, which may usefully be used to obtain a quick overview of a text. Indeed, memorizing may for some people in some circumstances be a first stage in achieving deep understanding. It becomes inappropriate, however, in cases where greater depth of understanding is required than can be obtained by skimming alone. Skim-reading may be a useful component of a learning strategy, but needs to be complemented at some stage by deeper, more reflective processing. Indeed, surface level approaches to studying in schools and universities have been identified as problematic insofar as they imply an approach geared to memorizing rather than understanding (Moon, 2013).

What, then, might be the practical implications for information professionals of these research findings? Well, firstly, it is important to be aware, as an experienced professional would be, that different people may engage in information processing (learning, problem solving and resultant information seeking) in very different ways.

The implications listed below come into play mainly in the case of relatively complex and protracted interactions between an information professional and a client over time – as opposed to relatively simple self-contained reference queries. The types of information seeking strategies of the types discussed above have been identified in relation to these types of complex learning and problem-solving situations. When engaging with a client over time in relation to a complex query, in relation to styles of information processing it may be useful for them:

- to be aware of the strategic approach being adopted by a client in relation to their problem (even if they are not explicitly aware of it as such), e.g. whether they seem at a stage of wanting to establish a broad wide-ranging (but possibly relatively superficial at this stage) overview of the task or topic they are exploring – or whether they are seeking detailed knowledge of a key aspect in order to build on.
- to be familiar with their own preferred information processing style if they have one – and whether there is any mismatch between what *they* think is the best way to go about information seeking and the way the client seems to want to go about it.
- to consider the fact that even the 'right' information presented at the 'wrong' time can hinder its perceived usefulness, acceptance and productive use by the client – e.g. if highly detailed information that would be extremely helpful in the procedure-building stage of a client's coming to understand a complex topic is presented when they are focusing on description building. Conversely, overview material mapping the inter-relationships between the main components of the topic may not be deemed useful if the client is focusing on carefully building up a step-by-step detailed understanding of a small part of the overall picture.

In relation to the quality (as opposed to the strategic style) of the client's approach to their problem, it may be useful to consider the extent to which the client appears successfully to be to subjecting information they are coming into contact with (as a result of interaction with the information professional) to appropriately deep critical scrutiny. This may be difficult to assess – but may become apparent if the client wishes to discuss their problem and the information they are receiving in relation to it. Whether it is relevant to the information professional's interaction with the client is dependent on the extent to which they feel that it is within their role to influence the client's level of critical thinking as part of their information literacy. This may be more clearly the case when dealing with young clients of school age. It will be important to avoid the possible danger of patronizing, or being thought to be patronizing the client.

Finally, the information professional must be aware of affective aspects of the information-seeking process and related processing of information with which the client is coming into contact as a result of interaction with them. A client may move between confidence and anxiety, satisfaction and frustration as they search for, find and evaluate information at different stages of their learning, problem solving and associated information behaviour over time. Awareness on the part of an information professional of this dimension of their interaction with a client arguably can only help improve the effectiveness of this interaction.

For further exploration of the issues covered above, the reader is referred to Chapters 4, 5 and 6 of Case (2012), and for an interesting discussion of information seeking in relation to information retrieval to Ingwersen and Järvelin (2005). The next chapter focuses on aspects of information behaviour that have received increasing research attention in recent years. At one level, information behaviour is a very logical cognitive (intellectual) activity. However, as we have seen in the work of Kuhlthau discussed above, there is also evidence that emotions are also involved, and that what might seem the most strictly logical way of going about things is not necessarily what people do.

References

Bates, M. J. (1989) The Design of Browsing and Berrypicking Techniques for the Online Search Interface, *Online Review*, **13** (5), 407–24.

Bates, M. J. (2002) Toward an Integrated Model of Information Seeking and Searching, *New Review of Information Behaviour Research*, **3**, 1–15. (Keynote Address, Fourth International Conference on Information Needs, Seeking and Use in Different Contexts, Lisbon, Portugal, 11 September, 2002.)

Case, D. (2012) *Looking for Information: a survey of research on information seeking, needs and behaviour*, Bingley, Emerald.

Choo, C. W., Detlor, B., and Turnbull, D. (1999) Information Seeking on the Web – an integrated model of browsing and searching. In Woods, L. (ed.), *Proceedings of the 62nd Annual Meeting of the American Society of Information Science (ASIS)*, *'Knowledge: creation, organisation and use'*, *Washington, DC, 1999*, Medford, NJ, Information Today, 187–99, http://choo.ischool.utoronto.ca/fis/respub/asis99.

Cole, C. (2012) *Information Need: a theory connecting information search to knowledge formation*, Medford, NJ, Information Today.

Daft, R. L. and Weick, K. E. (1984) Toward a Model of Organizations as Interpretation Systems, *Academy of Management Review*, **9** (2), 284–95.

Ellis, D. (1989) A Behavioural Model for Information Retrieval System Design, *Journal of Information Science*, **15** (4/5), 237–47.

Ellis, D. and Haugan, M. (1997) Modelling the Information Seeking Patterns of Engineers and Research Scientists in an Industrial Environment, *Journal of Documentation*, **53** (4), 384–403.

Ellis, D., Cox, D. and Hall, K. (1993) A Comparison of the Information Seeking Patterns of Researchers in the Physical and Social Sciences, *Journal of Documentation*, **49** (4), 356–69.

Erdelez, S. (1999) Information Encountering: it's more than just bumping into information, *Bulletin of the American Society for Information Science*, **25** (3), 26–9. www.asis.org/Bulletin/Feb-99/erdelez.html.

Ford, N. (1985) Learning Styles and Strategies of Postgraduate Students, *British Journal of Educational Technology*, **16** (1), 65–77.

Ford, N. (2002) *The Essential Guide to Using the Web for Research*, London, Sage.

Ford, N. and Ford, R. (1993) Towards a Cognitive Theory of Information Accessing: an empirical study, *Information Processing & Management*, **29** (5), 569–85.

Foster, A. (2004) A Nonlinear Model of Information-seeking Behaviour, *Journal of the American Society for Information Science and Technology*, **55** (3), 228–37.

Foster, A. and Ford, N. (2003) Serendipity and Information Seeking: an empirical study, *Journal of Documentation*, **59** (3), 321–40.

Greifeneder, E. (2014) Trends in Information Behaviour Research. In *Proceedings of ISIC, the Information Behaviour Conference, Leeds, 2–5 September 2014: Part 1*, (paper isic13), http://InformationR.net/ir/19-4/isic/isic13.html.

Heinström, J. (2002) *Fast Surfers, Broad Scanners and Deep Divers – Personality and Information Seeking Behaviour*, Doctoral dissertation, Information Studies, Abo Akademi University Press, Abo, www.abo.fi/fakultet/media/21373/thesis_Heinström.pdf.

Ingwersen, P. and Järvelin, K. (2005) *The Turn: integration of information seeking and retrieval in context*, Dordrecht, Springer.

Kuhlthau, C. C. (2004) *Seeking Meaning: a process approach to library and information services*, 2nd edn, London, Libraries Unlimited.

Mansourian, Y. and Ford, N. (2007) Search Persistence and Failure on the Web: a 'bounded rationality' and 'satisficing' analysis, *Journal of Documentation*, **63** (5), 680–701.

Marchionini, G. M. (1995) *Information Seeking in Electronic Environments*, Cambridge, Cambridge University Press.

Marchionini, G. M. and White, R. (2007) Find What You Need, Understand What You Find, *International Journal of Human-Computer Interaction*, **23** (3), 205–37.

Moon, J. (2013) *A Handbook of Reflective and Experiential Learning: theory and practice*, Abingdon, Routledge.

Pask, G. (1976a) Conversational Techniques in the Study and Practice of Education, *British Journal of Educational Psychology*, **46** (1), 12–25.

Pask, G. (1976b) Styles and Strategies of Learning, *British Journal of Educational Psychology*, **46** (2), 128–48.

Pask, G. (1988) Learning Strategies, Teaching Strategies and Conceptual or Learning Style. In Schmeck, R. R. (ed.), *Learning Strategies and Learning Styles*, New York, NY, Plenum Press.

Pirolli, P. and Card, S. (1995) Information Foraging in Information Access Environments. In *Proceedings of the SIGCHI Conference on Human Factors in Computing Systems 1995 (CHI 95)*, New York, NY, ACM Press/Addison-Wesley, 51–8.

Sutcliffe, A. and Ennis, M. (1998) Towards a Cognitive Theory of Information Retrieval, *Interacting with Computers*, **10**, 321–51.

Taylor, R. S. (1968) Question-negotiation and Information Seeking in Libraries, *College and Research Libraries*, **29**, 178–94.

University College London (2008) *Information Behaviour of the Researcher of the Future*, (The CIBER Report, commissioned by the British Library and Jisc), London, UCL.

Weick, K. E. and Daft, R. L. (1983) The Effectiveness of Interpretation Systems. In Cameron, K. S. and Whetton, D. A. (eds), *Organizational Effectiveness: a comparison of multiple models*, New York, NY, Academic Press, 71–93.

Wilson, T. D. (1997) Information Behaviour: an interdisciplinary perspective, *Information Processing & Management*, **33** (4), 551–72.

Wilson, T. D. (1999) Models in Information Behaviour Research, *Journal of Documentation*, **55** (3), 249–70, http://informationr.net/tdw/publ/papers/1999JDoc.html.

5

Information behaviour can be collaborative

Introduction

Although working together has always been central to work across the natural and social sciences and the arts and humanities, collaborative information behaviour is becoming increasingly common and important. Karunakaran, Reddy and Spence (2013) note that:

> . . . organizations have become information-intensive, but information is also fragmented across multiple actors, artifacts, and systems (Hansen and Järvelin, 2000, 2005). Therefore, collaboratively seeking, retrieving, and using work-related information have become common practices within organizations (Reddy and Dourish, 2002).

Yet Reddy and Jansen in their 2008 review of research concluded that relatively little attention had been paid to collaborative as opposed to individual aspects of information behaviour. Most models of information behaviour have related to the individual. Also, many information systems designed to support information seeking have operated on the model of the individual user, and are not well suited to supporting collaborative activity in organizations.

The sharing of information is by definition an act of collaboration. However, the degree to which 'sender' and 'receiver' of shared information actually engage in collaboration over and above sending and receiving the information may vary greatly. In one sense information is shared if it is published and other people can access it. However, 'information sharing' is used in this chapter to indicate sharing within an actual collaboration as defined below.

Before we go on to explore collaborative information behaviour in more detail, it is worth noting that as an increasing number of research studies focus on information behaviour as a collaborative social activity, it is important to acknowledge the complementary nature of both individual and social aspects and perspectives.

Ultimately, as noted by Bawden and Robinson (2011, 128), 'information behaviour is, by definition, individual'. This is not to deny the usefulness of studying the effects on information behaviour of social forces and influences, and seeking knowledge of the characteristics of shared information behaviour insofar as it might differ from individual information behaviour. Bawden and Robinson later asserted that:

> What we emphasize is the uniqueness and individuality of each person, which should not be minimized, even in view of the pragmatic advantages of studying information behavior primarily in group and social terms, and a recognition of the importance on many occasions of social context and collaboration. This is not at all inconsistent with a desire to identify and study interesting emergent information behaviors that are not predicable from individual cases. Identification of such features would surely be a major advance in the topic.
>
> Bawden and Robinson, 2013, 2589–90

Definitions

As with any concept we wish to study, it is important to establish a clear definition of collaborative information behaviour. González-Ibáñez, Haseki and Shah (2013) define 'collaboration' as:

> a social process in which two or more individuals intentionally and explicitly work together with the aim of cooperating to accomplish common goals, either synchronously or asynchronously, co-located or remotely located, using communication to interact with as well as to coordinate actions among group members
>
> González-Ibáñez, Haseki and Shah, 2013, 1166

whilst 'collaborative information behaviour' is defined by Karunakaran, Reddy and Spence as:

> the totality of behavior exhibited when people work together to (a) understand and formulate an information need through the help of shared representations;

(b) seek the needed information through a cyclical process of searching, retrieving, and sharing; and (c) put the found information to use.

Karunakaran, Reddy and Spence, 2013, 2438

Many studies have focused on the individual elements of collaborative information behaviour, some aspects receiving more attention than others – in particular collaborative information *seeking*. Indeed, a number of studies have focused on collaborative information seeking rather than collaborative information behaviour. Foster (2006, 330), for example, defines collaborative information seeking as 'the study of the systems and practices that enable individuals to collaborate during the seeking, searching, and retrieval of information.' Shah provides a little more detail when he defines it as:

> . . . an information-seeking process that takes place in a collaborative project (possibly a complex task) among a small group of participants (potentially with different set[s] of skills and/or roles), which is intentional, interactive, and mutually beneficial. Note that such a collaborative project could itself be an information-seeking endeavor (e.g., siblings looking for diabetes-friendly recipes for their mother), or it could encompass information seeking as one of its components (e.g., coauthors searching for and sharing relevant literature as a part of writing an article). Also, note that information seeking here refers not only to searching and retrieving but also to browsing, sharing, evaluating, and synthesizing information.
>
> Shah, 2014, 219

Note that both Foster and Shah include information retrieval within information seeking in their definitions. Also note that Shah includes sharing, evaluating and synthesizing information within his definition of information seeking. In this book, as commonly elsewhere in the literature, information seeking, sharing, evaluating and using are distinct from information retrieval, and are all components making up information behaviour.

THINK!

Is there a difference between information seeking and information retrieval? If so, what precisely is it?

There are two common meanings attributed to the term 'information retrieval'. It is most often used in the research literature to refer to the design, evaluation and use of information systems. However, it can also refer to the end result of searching for information – namely, the retrieval of information by an information seeker.

dif.

One simple way to distinguish between searching and retrieval is to consider retrieval to be most often associated with a focus on the behaviour and performance of an information *system*, whilst searching is most often associated with a focus on the behaviour and performance of a person when using such a system. These are two sides of the same coin – a person engages in searching behaviour and the system retrieves information for him or her.

Wilson (1999) draws a more complex distinction between the two terms. He considers information retrieval to be a subset of the broader concept of information searching. Searching is associated with the use of a range of possible types of search tool – of which information retrieval systems, which are generally associated with textual information sources, represent just one (other types including, for example, relational databases). He defines searching behaviour as:

> . . . a sub-set of information-seeking, particularly concerned with the interactions between information user (with or without an intermediary) and computer-based information systems, of which information retrieval systems for textual data may be seen as one type.
>
> Wilson, 1999, 263

Throughout this book, since we are primarily concerned with the behaviour of people rather than the behaviour of systems, the discussion focuses on seeking and searching rather than retrieval.

Whether we include the evaluation, synthesis and evaluation as part of – or as separate from – the information-seeking process is arguably a moot point which depends on the level of granularity we wish to adopt in our terminology. Viewed holistically, we can consider evaluation, synthesis and sharing of information as integral to the information-seeking process.

Arguably these activities *do* form an integral part of information seeking where this includes an iterative cycle in which information that has been found is shared with other members of a collaborating group of people, so that it can be synthesized with other retrieved information in order to evaluate the extent to which it does and does not satisfy the information need. To the extent that it does not provide a solution, further information is sought in an iterative information-seeking cycle. However, if we adopt a more fine-grained analysis, we can consider information seeking to be separate from sharing, synthesizing and evaluating it. Clearly, from this narrower perspective seeking is not strictly the same process as evaluating, or sharing, or synthesizing.

These may seem somewhat esoteric concerns, but being clear and consistent about the terminology we are using to describe complex concepts is extremely important. It is important to be clear about precisely what you mean (and what you do not mean) when using terms to describe complex concepts. In this context it is relevant to note that Shah (2014) emphasizes that there is much variation in terminology in the literature relating to collaborative information seeking. He notes the use of many apparently very similar terms such as collaborative search, collaborative information retrieval, social searching, concurrent search, collaborative exploratory search, co-browsing, collaborative navigation, collaborative information behaviour, collaborative information synthesis and collaborative information seeking.

In this book, I use the term 'information seeking' in its more holistic sense to embrace a potentially iterative cycle, including looking for information, evaluating the information retrieved and if necessary refining the information need and searching again. Particularly in a collaborative information-seeking context, this cycle may entail the sharing and synthesis of information – for example, to enable other group members to evaluate it, and to assess the extent to which the synthesis of new and already found information provides a solution to the problem being worked on.

'Information behaviour' includes not only information seeking, but also coming into contact with information in other ways, failing to come into contact with or avoiding information, and using/applying information. It may also include evaluating, synthesizing and sharing information *where these processes are not part of an iterative information-seeking cycle described above* – for example, where these activities take place as discrete steps *after* information has been sought and gathered.

Characteristics of collaborative information behaviour

THINK!

Have you ever engaged in collaborative information seeking with anyone else? If so, why did you choose to collaborate rather than act alone? Was there anything about the nature of the task or circumstances that made it appropriate to collaborate?

On the basis of an analysis of the literature, Shah (2014) notes a number of features about the task and circumstances that characterize collaborative as opposed to individual information seeking:

- It is often working towards a common goal and the prospect of mutual benefit that brings people together to engage in collaborative information seeking.

- Generally, to be worth the effort of collaboration a complex task is involved. Such a task may often be 'messy', with no immediately clear solution.
- Collaboration entails overheads such as additional cognitive load, and to be worthwhile the potential benefits should justify these overheads.
- Collaboration tends to occur where the individuals who need to solve a complex problem lack the knowledge or skills to be able to do so on their own. By collaborating they may achieve a whole that is more than just the sum of the parts.

London (1995), quoted in Shah (2014) identified a number of limitations associated with collaboration:

- It is a time-consuming process and therefore ill-suited to problems requiring a quick solution.
- The success of collaboration can be detrimentally affected by power inequalities amongst the collaborators.
- The process may be unsuccessful if all collaborators do not embrace an ethos in which the common good must take precedence over the interests of the minority.
- The size of the collaborating group can be critical, collaboration tending to break down in over-large groups.
- The process will not be successful unless there is power to implement decisions resulting from the collaboration.

According to Activity Theory, 'collaboration' can be considered at three levels: as a co-ordinated, a co-operative, or a co-constructive activity (Bardram, 1998).

Co-ordinated collaboration entails participants working independently but contributing to a shared goal. But none is party to the setting of this goal, or deciding on how it might best be achieved. The work of each is self-contained but designed (not by them) to fit in so that it contributes to the common goal in a coherent way, complementing the contributions of other collaborators. As Bardram (1998) notes, participants are acting on a common object, but do not share a common goal. For example, workers on a vehicle factory production line may all be working on the same car, but none has ownership of the goal of producing the finished product.

In **co-operative** collaboration participants not only work on a common object, but also share the common goal. They will engage interactively with each other to work out how the goal might best be achieved by the group. This may entail discussion and negotiation of their relative roles.

Co-constructive collaboration involves the group in discussing and negotiating what the goal should be as well as how it might best be achieved. Both the goal and the means to achieve it are open to reconceptualization by the participants. As Bardram notes:

> At this level of collaborative activity the object of work is not stable – or is not even existing – and hence has to be collectively constructed, i.e. co-constructed. The community asks questions like: 'What is the meaning of this problem in the first place? Why are we trying to solve it – and who benefits from its solution? How did the problem emerge – who created it and for what purpose? Is the objective still relevant or has the whole activity become obsolete?
>
> Bardram, 1998, 38–9

Central to collaborative information behaviour is information sharing. Tajla defined this as:

> . . . an umbrella concept that covers a wide range of collaborative behaviors from sharing accidentally encountered information to collaborative query formulation and retrieval. Collaboration means that information sharing is not an individual behavior but a collective and collaborative effort occurring in social networks (i.e., communities of practice or communities of sharing.
>
> Tajla, 2002, 147

Bao and Bouthillier (2007) apply the Activity Theory-based framework of collaboration described above, which entails three levels of activity (co-ordinated, co-operative and co-constructive) to information sharing.

At a **co-ordinated** collaborative level, although they share information, participants do not do so on the basis of having a shared goal. At this level, sharing is often random and informal. For example, a university researcher might come across and share information that they think might be useful to a colleague working on another project.

At a **co-operative** collaborative level, where participants share a common goal, information tends to be shared routinely and formally. An example would be of participants sharing information in order to explore an issue and come to a decision.

At a **co-constructive** collaborative level, information flows and use are collectively reconceptualized and reorganized (rather than just being executed) in order to achieve a common goal. Bao and Bouthillier give the example of setting up a 'just in time' production system in which:

> . . . businesses along the supply chain must establish an industry-wide

information-sharing mechanism to share real-time information seamlessly, which requires businesses integrating their information systems, reengineering business processes related to inventory management and production schedule, and retraining relevant employees, etc.

Bao and Bouthillier, 2007, 3

A number of studies have sought to discover how collaborative might differ from individual information behaviour. Recall Kuhlthau's Information Search Process model of information seeking introduced in Chapter 4 (p. 52). The extent to which Kuhlthau's relatively well established model of individual information behaviour can be applied to collaborative information behaviour was the focus of a study by Hyldegård (2006). She explored the collaborative working of a group of university students working on a group project over a seven-week period.

In Chapter 4, only the basic activity associated with each stage of Kuhlthau's model was presented. However, the model also included other cognitive and affective aspects, as shown in Table 5.1. As can be seen in the table, Kuhlthau associated each stage with thoughts, feelings and actions. She was one of the first researchers systematically to include feelings (affective aspects) in a model of information seeking to complement the previous relatively exclusive emphasis on thoughts (cognitive aspects).

According to Kuhlthau, in the early stages of information seeking[1] the individual experiences a degree of cognitive imprecision in that s/he has a need to know something that s/he does not yet know. The stages of initiation, selection and exploration are characterized, respectively, by affective feelings of uncertainty, optimism, and confusion/frustration/doubt.

At the formulation stage, in which a clearer focus is formed for the problem, the individual begins to feel less uncertainty. Confidence and a sense of direction are experienced during the collection stage, and from this point the

Table 5.1 Links between stages and affective elements in Kuhlthau's Information Search Process model

Stage	Cognitive aspects	Affective aspects
Initiation	General and vague	Uncertainty
Selection		Optimism
Exploration		Confusion, frustration and doubt
Formulation	Narrowed and clearer	Clarity
Collection	Increased interest	Sense of direction and confidence
Presentation	Clearer or focused	Relief and satisfaction if information seeking has gone well; disappointment if it has not

balance between seeking new information, and making sense of and synthesizing information found, shifts as the presentation stage is entered. Depending on the perceived success of the information seeking at this stage, the individual may feel relief and satisfaction, or disappointment.

Hyldegård's (2006) research found that:

- the group members' cognitive experiences were to an extent similar to those proposed in Kuhlthau's model. However, they resulted not just from information-seeking activities but also from factors such as social interaction, reading and writing.
- relating to affective experiences, the increased certainty accompanied by clarity, confidence and relief identified in the latter stages of Kuhlthau's model did not appear in Hyldegård's data. Even at the end of the information-seeking process, some group members were still experiencing uncertainty, frustration and disappointment. Hyldegård (2006, 276) attributes this partly to 'a mis-match in group members' motivations, ambitions and project focus'.
- the individual members of each group did not display similar behaviour, casting doubt on the suggestion that a group can be modelled as one in terms of behaviour.

Hyldegård proposes that models relevant to collaborative as opposed to individual information seeking should take account of the effects of contextual, social and psychological factors such as the dynamics of the work task factors and intra-group interactions. The role of affective aspects of information behaviour is discussed more fully in Chapter 6.

Reddy and Jansen (2008) also found significant differences between collaborative and individual information behaviour. They conducted studies of collaborative information behaviour in two hospitals, and concluded that:

- Collaborative information behaviour is different from individual information behaviour in relation to
  — the ways in which individuals interact
  — the complexity of information needs, and
  — the role played by information technology.
- A number of factors may trigger a transition from individual to collaborative information behaviour.
- Information retrieval systems may be used at different stages of the problem-solving process and may play a different role in collaborative and individual information behaviour.

They went on to propose a model of information behaviour that includes both individual and collaborative aspects. The model distinguishes between information searching and information seeking. Recall from Chapter 2 that Wilson proposed that these concepts are hierarchical, information behaviour embracing information seeking, and information seeking embracing information searching. Reddy and Jansen (2008) consider information searching to entail tactical manoeuvring and information seeking to entail strategic manoeuvring. People may move between these different forms of information behaviour at different stages of working.

Information searching and information seeking can take place within the contexts of individual and collaborative activity. Reddy and Jansen differentiate individual and collaborative information behaviour in terms of the complexity of the problem being worked on, the number of agents involved, and the nature of interactions between agents (people and systems). Individual information behaviour tends to entail a relatively simple problem. It involves a small number of agents – one person and one or more information systems, interacting in fact-finding or question-answering mode.

Collaborative information behaviour entails a number of people and systems, generally different people having different expertise. Interaction is different between the two types of information behaviour. Typically in individual information behaviour a person directs a query to an information system (or person) in a direct question–answer mode. They tend to rely on the system as the main method of finding information and often the information is found from the system.

Interaction at the collaborative level is typically more complex, entailing the need to engage in multi-directional conversations with (rather than just question) a number of people. Collaborative information behaviour is usually characterized by a more complex problem being worked on, and the exploratory use of information systems (as opposed to more simple fact-finding /question-answering). Typically people have to search for information in a wide range of resources due to the complexity of the problem they are working on.

People may switch between individual and collaborative information behaviour as a result of a range of factors or triggers. These triggers include what Reddy and Jansen have called 'environmental factors' – the nature of the problem, which may be relatively simple or more complex; the number of different agents involved (people and systems); and the nature of the interactions between these people and systems. Reddy and Jansen explain that:

The interplay of the complexity of the problem, the number of agents interacting, and the nature of these interactions initiates a trigger that transforms the context from IIB to CIB. At the individual level, the information problem is relatively simple when compared to the collaborative level. As the information problem becomes more complex and nuanced, the need to collaborate becomes more pronounced. This is especially true in domains where multiple areas of expertise are needed to address the information problem. In these domains, several agents must interact.

Reddy and Jansen, 2008, 266

Triggers include (but are not limited to):

- the complexity of the problem and consequently of the information need
- the dispersed and fragmented nature of relevant information sources
- a lack of prerequisite domain expertise, resulting in a person having to turn to others for help in finding a solution
- a lack of immediately or easily accessible information, making collaboration a potentially productive option.

Karunakaran, Reddy and Spence (2013), went on to present a more holistic model of collaborative information behaviour in organizations, which extends the previously discussed Reddy and Jansen (2008) model. It is based on both empirical data from studies by the authors and a review of relevant literature. They proposed that collaborative information behaviour consists of three broad phases: problem formulation, collaborative information seeking, and information use:

1 **Problem formulation** starts with individuals becoming aware of a problem and attempting to define it. Triggers – such as the complexity of the problem – result in this stage becoming collaborative as the need arises for different people to agree on the nature of the problem and how it might be tackled.
2 **Collaborative information seeking** entails searching for, retrieving, and sharing information. This is a cyclical process in which people find and share information relating to the problem, repeating the process until they feel they have sufficient to evaluate and use.
3 **Information use** entails evaluating, synthesizing and putting to use the information gathered in the previous information-seeking phase. Within this collaborative information behaviour model, evaluation and synthesis take place collaboratively but the use of information may be individual.

A number of activities apply across all of these phases. These include *information sharing and evaluation* and *collaborative sense-making*. Information sharing and evaluation take place both within and across the three main phases. Collaborative sense-making entails different people with different perspectives establishing shared understanding.

The authors acknowledge a number of limitations of the model. The activities addressed by the model are short term in that they typically take a few hours or less. The model does not take on board activities which take place over longer time frames – as in the case of, for example, students collaborating on a project over a semester. Recall that Hyldegård's research – which investigated students working on a project over seven weeks – identified factors such as intra-group social and psychological factors not reflected in the model of Karunakaran, Reddy and Spence (though the nature and context of the research were very different).

The authors also note that most (though by no means all) research work into collaborative information behaviour has taken place in healthcare settings – and their own model draws heavily on their work in hospitals. However, the extent to which findings of studies conducted in this context are generalizable or transferable to other settings is unclear. Finally, the authors acknowledge that the demarcations and relationships between the different activities entailed in collaborative information behaviour shown in their model are not complete, and further studies will be necessary to refine our understanding of these.

On the basis of an extensive review of the literature, Wilson (2010) identified a number of dimensions of information sharing, and went on to hypothesized relationships between them as a basis for future research. Two factors were the likely benefit that will result from sharing, and the level of risk that a participant perceives will result from sharing information.

Wilson considered that the greater the benefits participants anticipate will result from information sharing and the less the associated risks, the more likely they will be to share information. Information is likely to be most readily shared in a low risk/high benefit situation. It is least likely in a high risk/low benefit situation. A high risk/high benefit situation is likely to result in what Wilson terms 'problematical' information sharing: a low risk/low benefit situation in a negotiated approach in which participants will more cautiously explore the possibilities of sharing.

Another key factor is trust, which Wilson considers is likely to interact with risk and benefit. Information is most likely to be readily shared when participants (a) perceive there to be a positive risk/benefit ratio (high benefit and low risk) and (b) have a high level of trust in their information-sharing potential participants. Sharing is least likely where the risk/benefit is negative (high risk and low benefit) and there is a low level of trust.

However, in intermediate positions, trust is likely to mediate the relationship. Negative risk/benefit situations will not necessarily lead to a lack of sharing. Rather, high levels of trust militate for participants being more likely to negotiate rather than simply reject the possibility of information sharing, even when the risk/benefit is negative. Conversely, even when the risk/benefit may be positive, low levels of trust are likely to result in negotiation of the possibility of sharing rather than going ahead less cautiously.

Collaborative information behaviour is a relatively new area of research and is still in its infancy. A number of papers including Foster (2006), Shah (2014) and Karunakaran, Reddy and Spence (2013) have provided reviews of the field and have come to a number of conclusions about what are key findings in the area, and what are important gaps in our knowledge that remain. The following list represents my own selection and summary of key findings and issues requiring further work, based on these authors.

- Research to date suggests that in order to understand collaborative information behaviour, we must take into account a range of factors including:
  — the nature of the tasks being worked on
  — the domain in which the activity is taking place (e.g. academic, industrial)
  — the nature of the organization involved
  — the nature and make-up of the groups who are collaborating
  — factors associated with person to person and human-computer interactions
  — the extent and nature of access to heterogeneous sources of information.
- All information-related tasks are capable of being conducted in collaborative mode. These include the specification of an information need, information seeking, filtering, navigation, evaluation and the formulation of relevance judgments.

In particular, we need to learn more about:

- collaborative information behaviour in a range of populations, situations and subject domains to add to the studies already done in relation to healthcare professionals, students, knowledge workers and others – for

example, families with health issues
- those contexts and situations in which collaboration may be helpful. People often do not perceive value in collaborating even when in reality it could be useful. We need to be able to devise knowledge and strategies to promote CIB where/when appropriate.
- how popular social networking sites could be used to promote and support aspects of collaboration
- the costs and benefits of collaboration
- how to extend models of individual information behaviour and its components to include collaborative seeking, synthesis and sense-making; and
- what type of information systems can most helpfully support collaborative information behaviour. Much collaboration at present takes place with tools that were not designed specifically with collaboration in mind.
- how the behaviour of different sizes of collaborating groups might differ (e.g. in groups of two, tens or hundreds of people)
- how best to define 'complex' in the context of findings that a transition from individual to collaborative information behaviour is dependent on the complexity of the problem
- more about the nature of triggers for individual and collaborative information behaviour, and how they might differ.

Case study: collaborative information behaviour

Let us now look at an example of a study of collaborative information behaviour entailing information sharing. Von Thaden (2008) conducted a study of distributed information behaviour in an extremely safety-critical environment – flying an aircraft. Information of a range of different types from a variety of sources must all be handled by the crew on the flight deck of the aeroplane. Information must be identified, gathered, made sense of and used. It must be shared and communicated within the team on the flight deck, with ground controllers, and with other aircraft.

The research investigated the information behaviour – when flying missions in a flight simulator – of 19 student pilots in an upper level flight course at the University of Illinois at Urbana Champaign's Institute of Aviation. Substantial differences were found in the information behaviour of high- and low-performing crews, and between those involved in 'accidents' and those not.

The sources of information available to flight-deck crews are many and varied, including cockpit navigation instruments displaying location, altitude, GPS-based moving map position, and paper-based charts giving details of the route and potential obstacles.

In order to keep the flight on course and preserve safety, crews must engage in a range of both relatively routine scanning and monitoring of information and more active and focused responding to developing and emergency situations. This entails constantly acquiring and collectively making sense of relevant information to generate an accurate picture of the aircraft's state, position and trajectory, and to enable effective decision making as the flight progresses:

> As in many safety-critical settings, flight crews often make consistent, procedural responses to clearly defined, predicable situations as a part of normal operations. But unforeseen and indeterminate circumstances also frequently occur. In this latter class of situation, flight crews must use personal skill, judgment, and interaction with other crew members to negotiate meanings, create interpretations, and act in response to them. Misinterpretation and miscommunication about the operating conditions and what they mean can, and frequently do, serve as precursors to accidents.
>
> von Thaden, 2008, 1555

The situation is usually one in which always having an ideal set of full information is not realistic. In these circumstances crews must engage in 'satisficing' – i.e. making 'good enough' rather than optimal decisions based on the best available information at the time.

Building on the information behaviour models of Ellis (Ellis, 1989; Ellis and Haugan, 1997) and Choo, Detlor and Turnbull (2000), von Thaden developed a model of distributed information behaviour appropriate to safety-critical situations – the Distributed Information Behaviour System.

In this model, they differentiated between information behaviours related to *exploration*, and those related to *exploitation*. Each type of behaviour applies to information needs, information seeking and information use. *Exploration* is associated with *conditioned* behaviour across information needs, seeking and use. *Exploitation* is associated with *methodological* behaviour.

- Conditioned behaviour entails having a general rather than specifically focused area of interest. It is not driven by a specific information need. Rather, it is characterized by the relatively passive habitual scanning of many and varied pre-selected information sources in order to detect early or ongoing changes. Information may be encountered

serendipitously, and changes which come to light may be noted and acknowledged in a passive or habitual way – or decisions made intuitively rather than formally, using personal rather than technical criteria.
• Methodological behaviour differs from conditioned behaviour in the extent to which behaviour is active, focused, systematic and formal. It is characterized by deliberate planned active information seeking to obtain information relating to a specific issue. This may entail focusing on a particular area or instrument, or browsing selected information sources using pre-established protocols (such as a checklist). Information may be acquired and systematically checked relating to a specific issue in order to decide on a particular course of action. Specific knowledge is actively communicated, and information is used formally in decision making.

In the experiments, 19 student pilots took part in 49 simulated cross-country flights. Each flight involved two students as crew, and 24 distinct crew pairings (different combinations of the 19 students) were recorded. Crews were categorized as high, low or average in performance, performance being assessed in terms of professionalism, preparedness and the extent to which they carried out 'heedful interactions'. Heedful interactions were characterized by care in communicating, thoughtful attention to issues, working effectively as a team in terms of 'tight coupling' between crew members and co-ordination of duties and activities, continual involvement in sense-making and taking account of the interrelatedness of activities. The information behaviour of the crews was classified according to the distributed information behaviour model. There were interesting differences in the information behaviour of high- and low-performing crews.

THINK!

Considering the description of the Distributed Information Behaviour System described above, what different types of behaviour do you think might distinguish between high- and low-performing crews?

Low-performing crews engaged in more conditioned behaviours and less methodical information behaviours than did their high-performing counterparts. High-performing crews displayed more effective distributed negotiation of the meaning of information between the crew. Low-performing crews also struggled with establishing information meaning.

Low performing crews were not able to establish an effective distribution of their work. Within this group, there were also differences between the information behaviour of those low-performing crews who succumbed to accidents and those who did not. A number of statistically significant differences in information behaviour correlated with successful or accident-resulting outcomes. Two types of pathology in low-performing crews could lead to accidents:

1 Over-reliance on methodological information behaviours at the expense of necessary conditioned behaviours could lead crews to overlook vital new information that could affect safety.
2 Over-reliance on casual conditioned information behaviours may be engaged in at the expense of vital methodological action sequences.

Von Thaden gives examples of both types of pathology:

> This crew employed a fair balance of conditioned and methodical information behaviors toward the first part of their observed mission. However, toward the end of the flight, they became increasingly engrossed in following checklists and understanding their landing configuration, and ignored the need to explore their overall situation for information they might have missed. [The crew] landed on the runway without clearance to do so and crashed into another airplane that occupied the same runway at the same time.

> This crew experienced reduced engine power in one of their engines and assessed it in a casual conditioned manner, trying a seemingly random set of approaches, instead of using a methodical means to diagnose their problem. At one point, they reduced the throttles in both engines hoping to gain information about the engine's governor (which regulates engine speed). They never put the throttles forward again because they began exploring other options and explanations for the power loss. This crew eventually turned the aircraft, which reduced airspeed to the point of causing a stall. By the time the crew realized they needed to put the throttles forward, the aircraft's attitude was unrecoverable and it spun all the way to impact.
>
> von Thaden, 2008, 1567

Effective performance requires engagement in a variety of distributed information behaviours across all categories of information behaviour shown above. High-performing crews displayed a relatively balanced approach employing both conditioned *exploring* behaviours and methodical *exploiting* behaviours – but weighted more towards the latter.

Much of the value of this work lies in the qualitative understanding of the information behaviours of flight-deck crews, since the sample size was too small to be able to demonstrate statistically significant differences between accident-prone and successful low-performing crews. But the researchers conclude (von Thaden, 2008, 1568) that: 'the research strongly suggests that it is not just coincidence that determines the incidence of accidents for low performing crews'.

Summary

Collaborative information behaviour can take many forms, ranging from the informal sharing of information that you come across with a friend or colleague who you think will find it useful or interesting, to information behaviour in the context of more formal arrangements jointly to address issues and solve problems in and/or between organizations.

Although it is relatively under-researched compared to individual information behaviour in terms of volume of research over the years, there is increasing research interest in studying collaborative information behaviour. Those studies that have been conducted paint a complex picture of factors involved in determining whether information is or is not shared, the nature of information-related activities, and the relative success or failure of tasks that are dependent on the successful and effective acquisition, interpreting and sharing of information.

The quality of shared as opposed to just individual information behaviour may be an important contributing factor influencing the success of tasks, operations and organizations. The flight-deck case study presented in this chapter illustrated this in the context of safety-critical activity. The systematic study of collaborative information behaviour is relatively new, and much remains to be understood in what is increasingly recognized as a very important area of human activity.

The increasing adoption of collaborative working in academia, industry and commerce has implications for the information professionals and information systems and services supporting organizations (Toze, 2014). Areas enabling and facilitating collaborative work are essential in the modern academic library (Sinclair, 2007), and the ability to work together in teams to seek, interpret, evaluate and use information is an increasingly important aspect of the information literacy required of information professionals. Information management has a key role to play in commerce and industry in supporting collaborative research and development (e.g. Sheriff, Bouchlaghem, El-Hamalawi and Yeomans, 2012).

The notion of collaborative information behaviour and its promotion is relevant also to library staff and services providing support to members of the public. This calls to mind Sonnenwald's concept of 'information horizons' (see p. 124). Part of the librarian's role in providing support for individuals who approach them for help in problem solving is to assess the extent to which there might be scope for them to benefit from collaboration in the form of contacts with other individuals and groups of which they might not be aware. Helping them where appropriate to expand their information horizons in this way may entail encouraging them to adopt – and facilitating – a collaborative approach to certain problems which they may not have considered. Insofar as this might be transferable to other problem situations in which they might find themselves, there is also an information literacy educational aspect here too. For further reading relating to collaborative information behaviour the reader is referred to Foster (2006; 2010).

References

Bao, X. and Bouthillier, F. (2007) Information Sharing as a Type of Information Behavior, paper presented at Information Sharing in a Fragmented World: 35th Annual Conference of the Canadian Association for Information Science, McGill University, 10–12 May, www.cais-acsi.ca/ojs/index.php/cais/article/viewFile/604/270.

Bardram, J. (1998) *Collaboration, Coordination and Computer Support: an activity theoretical aproach to the design of computer supported cooperative work*, PhD thesis, University of Aarhus.

Bawden, D. and Robinson, L. (2011) Individual Differences in Information-Related Behaviour: what do we know about information styles? In Spink, A. and Heinström, J. (eds), *New Directions in Information Behaviour*, Library and Information Science, Volume 1, Bingley: Emerald, 127–58.

Bawden, D. and Robinson, L. (2013) No Such Thing as Society? On the individuality of information behaviour, *Journal of the American Society for Information Science and Technology*, **64** (12), 2587–90.

Choo, C. W., Detlor, B. and Turnbull, D. (2000) Information Seeking on the Web: an integrated model of browsing and searching, *First Monday*, **5** (2), http://journals.uic.edu/ojs/index.php/fm/article/view/729.

Ellis, D. (1989) A Behavioral Model for Information Retrieval System Design, *Journal of Information Science*, **13** (4/5), 237–47.

Ellis, D. and Haugan, M. (1997) Modeling the Information Seeking Patterns of Engineers and Research Scientists in an Industrial Environment, *Journal of Documentation*, **53** (4), 384–403.

Foster, J. (2006) Collaborative Information Seeking and Retrieval, *Annual Review of*

Information Science and Technology, **40**, Chapter 8, 329–56.

Foster. J. (ed.) (2010) *Collaborative Information Behavior: user engagement and communication sharing*, Hershey, PA, IGI Global.

González-Ibáñez, R., Haseki, M. and Shah, C. (2013) Let's Search Together, But Not Too Close! An analysis of communication and performance in collaborative information seeking, *Information Processing & Management*, **49** (5), 1165–79.

Hansen, P. and Järvelin, K. (2000) The Information Seeking and Retrieval Process at the Swedish Patent and Registration Office: moving from lab-based to real life work task environment. In *Proceedings of the 23rd Annual International ACM SIGIR Workshop on Patent Retrieval*, 43–53. Presented at the ACM SIGIR Conference on Research and Development in Information Retrieval, Athens, Greece.

Hansen, P. and Järvelin, K. (2005) Collaborative Information Retrieval in an Information-intensive Domain, *Information Processing & Management*, 41 (5), 1101–19.

Hyldegård, J. (2006) Collaborative Information Behaviour: exploring Kuhlthau's Information Search Process model in a group-based educational setting, *Information Processing & Management*, **42** (1), 276–98.

Karunakaran, A., Reddy, M. C. and Spence, P. R. (2013) Toward a Model of Collaborative Information Behavior in Organizations, *Journal of the American Society for Information Science and Technology*, **64** (12), 2437–51, doi:10.1002/asi.22943.

London, S. (1995) Collaboration and Community, www.scottlondon.com/articles/oncollaboration.html.

Reddy, M. and Dourish, P. (2002) A Finger on the Pulse: temporal rhythms and information seeking in medical work. In *Proceedings of the 2002 ACM Conference on Computer Supported Cooperative Work*, 344–53, presented at the CSCW '02 Computer Supported Cooperative Work, New Orleans, LA.

Reddy, M. and Jansen, B. J. (2008) A Model for Understanding Collaborative Information Behavior in Context: a study of two healthcare teams, *Information Processing & Management*, **44** (1), 256–73.

Shah, C. (2014) Collaborative Information Seeking, *Journal of the Association for Information Science and Technology*, **65** (2), 215–36.

Sheriff, A., Bouchlaghem, D., El-Hamalawi, A. and Yeomans, S. (2012) Information Management in UK-based Architecture and Engineering Organizations: drivers, constraining factors, and barriers, *Journal of Management in Engineering*, **28** (2), 170–80.

Sinclair, B. (2007) Commons 2.0: library spaces designed for collaborative learning, *Educause Quarterly*, **4**, 4–6, https://net.educause.edu/ir/library/pdf/EQM0740.pdf.

Tajla, S. (2002) Information Sharing in Academic Communities: types and levels of collaboration in information seeking and use. In *Information Seeking in Context, the*

Fourth International Conference on Information Seeking in Context, September, 11–13.

Toze, S. (2014) *Examining Group Process Through an Information Behaviour Lens: how student groups work with information to accomplish tasks*, Doctoral thesis, University of Halifax, Nova Scotia.

von Thaden, T. L. (2008) Distributed Information Behavior: a study of dynamic practice in a safety critical environment, *Journal of the American Society for Information Science and Technology*, **59** (10), 1555–69.

Wilson, T. D. (1999) Models in Information Behaviour Research, *Journal of Documentation*, **55** (3), 249–70.

Wilson, T. D. (2010) Information Sharing: an exploration of the literature and some propositions, *Information Research*, **15** (4) paper 440, http://InformationR.net/ir/15-4/paper440.html.

Note

1   A number of researchers, including Hyldegård, have noted that what Kuhlthau refers to in her model as information *searching* is what many researchers would term information *seeking*. For consistency in this book I use 'information seeking' when describing Kuhlthau's Information Search Process model.

6

Factors influencing information behaviour

Introduction

In the previous chapters we have explored a variety of types of information behaviour ranging from relatively active to more passive, and relatively focused to less directed forms of information seeking and acquisition, as well as serendipitous information encountering.

An important area of research is to explore what factors influence people to adopt particular types of information behaviour. Clearly, different tasks may require different information-seeking strategies, and specific types of information evaluation and use. But there is also evidence that different people may engage in very different types of information behaviour even when faced with apparently similar tasks and circumstances.

Understanding such influences may be helpful in a number of ways. If we can identify factors that may lead to relatively ineffective behaviour, then we may be able to exert counter-influences – whether in the form of training, education and self-understanding, or devising information systems that can help and support people as they search for, evaluate and use information. Research into information behaviour can help us not only identify factors that may constrain the effectiveness of the behaviour of individuals, groups and organizations, but also identify factors associated with particularly successful behaviour which we can use in attempting to lessen the influence of constraining influences.

There is a multiplicity of factors which can affect our information behaviour. Research suggests that an individual's information behaviour may be determined and influenced by a wide range of factors, both internal and external to that individual (Figure 6.1). 'Internal' includes:

- **demographic** factors, such as age and gender
- **cognitive** factors, including their level of knowledge in a topic which is the focus of their information behaviour, levels of experience of searching, evaluating and using information, linguistic ability and flexibility of mind, and learning/problem solving style
- **affective** factors (feelings and emotions), such as level of anxiety relating to a topic which is the subject of their information behaviour.

Factors 'external' to the individual refer here to features of the contexts in which they are operating, which include:

- work
- education
- leisure

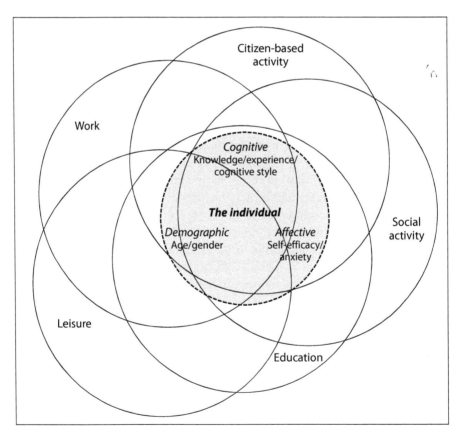

Figure 6.1 Factors that can influence information behaviour

- social relationships
- one's role as a citizen.

However, it is important to note that maintaining any clear distinction between 'internal' and 'external' factors is the subject of differing views and therefore a potential issue which has itself received research attention. This issue is explored later in this chapter.

A number of models of information behaviour have reflected the importance of contextual factors, some providing a good overall picture of factors from multiple contexts, others focusing in on one or other of these contexts.

Wilson (Wilson and Walsh, 1996) published a relatively holistic model (Figure 6.2) in which he also outlined a wide range of factors including those internal and external to individuals, spanning demographic, psychological, role-related and sociological. Wilson built on his earlier identification of different types of information-seeking behaviour (see 'Basic information-seeking processes and activities' in Chapter 4), embedding them into a model which sought to describe key mechanisms entailed in information seeking. This model begins to map the role of different factors in influencing information-seeking processes.

Wilson highlights the role of a wide range of factors in influencing information behaviour, including psychological, social, environmental and demographic factors. These act as what he terms 'activating mechanisms' and 'intervening variables'. Activating mechanisms are what prompt us to engage in activities. Intervening variables are factors which may influence the nature of those activities. So, for example, a person needing information in order to cope with an urgent and stressful situation is likely to engage in active search. A person with a less urgent and stressful need, however, may engage in more passive ways of acquiring information in the form of monitoring and browsing over time. Figure 6.2 shows Wilson's model.

'Internal' factors

A number of factors which may be thought of as relatively internal to the individual have been the subject of research for a considerable time, including gender, age, self-efficacy, cognitive styles and personality.

Gender

Gender has been found to be an influential variable in a number of studies of information behaviour. For example, in a study of academic and research

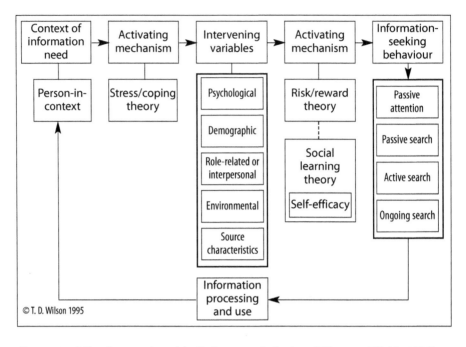

Figure 6.2 Wilson's general model of information behaviour (Wilson and Walsh, 1996)

library users (Steinerová and Šušol, 2007) found that males preferred individual information seeking in contrast to females' preference for a collaborative approach. Males also tended to adopt an analytic approach compared to the more pragmatic approach of females. The authors conclude that:

> Gender as a variable can be productive for better understanding of cognitive and social background of human information processing. Findings can inform design of services and systems and information literacy policies.
>
> Steinerová and Šušol, 2007

Zoe and DiMartino (2000) found that women preferred a more informal search environment in which instruction was characterized by participation and interaction. Agosto (2001), on the basis of reviewing the literature, concluded that:

> The most commonly discussed gender-specific aspect of information-seeking behavior is collaboration. In general, women tend to prefer learning through collaboration; men generally prefer learning through competition.
>
> Agosto, 2001, 2

Ford and Miller (1996) and Ford, Miller and Moss (2001) found evidence of females feeling, relative to males, greater disorientation, perceptions of inability to find their way around the web, of getting lost and not feeling in control. In studies by Jackson, Ervin, Gardner and Schmitt (2001) and Schumacher and Morahan-Martin (2001) females reported greater computer-related anxiety and discomfort and less computer-related self-efficacy. Karavidas, Lim and Katsikas (2004) found that males displayed less computer-related anxiety as well as better performance. Such affective differences have also been reported in relation to information seeking. Ybarra and Suman (2008), for example, report that men are more likely to report a positive experience when seeking health information on the web than women.

However, there are a number of studies reporting no significant gender difference (e.g. Fallows, 2005; Hupfer and Detlor, 2006; Kim, Lehto and Morrison, 2007; Liang and Tsai, 2009), and arguing that the gender divide is becoming extinct (e.g. Enochsson, 2005). There are also research findings that suggest that females tend to underestimate their level of web-based information-seeking ability despite there being no apparent difference between the genders (Hargittai and Shafer, 2006). However, Chen and Macredie (2010), in their review of human factors, conclude that:

> Although some studies show that there is no gender difference in Web-based interaction, the majority of studies indicate that gender is an influential variable. This implies that males and females might need different levels of support when they interact with the Web.
>
> Chen and Macredie, 2010, 381

Age

Age is another variable that has been studied in relation to both information seeking and more general computing-related activity.

THINK!

If you have recently observed someone older or younger than yourself looking for information (maybe a parent, or child – or a client, if you are an information professional) are you aware of any differences in the way *they* went about it compared with how *you* would have approached the task that you think might be age-related?

Czaja and Lee (2001), on the basis of a review of the literature, conclude that:

> Generally, the available literature suggests that older adults are able to search

and retrieve information within 'electronic environments'. However, they appear to have more difficulty than do younger adults and tend to use less efficient navigation strategies.

Czaja and Lee, 2001, 74–5

Sutcliffe and Ennis (1998) also found that older adults were less efficient and effective in web searching, and Ybarra and Suman (2008) conclude that reported frustration with the experience of searching for health-related information on the web increases with age.

A number of researchers have suggested that inferior performance by older people may be due to a decline in their fluid cognitive functions and consequent reliance on crystallized knowledge and abilities (Czaja, Charness, Fisk, Hertzog, Nari, Rogers and Sharit, 2006; Stine-Morrow, Miller, Gagne and Hertzog, 2008). However, task differences have also been found to affect performance in relation to age. For example, Cohen, Cohen and Aiken (2003) found that older people were better at finding online information than younger adults in open-ended exploratory search tasks. Younger people outperformed older people in relation to closed tasks in which they had to retrieve specific information. Chen and Fu (2009) also found that younger people displayed superior performance in relation to well defined search tasks, whilst older people performed better in more open-ended exploratory search tasks.

Task structure has been found to interact with type of interface in relation to age. For example, Chen and Fu (2009) studied the information searching of younger and older adults in a medical decision-making task. They investigated the effects of two different interfaces with varying information structures and different tasks. They found that younger people were more flexible in terms of employing different search strategies in response to different combinations of tasks and interfaces. Older people tended to use the same strategies despite differences in task and interface. The authors conclude that the knowledge structures of younger adults were changed in the interaction with the different systems interfaces, but older adults were more resilient in their knowledge structures. Corsi (1972) also found younger people to be more flexible in terms of adapting their strategies to fit task requirements.

Self-efficacy

Self-efficacy is an individual's belief in his or her ability successfully to perform some task (Bandura, 1986; 1993; 1997). There is evidence that high self-efficacy impacts positively on work performance across a range of contexts (Bandura, 1986; 1993; 1997). Self-efficacy is thought to affect individuals' goal setting, planning, motivation, the level of effort they put into a task, and their persistence in the face of setbacks (Stajkovic and Luthans, 1998).

Brown, Ganesan and Challagalla (2001) studied information seeking, from their supervisors or colleagues, of employees involved in industrial selling in order to improve the clarity with which they understood their role expectations. Information seeking was linked to increased role clarity – but this effect was moderated by self-efficacy. People with high levels of self-efficacy were more able to use information to clarify their roles than those with lower self-efficacy.

Hsu, Ju, Yen and Chang (2007) studied the role of self-efficacy in knowledge-sharing behaviour, concluding that that self-efficacy is a significant predictor. They note that their results accord with a number of other studies of the effects of self-efficacy on knowledge-sharing behaviour (Bock and Kim, 2002; Kankanhalli, Tan and Wei, 2005) and computer-related behaviour more generally (e.g. Compeau and Higgins, 1995; 1999; Easley, Devaraj and Crant, 2003; Hsu and Chiu, 2004).

Kuo, Chu, Hsu and Hsieh (2004), in a study of web use relating to e-commerce, explored whether there is a trade-off between economy of effort and accuracy in web searching. They found that whilst the level of accuracy was affected by the level of effort on the part of people with low levels of self-efficacy, there was no such trade-off for people with high self-efficacy.

Self-efficacy is linked to the notion of 'attribution', which has been the focus of a number of studies of information behaviour. The way in which a person attributes the causes of failure and success to factors within or beyond their control can affect self-efficacy positively or negatively, and attribution theories can contribute to our understanding of people's motivations for information seeking and avoidance. Savolainen (2013) notes that the main causes of success and failure in information seeking are ability, effort, task difficulty, and luck. However, these may be considered by different people to be internal or external, stable or unstable, and controllable or uncontrollable.

Mansourian and Ford (2007b) found empirical evidence of differences in information seekers' attributions. In a sample of university researchers, they found five types of attribution relating to success and failure in information seeking in which:

- both failure and success were attributed to external forces outside their control (e.g. luck)

- success was attributed to relatively external factors, whilst failure was attributed to relatively internal factors (e.g. effort or ability)
- internal and external attributions were not linked to search success or failure
- success was attributed to relatively internal factors, whilst failure was attributed to relatively external factors
- not only success but also failure were attributed to internal factors.

They speculated on possible implications for training and education in information seeking to the extent that:

> The more extreme low self-efficacy individual – if tending to attribute both success and failure to external factors to a greater extent than is warranted by a more objective assessment of the reality of the situation – may underestimate the potential benefits, in terms of increasing success and reducing failure, of engaging in training/self-learning, perceiving little to be gained by attempting to enhance internal factors such as knowledge and skills if both success and failure are due to external factors beyond his/her control.

> Conversely, the extreme high self-efficacy individual – again, assuming that his or her tendency distorts a more objective assessment of search attributions – may be excessively self-critical over search failures, and possibly expect too much in terms of the capacity of training to remedy them where in reality they are the result of external factors.

> Mansourian and Ford, 2007a, 674

Cognitive styles

A cognitive style is a tendency to adopt a particular approach to information processing across different tasks. This may relate to the way people go about acquiring, perceiving and understanding information. A number of cognitive styles have been the focus of much research in relation to learning and education, and more recently information behaviour.

Examples of cognitive styles include: verbal/visual; wholist/analytic; impulsive/reflective; parallel processing/sequential. Although there are many such styles visible in the research literature, Riding and Cheema (1991) consider that there are two fundamental dimensions of style: visual/verbal and wholist/analytic. Whilst both of these have been the focus of studies of information behaviour, the wholist/analytic dimension of style has received particular attention. This wholist/analytic dimension of cognitive style (Riding and Cheema, 1991; Riding and Rayner, 1998) is also known as field-dependence/independence (Witkin, 1976; Witkin and Goodenough 1981, Witkin, Moore, Goodenough and Cox, 1977). Riding's terminology of 'wholist' and 'analytic' is used here as opposed to Witkin's 'field-dependent' and 'field-independent', though as Riding and Cheema (1991) note, the constructs are essentially equivalent.

This style has been the focus of research study in psychology and education for over 40 years, and has been found to influence a wide range of human activity, from basic perception to career choice. Relatively wholist individuals have also been found to be more socially oriented, and less independent, in terms of needing more help in structuring unstructured situations, than their analytic counterparts. More recently it has been the focus of a number of studies of information behaviour. The cognitive style literature suggests that differences in people's cognitive styles may affect not only the strategies they adopt in learning or information seeking, but also the nature and effectiveness of the results of these cognitive processes – whether in learning (Ford, 1995; Ford and Chen, 2001; Pask, 1988; Witkin et al., 1977) or information seeking (Ford, 2001).

Witkin et al. (1977) published a detailed review of research describing the essential features characterizing this style. Relatively analytic individuals are better at structuring and analytical activity when compared with their wholist counterparts. Wholist individuals thrive more in situations where information is structured and analysed for them. Relatively analytic individuals tend to experience the components of a structured field analytically, as discrete from their background, and to impose structure on a relatively unstructured field. By contrast, relatively wholist individuals tend to be less good at such structuring and analytic activity, and to perceive a complex stimulus holistically as a gestalt.

A number of studies have explored the implications of this cognitive style dimension for information behaviour. There is evidence that the wholist/analytic cognitive style dimension can affect web-based information search strategies. Studies by Ford, Wood and Walsh (1994) and Wood, Ford and Walsh (1992), for example, revealed significant links between these styles and search behaviour. Postgraduate university students conducted searches on a database on subjects related to their coursework. The searching strategies of postgraduate university students searching Silver Platter's CD ROM-based Library and Information Science Abstracts (LISA) were classified in terms of relative breadth and depth. A high use of 'OR' to link keywords represents a relatively broad strategy: a high use of 'AND' a relatively narrow strategy. Other measures included use of truncation and generic descriptors (which broaden a search) and use of date or language qualifiers (which tend to narrow a search). It was found that relatively wholist individuals used significantly broader search strategies than their analytic counterparts.

Wang, Hawk and Tenopir (2000) investigated cognitive and affective aspects of web searching by Masters students. They found interactions between cognitive style and both difficulty and confusion. Wholist students experienced greater difficulty and confusion than analytic students. Levels of anxiety were linked to negative feelings, which in turn, could affect levels of persistence in searching.

Palmquist and Kim (2000) investigated searching by undergraduate college students of a university website. They found that cognitive style interacted with search experience. Wholist novice searchers took longer and traversed more nodes when finding information than analytic novices. Wholist novices also made greater use of embedded links. The authors concluded that wholist searchers prefer a well structured set of stimuli, and do not enjoy imposing a structure by themselves, therefore tending to follow links prescribed by web page authors. No significant cognitive style differences were found among experienced searchers.

Differences do not relate only to information seeking. Ford et al. (2002), for example, found that analytic researchers were more active and analytic than wholist in relation to their problem-solving and information-seeking behaviour. They report more of Ellis' (Ellis, 1989; Ellis and Haugan, 1997) 'differentiating' activity (see 'Basic information-seeking processes and activities' in Chapter 4) and higher levels of change in their perception of the problem they are working on. This tends to support the view that analytic individuals engage more actively and critically as they process new information.

Chen and Macredie (2002) reviewed a number of studies of the wholist/analytic dimension in relation to information processing. They concluded that the research suggests that when navigating an intellectual space relatively wholist individuals prefer more structured linear pathways while more analytic learners prefer freer, more exploratory, non-linear pathways through hypermedia systems (e.g. Andris, 1996; Chang, 1995; Durfresne and Turcotte, 1997; Reed and Oughton, 1997). They also concluded that wholists had a greater need to be provided with structure and guidance. This last point is supported by a study by Heinström (2002), which found that wholists appeared more to become lost and to be distracted on the web.

Chen, Magoulas and Dimakopoulos (2005) investigated people's preferences for different ways in which information in subject categories was presented in a web directory. They found that wholist individuals preferred more main categories, with fewer levels of subcategory and web pages that presented subcategories first, followed by the corresponding results. Conversely, analytics individuals preferred to have results presented first, followed by subcategories. Where categories and subcategories were presented before specific results, wholists preferred to have main and subcategories presented on separate pages whilst analytics preferred both to be presented on the same page.

The results of these studies imply that analytic individuals prefer to adopt an approach in which they pay early attention to relatively detailed lower-level content when processing information in order to learn or problem-solve. Wholists prefer to pay early attention to establishing a good global overview of a new topic to gain a good understanding of its main elements and how these interrelate before committing energy to narrower, more detailed analysis.

Personality

Recall from the section on 'Information-seeking strategies' in Chapter 4 that Heinström (2002) identified different information-seeking strategies: fast surfing, broad scanning and deep diving. Her research linked the adoption of different strategies with different personality features and also study approaches:

- A deep approach entails having the intention really to understand material being learned, including appreciating the main argument and examining the supporting evidence presented.
- A surface approach is characterized by a focus on memorizing information in order to be able to reproduce it without understanding it more deeply.
- A strategic approach to studying may be adopted by some individuals, in which they are able flexibly to adopt either a deep or surface strategy as they deem appropriate for a particular task and context.

Heinström's study also measured five personality traits, comprising the following:

1 **Neuroticism:** people high in neuroticism, compared to their less neurotic counterparts, are more emotionally unstable and likely to experience anger, anxiety, envy and guilt.
2 **Extraversion:** relatively extravert individuals tend to be outgoing, and more physically and verbally active. Their introverted counterparts tend

to be reserved, withdrawn and solitary.

3 **Openness to experience:** as the label indicates, individuals who display this trait are relatively open to new ideas and experiences. People who are low in this trait prefer more familiar ideas and experiences and are more conventional and conservative.

4 **Agreeableness:** individuals scoring high on agreeableness tend to have a caring, altruistic personality and a willingness to give emotional support. People who score low on this scale tend to be more self-centred and indifferent to others.

5 **Conscientiousness:** this is a trait characterized by being competent, organized and systematic, with a desire to perform a task well.

Interestingly, Heinström found links between information-seeking behaviour and both study approach and personality traits. Specifically, she found associations between:

- Fast surfing and
  — a surface study approach
  — neuroticism
  — low openness to experience
  — low conscientiousness.
  Fast surfing was correlated with poor study results. This combination of a nervous personality and surface study approach was also linked to problems relating to both seeking and analysing information in terms of 'difficulties in relevance judgement, experience of time pressure and problems with critical information judgement'.

- Broad scanning was associated with
  — extraversion
  — openness
  — competitiveness.
  Broad scanning was most prevalent amongst students in the Department of Economics and Social Sciences, thought by Heinström probably to be due to the 'soft discipline' nature of these subjects, in which information can be found in a wide range of sources.

- Deep diving was linked to
  — openness to experience
  — a combination of deep and strategic approaches to studying.
  Openness to experience and a deep study approach were linked to

preferring documents which promote relatively divergent thought processes entailing new ideas rather than those which confirm existing ideas in a more convergent way.

Heinström concluded that:

> personality or study approach influence information seeking by interacting with other variables, such as … faculty, stage of research process, task or knowledge etc. The core personality is likely to remain the same across situations although the way it is expressed and how much it influences behaviour varies according to context.
>
> Heinström, 2002, 256

Heinström acknowledges that the adoption of a particular approach to information processing may result from interaction between a number of factors – both internal and external to the individual. Aspects of personality may interact with habitual study approach, and both may interact with contextual elements such as a fast-approaching deadline, and disciplinary differences in what people are studying.

More recently Heinström, Sormunen and Kaunisto-Laine (2014) studied the effects of both personality (intellectual curiosity, conscientiousness and negative emotionality) and study approach (deep, strategic and surface) on information behaviour amongst high school students. They found that these individual differences were more influential on the students' information behaviour than high school grade. Specifically, they found that:

> . . . each of the traits had their own particular influence at various stages of the process. Personality traits had a stronger impact at the task construction phase, while study approaches were more influential at task performance and task completion. Overall, individual traits were most influential on the task completion stage, when students read information sources and wrote their own texts, in other words when they used information. Information use has not been much studied in earlier information research. We, therefore, regard this finding as particularly noteworthy.
>
> Heinström, Sormunen and Kaunisto-Laine, 2014, 1092

As we will see later in this chapter, Mansourian focused more directly on factors that may influence approaches to information processing, and the interaction between internal and external factors.

Emotions

The personality traits researched by Heinström are broad, underlying features which affect the behaviour and attitudes of a person across a wide range of activity, including information behaviour. Another broad, underlying characteristic affecting a wide range of our attitudes and behaviours – and studied in the context of information behaviour by Savolainen – is a tendency to approach life with a feeling of basic optimism or pessimism. Pessimism has been found to be linked with neuroticism, one of the 'big five' personality traits studied by Heinström.

Information needs as conceived by Savolainen were discussed in Chapter 3 in the section on 'Information needs', and relate to the need to achieve 'mastery of life'. Savolainen (1995) went on to propose a typology of mastery of life in terms of different styles in which different people go about problem solving and associated aspects of information-seeking behaviour. He categorizes these styles across two dimensions: (1) cognitive/affective; and (2) pessimistic/optimistic (shown in Table 6.1). Degrees of optimism and pessimism are present in Savolainen's classification, which comprises:

- unreserved optimism (in which the person expects no setbacks in problem solving)
- reserved optimism (in which s/he does expect some setbacks)
- reserved pessimism (in which s/he does expect some failures)
- unreserved pessimism (in which s/he expects to fail).

Table 6.1 Savolainen's 'mastery of life' styles

	Cognitive (analytic and systematic)	Affective (emotion-based)
Pessimistic (expectation of failure)	The person accepts the possibility that s/he will not find an optimal solution to the problem. S/he is less ambitious in the way s/he sets problem-solving objectives. Nevertheless, the person may still be systematic in his/her problem solving and related information seeking.	'Learned helplessness' characterizes this style, in which problem solving is dominated by emotional reactions and a short-sighted perspective. The person avoids systematically trying to improve his/her situation. Systematic information seeking to support problem solving is not particularly appropriate in these circumstances.
Optimistic (expectation of success)	The person believes that problems are mainly cognitive (intellectual) rather than affective (emotion-influenced), and is confident that most problems can be solved by systematic analysis. Information seeking is key to this process.	Affective factors are influential in problem solving and information seeking. Although his/her feeling may vary from situation to situation, s/he is primarily optimistic about problem solving and confident in his/her cognitive abilities. However, the person may tend to avoid situations in which s/he thinks there is a risk of failure, and this may deteriorate into wishful thinking.

Savolainen went on to link these basic orientations with their cognitive and affective implications, as shown in Table 6.1.

Savolainen (2012) further explored the role of affective as well as cognitive factors, and the interaction between the two in information seeking. He adopted an expectancy-value perspective on motivation, in which individuals are motivated to engage in task activity based on an interaction between *expectancy* (the belief that one is able to perform the task), *value* (the perceived benefit of performing the task) and *emotions* (how the person feels about performing the task). Savolainen notes that cognitive and affective factors interact with each other and with contextual factors (including situational, social and task-related) to affect information seeking. He gives the following example:

> Ultimately, how the cognitive and affective factors are related depend on the nature of contextual factors of these kinds. For example, at the phase of topic selection, the weighing of topics against project requirements (cognitive attribute) may be associated with a higher level of anxiety (affective attribute) if the time frame of the project (contextual factor) is very narrow.
>
> Savolainen, 2012

Savolainen (2014) has conducted a conceptual analysis based on relevant research literature of one of eight information-related viewpoints relating to emotions included in Dervin and Reinhard's (2007) outline conceptual framework. He selected as a key viewpoint the relationship between emotions and both activating and inhibiting motivations for information seeking. The analysis suggested that emotions may affect motivation to seek information in terms of starting, expanding, limiting, terminating or avoiding information seeking. He concludes that:

> Some emotions, for example anxiety, may motivate in multiple ways, ranging from starting information seeking to information avoidance, while other emotions such as joy are typically experienced while starting or expanding information seeking.
>
> Savolainen, 2014, 64

Savolainen also notes that research in information science has focused on negative emotions such as anxiety to the relative exclusion of positive emotions such as pleasure.

An example of the effects of negative emotions is provided in a doctoral study by Namuleme (2013). Her study showed how affective factors may affect a person's willingness to accept that they have an information need. Namuleme found, for example, that affective factors may in certain circumstances influence a person's decision to acknowledge the need for information. She found instances of people soon after being diagnosed with a serious illness being unwilling to engage in information seeking through fear of what they might find and be confronted with. Others appeared to be in denial, again possibly wanting to shield themselves from what they perceived might be distressing consequences of accepting that they needed to learn more about how the disease might progress, and how they might most effectively manage it. For some people, this situation changed as they became more used to their situation and became anxious to learn more about their illness.

Kuhlthau (2004) also explored affective factors in information seeking. She focused on positive and negative feelings that are associated with increasing and decreasing uncertainty as people search for information. Her model associated changing negative and positive feelings with different stages in the progress of information seeking. Progress through the various stages are characterized by a move from vagueness to greater focus, and from uncertainty, confusion and doubt to clarity and a sense of direction. Although Kuhlthau includes these as *feelings* (affective), arguably the dimensions of uncertainty/certainty, clarity/vagueness and having a sense of direction/ disorientation are *cognitive*. Cognitive uncertainty can generate affective responses (such as anxiety or satisfaction). Nahl (2007) writes of affective reactions (such as frustration and anxiety) to cognitive uncertainty. Savolainen (2012) also notes that uncertainty should be regarded as cognitive rather than affective, noting in relation to Kuhlthau's model:

> Interestingly, in the graphical illustration of the model, uncertainty is placed in the field of feelings denoting the affective attribute (Kuhlthau 1993: 343). Logically, this conflicts with the principle of uncertainty proposing that uncertainty is primarily a cognitive state that can cause affective symptoms of anxiety and lack of confidence.
>
> Savolainen, 2012

Kuhlthau's model shows how different feelings, both positive and negative, are associated with different stages of information seeking – from optimism, through frustration, to disappointment or satisfaction and a sense of accomplishment to confidence.

Wilson (1981) also notes the possible effects of affective factors in influencing choice of information sources during information seeking:

. . . the channel of communication, particularly the choice of oral channels over written channels, may well be guided by affective needs as much, if not more than, by cognitive needs. For example, in seeking information from a superior, someone may be more interested in being recognized and accepted as a particular kind of person than in the actual subject content of the message; in other words, he may be seeking approval or recognition. The oral transfer of information to others may also be done for affective reasons; for example, to establish dominance over others by reminding them that you are better informed and, therefore, in some sense superior.

Wilson, 1981

Affective factors may influence not only information seeking, but also engagement with and the evaluation and use of information. Namuleme's study of people infected and/or affected by HIV/AIDS found cases of people choosing not to read and assess the usefulness of information with which they come into contact. This could be due to fear of discovering unpalatable information, or fear of the unwanted revelation of their HIV/AIDS status and consequent stigma if they were observed reading information about the disease – fear which on occasion caused people to hide and even destroy information. This could mean that even information which was potentially extremely useful to them was not in fact used.

Wilson (1981) notes that the work context may give rise to affective as well as cognitive needs. The need to solve a particular problem, plan, perform some analysis or compile a report may lead to the need to acquire information. But within an organization, a person may also feel the need to be appreciated and/or to experience self-actualization. Such affective considerations may affect, for example, the sources of information to which a person may turn, maybe as first resort consulting a senior colleague in order to impress.

Case study: the relationship between cognitive and affective factors

Howell and Shepperd (2013) report a novel and interesting study which investigated the relationship between cognitive (rational) and affective (emotion-based) thinking on information seeking and information avoidance in a health information context.

There is considerable research evidence to suggest that some people prefer to avoid information when they think that the information may prove frightening, may counter deeply held beliefs, or may result in their having to undergo something unpleasant. This may often be the case when people are faced with a diagnosis. For example, many people who are tested for HIV fail to return to receive the results of their test. There is other evidence (e.g. Namuleme, 2013) that people may enter a period of denial in which they avoid information which objectively would be of great benefit to them.

As the authors note in their review of relevant literature, there is evidence to suggest that people may process information and make decisions using two very different mental systems. One is cognitive – logical and analytic, entailing careful rational thinking. The other is intuitive and affective, based on emotion. The two systems may produce very different results. In particular, what objectively is a more sensible decision may be rejected by someone operating in emotion-based thinking. The authors also reviewed research into meta-cognition, suggesting that thinking about one's own cognitive processes (meta-cognition) may enable us to take more control of our thinking, and to switch from intuitive to analytic modes (Alter, Oppenheimer, Epley, and Eyre, 2007).

People may respond to health threats either by attempting to reduce fear of the threat, or by attempting to reduce the threat itself. Fear control tends to be emotionally driven. Threat control tends to be cognitive, and there is evidence that when operating in this mode people respond with health-promoting behaviours (Witte, 1994, quoted in Howell and Shepperd, 2013). Thus people may seek, evaluate and use information relevant to their health condition rather than engage in information avoidance.

Howell and Shepperd (2013) also noted that research into meta-cognition suggests that it may be possible to induce people to switch from emotion-based to cognitive responses. They proposed that health-related information avoidance reflects a defensive emotion-based response. They went on to conduct a series of three experiments designed to assess the extent to which it may be possible – via engagement in meta-cognitive reflection – to induce people to engage in rational (cognitive) as opposed to emotional (affective) health-related information behaviour. They went on to design a series of three experiments to test the following hypotheses:

- Thinking about one's own thinking (meta-cognition) relating to health information – specifically, thinking about their reasons for seeking and avoiding information – will tend to reduce information avoidance.
- But this will happen only when the benefits of engaging with the information are considered logically to outweigh the disadvantages. Where the information is considered not to offer a benefit, information avoidance will not be reduced by meta-cognition.

In the first study 146 undergraduates (mixed male and female, with a mean age of 19) were asked to choose whether or not they wished to learn their risk level (using an online risk calculator) for type 2 diabetes. They answered a series of questions relating to potential motives for seeking and avoiding information about their risk. One group answered the questions *before* deciding: the other made their decision *after* answering the questions. The questions prompted the participants to think about what would be the cognitive, affective, and behavioural consequences of learning that they had a high risk of type 2 diabetes. The participants were also asked about their personal coping abilities and their general thoughts about this disease. After deciding whether to learn about their own risk, the participants calculated the likelihood of their developing the disease.

The result of the study was as hypothesized. Significantly fewer participants engaged in information avoidance when they had engaged in the meta-cognitive reflection before making their decision. This effect was found regardless of whether the participants' levels of personal likelihood of developing the disease were rated as high or low.

In the second study, 130 adults (mixed male and female, with a mean age of 35.4) had to decide whether they wished to learn about their risk of developing cardiovascular disease. The participants input data to an online risk calculator, and were told that the calculator would assess their risk of developing the disease whilst they completed another task. After completing this task, they would be asked to decide whether or not to access the information relating to their own risk.

They were divided into two groups. The first, prior to making their decision, were asked to list and rate the strength of their reasons for seeking or avoiding information about their risk of developing cardiovascular disease. They were asked to list four reasons why they should learn about their risk and four reasons why they should avoid learning about it. They then rated the importance, in making their decision, of each of these reasons. The second group was asked to engage in an activity which did not provoke meta-cognitive reflection (reflection on their own thought processes). They were asked simply to list eight facts they knew about the disease. As in the first study, participants were also asked to rate the likelihood of their developing the disease.

As in the first study, significantly fewer participants displayed information avoidance when they had engaged in the meta-cognitive reflective activity. Furthermore, the more the participants rated reasons for learning about their risk as more important than reasons for avoiding it the less likely they were to display information avoidance.

THINK!

Recall that the researchers hypothesized that reflection would result in less information avoidance *only if* accessing rather than avoiding the information was considered to be the superior intellectual choice.

Do you think they successfully tested this hypothesis? Did those people who accessed as opposed to avoiding the information perceive this to be the superior intellectual choice?

If they did – how do you know they did?

Both studies described above showed that reflection seemed to reduce information avoidance. But the hypothesis suggests that this effect would *not* be observed if information avoidance was not a clearly inferior option. Neither study compared the situation where information seeking was clearly not logically superior to information avoidance.

In order explicitly to test this part of the hypothesis, the researchers set up a third experiment. This time, 166 undergraduates (mixed gender and a mean age of 18.6) participants were told that an enzyme deficiency was either treatable or untreatable. They were shown a video about a fictitious disease called thioamine acetylase deficiency. They were told that 20% of college students have this deficiency and that it could result in severe medical complications despite an absence of early symptoms. Participants were divided into two groups – one of which was told that the condition was untreatable, the other that it was. Participants were further grouped into those who engaged in the reflective exercise in which they thought of and rated reasons for information seeking and avoidance, and those who were asked simply to list eight facts that they had learned about the condition. They then estimated their personal likelihood of developing it.

The researchers argued that information seeking would be a clearly superior choice when the disease was treatable – but not when it was untreatable. There is arguably no great logical advantage in knowing one's risk of a disease if there is nothing one can do about it in terms of treatment. If the hypothesis being tested was true, then information avoidance would reduce as a result of meta-cognitive reflection only in those cases where the condition was treatable.

When the condition was described as treatable, there was significantly less information avoidance in the meta-cognitive reflection group than the group who did not reflect. Also, the participants rated their reasons for seeking information as more important than their reasons for avoiding it. However, when the condition was described as untreatable, there was no difference in information avoidance between the reflection and no-reflection groups. The participants also gave equal importance to their reasons for seeking and avoiding the information. As in the first study, the estimated level of personal likelihood of developing the condition had no effect. Recall that in the second study, the more the participants rated reasons for learning about their risk as more important than reasons for avoiding it the less likely they were to display information avoidance. This effect was not found in the third experiment.

The study illustrates differences between logical cognitive information processing and emotion-based affective information processing. Not only are these very different forms of mental activity, but they may also have very differing results in terms of a person's behaviour and response to a given situation. Moreover, the study suggests that it may be possible to influence people to switch between these different forms of thinking – and therefore potentially to affect the nature and quality of their responses to a given situation. Specifically, the study suggests that reflection can encourage people to move from emotion-based to more rational decision making. In a health context where acquiring information about a condition and relevant treatment may be logically the most beneficial option, it may be that simply by asking people to reflect on the reasons underlying the decisions they make may reduce levels of information avoidance.

However, such conclusions are subject to caution, since this study has, as do all studies, certain limitations. It is based on observing people in an artificial experimental situation. As the researchers acknowledge, participants were deciding whether or not to learn their level of health risk using an online calculator, and the extent to which they might behave in the same way in a real-life situation in which they had to return to a doctor's office to receive test results for a condition which really applied to them is not clear.

External influences

Researchers have increasingly widened their focus to include factors which might be considered relatively 'external' to the individual in that they do not relate directly to the mental processes (cognitive and affective) of the information seeker/user.

People live and work within a range of different contexts. An early researcher who recognized this in the work context was Paisley. In his research into scientific information users (Paisley, 1968), he emphasized that people operate within, and are influenced by, a range of different contexts – some embedded within others. He differentiated between:

- the cultural context
- the political context

- membership groups to which the scientist may belong
- his or her reference group
- the invisible college within which s/he may operate
- the formal organization within which s/he may work
- his or her work team
- the scientist 'within his own head'
- the legal and economical context.

Since Paisley's work, awareness of the importance for understanding their information behaviour of the context in which individuals or groups of people are operating has grown steadily. 1996 saw the first Information Seeking in Context (ISIC) biennial conference, which has continued to grow to the present time. Increasing research efforts have focused on contextual aspects of information behaviour, and the field has embraced social science research methods, acknowledging the interconnectedness of a broad range of factors which both influence and are essential constituents of information behaviour.

Work-related and organizational factors

A major focus of research into influences on information behaviour has been the nature of the work in which people are engaged which gives rise to information needs, including the particular tasks they are performing and characteristics of the organizations within which they are working.

Leckie and Pettigrew (1997) consider that information practices are primarily influenced by people's work roles, which in turn influence the tasks they are expected to perform, in turn determining information needs. The way in which individuals go about trying to satisfy these needs are influenced by *inter alia* organizational culture, the availability of relevant information, and characteristics of the individual.

Research suggests that task complexity can affect information behaviour. Byström (2002) made a number of observations based on a review of the literature on task complexity and information behaviour:

- As task complexity increases, the use of information sources may increase or decrease depending on the nature of the work context. It increases in the case of administrative- and technical-related tasks, and decreases in the case of engineering and management (Zeffane and Gul, 1993).
- In other areas there are conflicting findings. The effects of an increase in task complexity on preference for people rather than documents as

sources of information are unclear, as are the effects of task complexity on the use of internal or external information sources.

- In an educational context, Kuhlthau's research indicated that the type of information used depends on the stage of a task. At the beginning of a task more general relevant information is required. Towards the end of the task more specialized, focused information is relevant (Kuhlthau, 1993).

- Also in an educational context, Vakkari (2000) found that university students generated more precise search terms as they progressed in a task, and that people (in the form of their tutors) were more important as information sources as they began their task. Documents were important throughout the process (Vakkari and Pennanen, 2001).

- Perceptions of task complexity and uncertainty differ between novices and experts in task performance (Kuhlthau, 1999).

- Tasks perceived as complex or uncertain are more frequent in educational contexts than professional ones (Byström, 1997; Wilson and Spink, 2000). However, task complexity is itself a complex concept, and can be defined from a number of perspectives (Liu and Li, 2012). From a *structuralist* viewpoint it may be thought of in terms of structural aspects, such as the number of task elements and relationships between them. Defined from a *resource requirement* viewpoint, task complexity relates to the level of resources needed to conduct the task, such as intellectual and physical effort and load, and time. From an *interaction* viewpoint task complexity is the product of interaction between characteristics of the task and of the person performing the task, such as prior knowledge and experience, and perception of the task. This definition introduces a subjective element, since a key component is the task performer's perception of the task and its complexity.

From an information behaviour research point of view, arguably an interaction perspective is particularly appropriate, since different people may interpret the same task in different ways, and ultimately a person's information behaviour is determined in large part by their perceptions of the task (Byström and Järvelin, 1995).

Some researchers, such as Kim (2008), have differentiated task complexity from task difficulty by considering complexity to be an objective measure related to the characteristics of the task (irrespective of searcher characteristics) whilst task difficulty relates to the perceptions of the information seeker, thus rendering it essentially subjective. Kim also differentiates between pre-task and post-task perceptions of task difficulty, pre-task difficulty being a measure of perceived likelihood of success, which is conceptually similar to self-efficacy (see the section on 'Internal' factors earlier in this chapter).

Wildemuth, Freund and Toms (2014) reviewed the array of definitions used in 106 research studies in interactive information retrieval. They explored the concepts of task complexity and difficulty in the context of research into information-searching experiments in which participants either choose their own or are given researcher-assigned topics on which to search for information. Based on an analysis of the research literature, the authors adopt an objective view of task complexity as 'an inherent attribute of the search task, independent of the task doer or the actions taken to carry out the task' (Wildemuth, Freund and Toms, 2014), defined in terms of:

- the multiplicity of steps or subtasks;
- the multiplicity of facets where facets represent the concepts or types of concepts represented in the task, e.g. dates or genre; and
- some degree of indeterminability or uncertainty (i.e. for a complex task, the search process or outcomes cannot be determined in advance of completing the task).

Wildemuth, Freund and Toms, 2014, 1132

Search task difficulty may include a subjective aspect, insofar as it is conceptualized as an interaction between attributes of the search task and characteristics of the searcher and the context in which they are operating. It may be defined in terms of:

- the extent to which a given set of people successfully perform the task
- an assessment of the degree to which the words used in the description of the task match keywords in the relevant documents to be retrieved
- the number of documents in the collection being used in the test that are relevant and potentially retrievable
- the perceptions of the level of difficulty perceived by the searchers and/or expert judges.

These complexities mean that unless (a) task complexity and difficulty are clearly and unambiguously defined and (b) an adequate range of factors that may affect the relationship between task complexity or difficulty and information behaviour are taken into account in a research study, research findings may be confounded. An example of the latter issue is given above, where conflicting results were found in relation to the relationship between task complexity and decreasing or increasing use of information sources. This was to some extent resolved by making explicit another influential variable, the inclusion of which renders these seemingly clashing results compatible, namely the work context (e.g. administrative or engineering).

Clearly there is much work to be done before we can establish clearly and robustly what are the effects on information behaviour of task complexity and difficulty. As Liu and Li (2012) note:

> . . . defining task complexity suffers from a confusion of individual and task
> characteristics . . . which leads to the confusion and misuse of the concepts of
> objective task complexity vs. subjective task complexity and of task complexity
> vs. task difficulty. As a consequence, it is difficult not only to generalize findings
> from one area to another, but also to generalize findings from laboratory tasks to
> real-life tasks.
>
> Liu and Li, 2012, 557

Wilson (1981) also draws attention to the effects of the economic and political contexts within which an organization may operate. Due to the level of resources at their disposal some may be relatively 'information rich' and others 'information poor', with consequences for the extent to which information is sought, and the sources used. Political considerations may also have their effect: in some countries certain materials not being approved and available for certain groups and organizations. In relation to both economic and political factors, the same may hold true for individuals as well as organizations.

Social and community integration

A number of researchers have explored the influences of what might broadly be termed social as opposed to work-related factors, in the sense of communities of people forming not specifically for work purposes.

For example, Fisher and her colleagues (Fisher et al., 2005; Fisher, Durrance and Hinton, 2004; Fisher et al., 2004; Pettigrew, 1999) developed the concept of an 'information ground' to describe the relatively informal and temporary coming together of groups of people around some goal or activity. This is described by Pettigrew (1999: 811) as:

> . . . an environment temporarily created when people come together for a
> singular purpose but from whose behavior emerges a social atmosphere that
> fosters the spontaneous and serendipitous sharing of information
>
> Pettigrew, 1999, 811

The concept arose in Fisher's study of how people at foot clinics shared information. She found that the fact that people found themselves in close proximity led to incidental information sharing about a range of issues. Information grounds entail certain social conventions, roles and norms.

'Small world' or 'life in the round' theory was developed by Chatman (1999) from studies of relatively vulnerable groups, such as elderly people living in assisted living environments, prisoners and low-income earners. The theory posits that such groups operate within their own norms and rules, which define 'insiders' and 'outsiders', and tend to constrain free-ranging information behaviour. 'Outside' information not relevant to daily concerns within the group is not regarded as important and thus is not sought unless there is a critical need to do so. What is regarded as important or trivial is determined by the group. Chatman argued that information behaviour is essentially constrained within a small world, and that a limited and parochial view of the potential usefulness of information is perpetuated within the group, which may lead to a situation of information poverty.

According to Sonnenwald's (1999) theory of 'information horizons', within any situation or context, information behaviour is limited to the view of possible solutions to a particular problem that is visible within the information horizons of the people involved. A 'situation' is defined by Sonnenwald as 'a set of related activities, or a set of related stories, that occur over time'. Situations take place within a 'context', which relates to a 'set' of past, present and future situations. A context is therefore a more general concept than the situations that occur within it. The context in which the situation just defined may occur is academia (as opposed to, say, everyday life or working as a doctor).

Information horizons consist of a range of human and non-human information resources, which include social networks, documents, information search tools and one's observations of the world. Some of these resources have knowledge of each other. The information horizons relevant to people in particular situations or contexts are what Sonnenwald calls 'densely populated solution spaces' in which many different solutions can be conceived. However, it can be difficult to see the solutions that are potentially available within the information sources.

From an information-seeking perspective, the problem shifts from one of trying to find information relating to an optimal solution to one of trying to make possible solutions visible, both to the individual and where relevant to other information resources. Sonnenwald (1999) surmises that:

> ... perhaps a digital information horizon could take into account an individual's

social network by also providing access to the social network and expanding it to include additional human experts who could either satisfy the need directly or provide pointers to appropriate resources. Thus the problem further shifts from the traditional focus of eliminating human intermediaries to providing access to many human intermediaries.

Sonnenwald, 1999, 10

The relationship between 'internal' and 'external' factors

THINK!

Have you ever done a 'quick and dirty' search for information? By this I mean a search that you know fell short of the maximum quality search you could have done in ideal circumstances.

If so – why did you do this type of search and not an ideal search? And in what way was the search not ideal – i.e. what did you do (or not do) that you would have done (or not done) in such an ideal search?

So-called 'internal' and 'external' factors may interact to influence information behaviour. Mansourian (Mansourian and Ford, 2007b), for example, explored factors influencing choice of search strategy in an academic context. He produced a model linking the strategies he had observed with potential explanatory factors, drawing on more general work by Agosto (2002), who had devised a framework for research into information seeking based on the theories of 'bounded rationality' and 'satisficing'. These concepts were originated by Simon (1955, 1956) and reflect observations that people often do not behave in the way that would be dictated by complete rationality. Satisficing strategies and factors possibly influencing the adoption of a bounded rationality approach – linked to his classification of types of searching – are shown in Figure 6.3.

In certain situations and circumstances, for example when time or resources are limited, people will 'satisfice' – that is, engage in behaviour that they perceive is 'good enough'. 'Satisficing' is a blend of the words 'satisfying' and 'sufficing'. Where it may be impossible, or excessively time- or effort-consuming, to arrive at the logically optimal outcome (having systematically considered all the options available), people may instead use shortcuts to limit the choices available and apply their rationality to this reduced set of choices. These concepts are similar in certain respects to Zipf's (1949) 'least effort' principle, whereby people try to minimize the amount of effort they expend on a task.

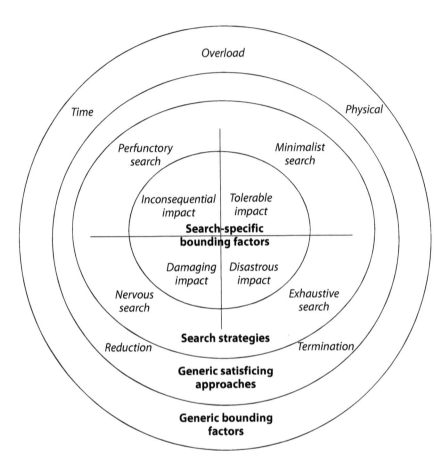

Figure 6.3 Mansourian's model of bounded rationality and satisficing (Mansourian and Ford, 2007b)

Thus, factors influencing people to adopt a satisficing approach may be internal and/or external, and may entail interaction between the two. For example, time constraints (external) and the volume of information available on the topic at hand (external), plus an individual's assessment that s/he is not able to process it adequately (internal cognitive) may lead to anxiety (internal affective), which may lead to a satisficing approach.

Agosto (2002) developed a conceptual framework to analyse interview data from young people relating to their web-based decision-making, based on the concepts of bounded rationality and satisficing. Mansourian used a slightly modified version of this framework to analyse data gathered from university researchers, and found evidence of Agosto's categories. These categories are shown in the two outer circles in Figure 6.3 and are described as follows.

Factors that may motivate individuals to attempt to shortcut a fully ration approach include:

- time constraints
- information overload
- and/or physical constraints (such as discomfort or amount of effort required).

Satisficing strategies that may be applied in order to limit the range of options include:

- **reduction** – reducing the search task, for example by only using known websites, by searching for abstracts, current contents or other summaries rather than the full versions of documents) and/or by narrowing down the sites to be used by category appropriate to the type of search (e.g. Pubmed for medical literature searches)
- **termination** via 'stop rules', which may include:
  — acceptance (stopping after a search produces results deemed acceptable)
  — discomfort (stopping when things are felt to be too uncomfortable to continue – for example, via a headache or other physical discomfort)
  — boredom
  — time limitations exceeded
  — 'snowballing' (experiencing repetition in search results, which suggests that the search is unlikely to throw up much new material).

Wilson (1981, 1994, 1997) has also developed models which integrate internal and external factors influencing information behaviour, later versions building on and extending previous ones. In his 1997 model, Wilson integrated work conducted within information science with a review of relevant literature from other fields to form an integrated explanatory framework relating to the processes of – and the factors that drive, inhibit and shape – information behaviour. He also built on his previous model, first published in 1981 and presented in updated form (Figure 6.4) in Wilson (1999). This model charts links between relatively internal and external factors that may affect information behaviour.

In the model, Wilson incorporates Ellis' types of information seeking (starting, chaining, browsing, etc. – see Chapter 7), explaining that this

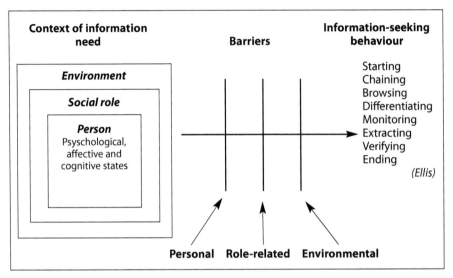

Figure 6.4 Wilson's revision of his 1981 'general model of information-seeking behaviour' (Wilson, 1999)

behaviour takes place in a broader context of influencing factors. Wilson acknowledges that an information need is not a need in itself, but rather derives from a more fundamental need. This is generated by interaction between a number of different internal and external factors (personal, social and environmental) which can also form barriers to a search for information.

Information needs arise in relation to different aspects of the contexts in which people live and work, which Wilson categorizes into personal, role-related and environmental. He proposes that information-seeking behaviour, which is a response to the need to acquire information to help resolve some problem or issue, is subject to a number of barriers which may also relate to personal, role-related and/or environmental factors.

Personal factors may include, for example, 'cognitive dissonance'. There is evidence that people tend to want to resolve conflicting views when confronted with them. One way is to seek information which confirms rather than challenges their existing views (via selective exposure to information) – or to justify the rejection of new views if they are dissonant with their existing ones. However, the extent to which different individuals are driven by this motivation to resolve cognitive dissonance may differ. People may also differ physiologically, cognitively and emotionally, and these differences may affect information behaviour. They may include physical barriers to accessing information, emotional factors such as fear, and cognitive characteristics such as their level of existing relevant knowledge base.

Social role-related factors may also influence information behaviour. Wilson notes that Connell and Crawford (1988), for example, found that women reported receiving more health information than men. They attributed this finding to women's traditional role as care-givers and lay health-care providers. Social issues such as privacy may also affect access to and the use of information. Social stigma, for example, may be a barrier to seeking information on certain diseases.

Environmental factors may also play a role. These include time (for example, the time available for a search), geographical location (people's geographical location sometimes affecting, for example, their access to medical information) and national cultures (which may affect access to innovations and their associated information).

The 'context of information need' section at the left in Wilson's previous model (Figure 6.4) is abbreviated to the single box shown at the top left in the new model presented in 1996 (Figure 6.5). Similarly, the 'information-seeking behaviour' section shown at the right of the earlier model is abbreviated to the 'information-seeking behaviour' box at the top right of the 1996 model.

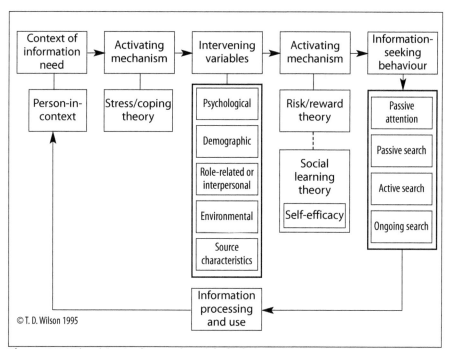

Figure 6.5 Wilson's 'revised general model of information behaviour' (Wilson and Walsh, 1996)

This model builds on the previous two. Developments include:

- Inclusion of an 'activating mechanism' which intervenes between the person in context and the decision to seek information. The model suggests stress/coping models as an example of such a mechanism, though others may equally apply.
- Expansion of the notion of intervening variables or barriers to include information source characteristics (such as ease of access, credibility and communication channel).
- Recognition that personal variables may include demographic as well as physiological, cognitive and affective factors.
- Inclusion of another activating mechanism stage between determining the nature of one's information need and acting to satisfy it. Risk/reward theory, social learning theory and self-efficacy are proposed as examples. Risk/reward theory is concerned with the balance between effort and gain. Social learning theory suggests that the degree to which a person is likely to expend effort and persistence in coping with a problem is related to their self-efficacy, or confidence in their ability to succeed.
- Expansion of types of information seeking to include passive as well as active approaches.
- Extension of the model's scope beyond information seeking to embrace other aspects of information behaviour, namely information processing and information use.
- Inclusion of a feedback loop whereby information processing and use feed back into the context in which an information need is generated.

Wilson explains that:

> The diagram has been simplified by showing the intervening variables at only one point, whereas at least some of the variables may intervene between context and activating mechanism, between activating mechanism and information-seeking behaviour and between information-seeking behaviour and information processing and use.
>
> Wilson, 1997, 569

Wilson's model is relatively broad in coverage. Being so broad, it is not intended to provide as deep an explanation of aspects of information behaviour as are some models that are narrower in scope. Its breadth means that it can accommodate more specific models and theories whilst not elaborating them in detail. Several are included in the model as examples, but it is capable of accommodating others in appropriate sections, such as Cole's theory of information need (see Chapter 3), Chatman's small world theory (see p. 124), etc.

Indeed, when considered in terms of not only the diagrammatic representation but also the textual description and explanation of key concepts, the extent to which Wilson's model represents a theory is far from clear cut. We will explore the differences and relationships between models and theories in the next chapter.

Summary

Research suggests that there is a wide range of potential influences on people's information behaviour. These include factors that may be considered relatively intrinsic to the individual, such as gender, age and various facets of their personality and intellectual approach to learning and problem solving. They also include factors that may be thought of as relatively external to the individual, relating to the context in which they are operating, such as their social roles and relationships, their jobs and working environment, including the tasks they need to perform and the problems they need to solve.

If we can better understand the extent to which – and how – such factors influence information behaviour, we may be better able to intervene in some way in order to help people, where appropriate and possible, to improve the efficiency and effectiveness of the way they go about seeking, evaluating and using information. In particular, if we can discover which features of information behaviour are likely to lead to relatively successful and which to relatively less successful information behaviour then this may help us to:

- design information systems capable of providing users with techniques and approaches better suited to their needs and better adapted to their information-related strengths and weaknesses
- provide more effective training and education designed to help people adopt and develop information behaviour that maximizes their strengths and compensates for their weaknesses
- interact more effectively as information professionals with clients in the process of helping them resolve their learning, problem-solving and leisure needs by finding, evaluating and using information more effectively.

However, we still lack robust models capable of being applied with confidence in real-life situations relevant to professional practice. In many cases research has produced conflicting results, or results that cannot yet be generalized with confidence to real-life information interactions, procedures and policies. But some general principles do emerge for practitioners. Whilst not affording guidelines for practice, research suggests a number of factors to be borne in mind when interacting with information seekers and developing information systems to help them. We need to be aware that:

- different individuals may approach what appears to be objectively the same problem or task in very different ways
- different individuals may want very different outcomes from an ostensibly similar problem or task depending on the context in which they are operating – for example, if they are time-limited or at different stages of their learning or problem solving
- it may be useful to think outside the parameters of the information need as initially presented by clients insofar as they may be constrained by their information horizons. But it is important to know when this would constitute a patronizing and inappropriate approach!

So far we have explored a number of themes characterizing our understanding of aspects of information behaviour in the form of a range of models and theories. To explore further issues relating to different groups of people by occupation, social role and demographic grouping, the reader is referred to Chapters 11 and 12 in Case (2012) and Fisher and Julien (2009). For an overview of individual differences in information behaviour attributable to personality and thinking styles see Bawden and Robinson (2011). In the next chapter we will explore in more detail the precise nature of models and theories in developing such understanding.

References

Agosto, D. E. (2001) Propelling Young Women into the Cyber Age: gender considerations in the evaluation of web-based information, *School Library Media Research*, **4**, 1–20, www.ala.org/aasl/sites/ala.org.aasl/files/content/ aaslpubsandjournals/slr/vol4/SLMR_PropellingYoungWomen_V4.pdf.

Agosto, D. E. (2002) Bounded Rationality and Satisficing in Young People's Web-Based Decision Making, *Journal of the American Society for Information Science and Technology*, **53** (1), 16–27.

Alter, A. L., Oppenheimer, D. M., Epley, N. and Eyre, R. N. (2007) Overcoming Intuition: metacognitive difficulty activates analytic reasoning, *Journal of*

Experimental Psychology: General, **136**, 569–576, doi:10.1037/0096- 3445.136.4.569.

Andris, J. (1996) The Relationship of Indices of Students Navigational Patterns in a Hypermedia Geology Lab Simulation to Two Measures of Learning Style, *Journal of Educational Multimedia and Hypermedia*, **15**, 303–15.

Bandura, A. (1986) *Social Foundations of Thought and Action*, Upper Saddle River, NJ, Prentice Hall.

Bandura, A. (1993) Perceived Self-efficacy in Cognitive Development and Functioning, *Education Psychologist*, **28** (2), 117–48.

Bandura, A. (1997) *Self-efficacy: the exercise of control*, New York, NY, Freeman.

Bawden, D. and Robinson, L. (2011) Individual Differences in Information-related Behaviour: what do we know about information styles? In Spink, A. and Heinström, J. (eds), *New Directions in Information Behaviour* (Library and Information Science, Volume 1), Emerald, 127–58.

Bock, G. W. and Kim, Y. G. (2002) Breaking the Myths of Rewards: an exploratory study of attitudes about knowledge sharing, *Information Resources Management Journal*, **15** (2), 14–21.

Brown, S. P., Ganesan, S. and Challagalla, G. (2001) Self-efficacy as a Moderator of Information-seeking Effectiveness, *Journal of Applied Psychology*, **86** (5), 1043–51.

Byström, K. (1997) Municipal Administrators at Work – Information Needs and Seeking (IN&S) in Relation to Task Complexity: a case-study amongst municipal officials. In Vakkari, P., Savolainen, R. and Dervin, B. (eds), *Information Seeking in Context*, London, Taylor Graham, 125–146.

Byström, K. (2002) Information and Information Sources in Tasks of Varying Complexity, *Journal of the American Society for Information Science and Technology*, **53** (7), 581–91.

Byström, K. and Järvelin, K. (1995) Task Complexity Affects Information Seeking and Use, *Information Processing & Management*, **31** (2), 191–213.

Case, D. (2012) *Looking for Information: a survey of research on information seeking, needs and behavior*, 3rd edn, Bingley, Emerald.

Chang, C. T. (1995) A *Study of Hypertext Document Structure and Individual Differences: effects on learning performance*, PhD dissertation, University of Illinois at Urbana-Champaign.

Chatman, E. A. (1999) A Theory of Life in the Round, *Journal of the American Society for Information Science*, **50** (3), 207–17.

Chen, S-Y. and Fu, Y-C. (2009) Internet Use and Academic Achievement: gender differences in early adolescence, *Adolescence*, **44** (176), 797–812.

Chen, S. Y. and Macredie, R. (2002) Cognitive Styles and Hypermedia Navigation: development of a learning model, *Journal of the American Society for Information Science and Technology*, **53** (1), 3–15.

Chen, S. Y. and Macredie, R. (2010) Web-based Interaction: a review of three important human factors, *International Journal of Information Management*, **30** (5), 379–87.

Chen, S. Y., Magoulas, G. D. and Dimakopoulos, D. (2005) A Flexible Interface Design for Web Directories to Accommodate Different Cognitive Styles, *Journal of the American Society for Information Science*, **56**, 70–83, doi: 10.1002/asi.20103.

Cohen, J. P., Cohen, W. S. and Aiken, L. S. (2003) *Applied Multiple Regression/Correlation Analysis for the Behavioral Sciences*, 3rd edn, NJ: Mahwah, Lawrence Erlbaum.

Compeau, D. R. and Higgins, C. A. (1995) Computer Self-efficacy Development of a Measure and Initial Test, *MIS Quarterly*, **19** (2), 189–211.

Compeau, D. R. and Higgins, C.A. (1999) Social Cognitive Theory and Individual Reactions to Computing Technology: a longitudinal study, *MIS Quarterly*, **23** (2), 145–58.

Connell, C. M. and Crawford, C. O. (1988) How People Obtain Their Health Information: a survey in two Pennsylvania counties, *Public Health Reports*, **103**, 189–95.

Corsi, P. M. (1972) *Human Memory and the Medial Temporal Region of the Brain*, PhD dissertation, McGill University.

Czaja, S. J. and Lee, C. C. (2001) The Internet and Older Adults: design challenges and opportunities. In Charness, N., Parks, D. C. and Sabel, B. A. (eds), *Communication, Technology and Aging: opportunities and challenges for the future*, New York, NY, Springer, 60–78.

Czaja, S. J., Charness, N., Fisk, A., Hertzog, C., Nari, S., Rogers, W. and Sharit, J. (2006) Factors Predicting the Use of Technology: findings from the Center for Research and Education on Aging and Technology Enhancement (CREATE), *Psychology and Aging*, **21** (2), 333–52.

Dervin, B. and Reinhard, C. D. (2007) How Emotional Dimensions of Situated Information Seeking Relate to User Evaluations of Help from Sources: an exemplar study informed by sense-making methodology. In Nahl, D. and Bilal, D. (eds), *Information and Emotion: the emergent affective paradigm in information behavior research and theory*, Medford, NJ, Information Today, 51–84.

Durfresne, A. and Turcotte, S. (1997) Cognitive Style and its Implications for Navigation Strategies. In Boulay, B. and Mizoguchi, R. (eds), *Artificial Intelligence in Education Knowledge and Media Learning Systems*, Kobe, Japan/Amsterdam, IOS Press, 287–93.

Easley, R. F., Devaraj, S. and Crant, J. M. (2003) Relating Collaborative Technology Use to Teamwork Quality and Performance: an empirical analysis, *Journal of Management Information Systems*, **19** (4), 247–68.

Ellis, D. (1989) A Behavioural Model for Information Retrieval System Design, *Journal of Information Science*, **15** (4/5), 237–47.

Ellis, D. and Haugan, M. (1997) Modelling the Information Seeking Patterns of Engineers and Research Scientists in an Industrial Environment, *Journal of Documentation*, **53** (4), 384–403.

Enochsson, A. (2005) A Gender Perspective on Internet Use: consequences for information seeking, *Information Research*, **10** (4), http://informationr.net/ir/10-4/paper237.html.

Fallows, D. (2005) How Women and Men Use the Internet, *Pew Internet and American Life Project*, Washington, DC, http://www.pewinternet.org/2005/12/28/how-women-and-men-use-the-internet.

Fisher, K. E. and Julien, H. (2009) Information Behavior, *Annual Review of Information Science and Technology*, **43** (1), 1–73.

Fisher, K. E., Durrance, J. C. and Hinton, M. B. (2004) Information Grounds and the Use of Need-Based Services by Immigrants in Queens, New York: a context-based, outcome evaluation approach, *Journal of the American Society for Information Science and Technology*, **55**, 754–66.

Fisher, K. E., Marcoux, E., Miller, L. S., Sánchez, A. and Ramirez Cunningham, E. (2004) Information Behaviour of Migrant Hispanic Farm Workers and Their Families in the Pacific Northwest, *Information Research*, **10**, www.informationr.net/ir/10-1/paper199.html.

Fisher, K. E., Naumer, C., Durrance, J., Stromski, L. and Christiansen, T. (2005) Something Old, Something New: preliminary findings from an exploratory study about people's information habits and information grounds, *Information Research*, **10**, http://InformationR.net/ir/10-2/paper223.html.

Ford, N. (1995) Levels and Types of Mediation in Instructional Systems: an individual difference approach, *International Journal of Human–Computer Studies*, **43**, 243–59.

Ford, N. (2001) The Increasing Relevance of Pask's Work to Modern Information Seeking and Use, *Kybernetes*, **30** (5/6), 603–30.

Ford, N. and Chen, S. Y. (2001) Matching/mismatching Revisited: an empirical study of learning and teaching styles, *British Journal of Educational Technology*, **32** (1), 5–22.

Ford, N. and Miller, D. (1996) Gender Differences in Internet Perceptions and Use, *Aslib Proceedings* **48** (7–8), 183–92.

Ford, N., Miller, D. and Moss, N. (2001) The Role of Individual Differences in Internet Searching: an empirical study, *Journal of the American Society for Information Science and Technology*, **52** (12), 1049–66.

Ford, N., Wood, F. and Walsh, C. (1994) Cognitive Styles and Online Searching, *Online and CD-ROM Review*, **18** (2), 79–86.

Ford, N., Wilson, T., Foster, A., Ellis, D. and Spink, A. (2002) Information Seeking and Mediated Searching: Part 4. Cognitive styles in information seeking, *Journal of the American Society for Information Science and Technology*, **53** (9), 728–35.

Hargittai, E. and Shafer, S. (2006) Differences in Actual and Perceived Online Skills: the role of gender, *Social Science Quarterly*, **87** (2), 432–48.

Heinström, J. (2002) *Fast Surfers, Broad Scanners and Deep Divers – Personality and Information Seeking Behaviour*, Doctoral dissertation, Information Studies, Abo Akademi University Press, Abo.
www.abo.fi/fakultet/media/21373/thesis_heinstrom.pdf.

Heinström, J., Sormunen, E. and Kaunisto-Laine, S. (2014) Spanning Information Behaviour Across the Stages of a Learning Task: where do personality and approach to studying matter?, *Journal of Documentation*, **70** (6), 1076–97.

Howell, J. L. and Shepperd, J. A. (2013) Reducing Health-information Avoidance Through Contemplation, *Psychological Science*, **24** (9), 1696–1703, doi: 10.1177/0956797613478616.

Hsu, M. H. and Chiu, C. M. (2004) Internet Self-efficacy and Electronic Service Acceptance, *Decision Support Systems*, **38** (3), 369–81.

Hsu, M-H., Ju, T. L., Yen, C-H. and Chang, C-M. (2007). Knowledge Sharing Behavior in Virtual Communities: the relationship between trust, self-efficacy, and outcome expectations, *International Journal of Human–Computer Studies*, **65** (2), 153–69.

Hupfer, M. E. and Detlor, B. (2006) Gender and Web Information Seeking: a self-concept orientation model: research articles source, *Journal of the American Society for Information Science and Technology*, **57** (8), 1105–15.

Jackson, L. A., Ervin, K. S., Gardner, P. D. and Schmitt, N. (2001) Gender and the Internet: women communicating and men searching, *Sex Roles*, **44** (5/6), 363–79.

Kankanhalli, A., Tan, C. Y. B. and Wei, K. K. (2005) Contributing Knowledge to Electronic Knowledge Repositories: an empirical investigation, *MIS Quarterly*, **29** (1), 113–43.

Karavidas, M., Lim, N. K. and Katsikas, S. L. (2004) The Effects of Computers on Older Adult Users, poster session presented at the American Psychological Association 112th Annual Convention, 28 July–1 August, Honolulu.

Kim, D.-Y., Lehto, X. Y. and Morrison, A. M. (2007) Gender Differences in Online Travel Information Search: implications for marketing communications on the internet, *Tourism Management*, **28** (2), 423–33.

Kim, J. (2008) Perceived Difficulty as a Determinant of Web Search Performance, *Information Research*, **13** (4), paper 379.

Kuhlthau, C. C. (1993) *Seeking Meaning: a process approach to library and information services*, Norwood, NJ, Ablex.

Kuhlthau, C. C. (1999) The Role of Experience in the Information Search Process of an Early Career Information Worker: perceptions of uncertainty, complexity, construction and sources, *Journal of the American Society for Information Science*,

50 (5), 399–412.

Kuhlthau, C. C. (2004) *Seeking Meaning: a process approach to library and information services*, 2nd edn, London, Libraries Unlimited.

Kuo, F.-Y., Chu, T.-H., Hsu, M.-H. and Hsieh, H.-S. (2004) An Investigation of Effort–Accuracy Trade-Off and the Impact of Self-Efficacy on Web Searching Behaviors, *Decision Support Systems*, **37** (3), 331–42.

Leckie, G. J. and Pettigrew, K. E. (1997) A General Model of the Information-seeking of Professionals: role theory through the back door? In Vakkari, P., Savolainen, R. and Dervin, B. (eds), *Proceedings of an International Conference on Research in Information Needs, Seeking and Use in Different Contexts, Tampere, Finland*, London, Taylor Graham.

Liang, J. and Tsai, C. (2009) The Information Commitments Toward Web Information Among Medical Students in Taiwan, *Educational Technology & Society*, **12** (1), 162–72.

Liu, P. and Li, Z. (2012) Task Complexity: a review and conceptualization framework, *International Journal of Industrial Ergonomics*, **42**, 553–68.

Mansourian, Y. and Ford, N. (2007a) Web Searchers' Attributions of Success and Failure: an empirical study, *Journal of Documentation*, **63** (5), 659–79.

Mansourian, Y. and Ford, N. (2007b) Search Persistence and Failure on the Web: a 'bounded rationality' and 'satisficing' analysis, *Journal of Documentation*, **63** (5), 680–701.

Nahl, D. (2007) The Centrality of the Affective in Information Behavior. In Nahl, D. and Bilal, D. (eds), *Information and Emotion: the emergent affective paradigm in information behavior research and theory*, Medford, NJ, Information Today, 3–37.

Namuleme, R. K. (2013) *Information and HIV/AIDS: an ethnographic study of information behaviour*, PhD thesis, University of Sheffield.

Paisley, W. (1968) Information Needs and Uses. In Cuadra, C. A. (ed.), *Annual Review of Information Science and Technology*, **3**, 1–30.

Palmquist, R. A. and Kim, K.-S. (2000) Cognitive Style and On-Line Database Search Experience as Predictors of Web Search Performance, *Journal of the American Society for Information Science*, **51** (6), 558–66.

Pask, G. (1988) Learning Strategies, Teaching Strategies, and Conceptual or Learning Style. In Schmeck, R. R. (ed.), *Learning Strategies and Learning Styles*, New York, NY, Plenum Press, 83–99.

Pettigrew, K. E. (1999) Waiting for Chiropody: contextual results from an ethnographic study of the information behaviour among attendees at community clinics, *Information Processing & Management*, **35**, 801–17.

Reed, W. M. and Oughton, J. M. (1997) Computer Experience and Interval Based Hypermedia Navigation, *Journal of Research on Computing in Education*, **30**, 38–52.

Riding, R. J. and Cheema, I. (1991) Cognitive Styles: an overview and integration,

Educational Psychology, **11**, 193–215.

Riding, R. and Rayner, S. G. (1998) *Cognitive Styles and Learning Strategies*, London, David Fulton.

Savolainen, R. (1995) Everyday Life Information Seeking: approaching information seeking in the context of 'way of life', *Library & Information Science Research*, **17** (3), 259–94.

Savolainen, R. (2012) Elaborating the Motivational Attributes of Information Need and Uncertainty, *Information Research*, **17** (2), paper 516, http://InformationR.net/ir/17-2/paper516.html.

Savolainen, R. (2013) Approaching the Motivators for Information Seeking: the viewpoint of attribution theories, *Library & Information Science Research*, **35**, 63–8.

Savolainen, R. (2014) Emotions as Motivators for Information Seeking: a conceptual analysis, *Library & Information Science Research*, **36**, 59–65.

Schumacher, P. and Morahan-Martin, J. (2001) Internet and Computer Experiences Related? Gender differences, *Computers and Human Behavior*, **17**, 92–110.

Simon, H. A. (1955) A Behavioral Model of Rational Choice, *Quarterly Journal of Economics*, **69**, 99–118.

Simon, H. A. (1956) Rational Choice and the Structure of the Environment, *Psychological Review*, **63**, 129–38.

Sonnenwald, D. H. (1999) Evolving Perspectives of Human Information Behavior: contexts, situations, social networks and information horizons. In Allen, D. K. and Wilson, T. D. (eds), *Exploring the Contexts of Information Behaviour: proceedings of the Second International Conference on Research in Information Needs, Seeking and Use in Different Contexts 13/15 August 1998, Sheffield, UK*, London, Taylor Graham.

Stajkovic, A. D. and Luthans, F. (1998) Self-efficacy and Work-related Performance: a meta-analysis, *Psychological Bulletin*, **124** (2), 240–61.

Steinerová, J. and Šušol, J. (2007) Users' Information Behaviour – a Gender Perspective, *Information Research*, **12** (3), paper 320, http://InformationR.net/ir/12-3/paper320.html.

Stine-Morrow, E. A. L., Miller, L. M. S., Gagne, D. D. and Hertzog, C. (2008) Self-regulated Reading in Adulthood, *Psychology and Aging*, **23** (1), 131–53.

Sutcliffe, A. and Ennis, M. (1998) Towards a Cognitive Theory of Information Retrieval, *Interacting with Computers*, **10** (3), 321–51.

Vakkari, P. (2000) Cognition and Changes of Search Terms and Tactics During Task Performance: a longitudinal study. In *Proceedings of the RIAO 2000 Conference*, Paris, C.I.D., 894–907.

Vakkari, P. and Pennanen, M. (2001) Sources, Relevance and Contributory Information of Documents in Writing a Research Proposal: a longitudinal case study. In Hoglund, L. and Wilson, T. D. (eds), *The New Review of Information Behaviour Studies*, vol. 2, Cambridge, Taylor Graham, 217–32.

Wang, P., Hawk, W. B., and Tenopir, C. (2000) Users' Interaction with World Wide Web Resources: an exploratory study using a holistic approach, *Information Processing & Management*, **36**, 229–51.

Wildemuth, B., Freund, L. and Toms, E. (2014) Untangling Search Task Complexity and Difficulty in the Context of Interactive Information Retrieval Studies, *Journal of Documentation*, **70** (6), 1118–40.

Wilson, T. D. (1981) On User Studies and Information Needs, *Journal of Documentation*, **37** (1), 3–15, http://informationr.net/tdw/publ/papers/1981infoneeds.html.

Wilson, T. D. (1994) Information Needs and Uses: fifty years of progress? In Vickory, B. C. (ed.), *Fifty Years of Information Progress: a Journal of Documentation review*, London, Aslib, 15–51.

Wilson, T. D. (1997) Information Behaviour: an interdisciplinary perspective, *Information Processing & Management*, **33** (4), 551–72.

Wilson, T. D. (1999) Models in Information Behaviour Research, *Journal of Documentation*, **55** (3), 249–70.

Wilson, T. D. and Spink, A. (2000) Uncertainty and Its Correlates. In Hoglund, L. and Wilson, T. D. (eds), *The New Review of Information Behaviour Studies*, vol. 1, Cambridge, Taylor Graham, 69–84.

Wilson, T. D. and Walsh, C. (1996) *Information Behaviour: an interdisciplinary perspective*, Sheffield, University of Sheffield Department of Information Studies (British Library Research and Innovation Report No. 10), http://informationr.net/tdw/publ/infbehav/index.html.

Witkin, H. A. (1976) Cognitive Style in Academic Performance and in Teacher–student Relations. In Messick, S. and associates (eds), *Individuality in Learning*, San Francisco, CA, Jossey-Bass, 38–72.

Witkin, H. A. and Goodenough, D. R. (1981) *Cognitive Styles: essence and origins*, New York, NY, International Universities Press.

Witkin, H. A., Moore, C .A., Goodenough, D. R. and Cox, P.W. (1977) Field-dependent and Field-independent Cognitive Styles and Their Educational Implications, *Review of Educational Research*, **47**, 1–64.

Witte, K. (1994) Fear Control and Danger Control: a test of the extended parallel process model (EPPM), *Communication Monographs*, **61**, 113–34, doi: 10.1080/03637759409376328.

Wood, F., Ford, N. and Walsh, C. (1992) *Online Searching and Cognitive Styles: final report to the British Library*, London, British Library.

Ybarra, M. and Suman, M. (2008) Reasons, Assessments and Actions Taken: sex and age differences in uses of Internet health information, *Health Education Research*, **23** (3), 512–21.

Zeffane, R. M. and Gul, F. A. (1993) The Effects of Task Characteristics and Sub-unit

Structure on Dimensions of Information Processing, *Information Processing & Management*, **29** (6), 703–19.

Zipf, G. K. (1949) *Human Behaviour and the Principle of Least Effort*, Reading, MA. Addison-Wesley.

Zoe, L. R. and DiMartino, D. (2000) Cultural Diversity and End-user Searching: an analysis by gender and language background, *Research Strategies*, **17** (4), 291–305.

7

Models and theories in information behaviour research

Introduction

One of our goals as we seek to increase our understanding in an area of human knowledge is to develop models and theories. Definitions of what constitutes a model and a theory are many, and the terms may be used with *Pt* varying degrees of stringency. But basically they are representations of our thinking about a phenomenon at a particular time and from a particular point of view. Different researchers and writers may define models and theories in different ways. However, the terms as used in this book are defined below.

Understanding of a phenomenon is often represented as a 'model' of that phenomenon. By 'model', I simply mean a representation (often, but not always, in diagrammatic form) of our understanding about something.

An 'explanatory' (or 'propositional') model seeks to explain some phenomenon by making explicit the key concepts that constitute it, and the relationships between these concepts. A 'descriptive' (rather than explanatory) model may simply map out the component parts of a phenomenon like a sort of 'road map', without going on to specify in much detail the nature of relationships between these concepts. Often there will be links between the concepts (often represented as lines or arrows between boxes in diagrammatic form) but the nature of the links is not elaborated in a lot of detail. These different terms ('explanatory' and 'descriptive') are used simply to differentiate models of different complexity, and the dividing line between the two is subject to interpretation.

Take, for example, Wilson's well known model of information behaviour (Wilson and Walsh, 1996), shown in Figure 7.2 on p. 144. The diagram appears as a descriptive model in which concepts appear in boxes linked by unlabelled arrows which do not make clear the precise relationships between the boxes. However, when the model is viewed in conjunction with reading the text provided by Wilson in the article presenting the model, where he elaborates and explains the various elements and their interrelationships, the model becomes less descriptive and more explanatory. Note that differences between 'descriptive' and 'explanatory' relate to the intent of a model rather than the strength of evidence to support it. Thus, the explanation represented in an explanatory model may be either hypothetical or based on substantial evidence.

Note that 'theory' is often used generally simply to indicate a contrast to 'practice'. The phrase 'theory versus practice' is sometimes used with pejorative overtones to imply a gap between the type of knowledge generated by researchers and what is applicable in the real world. However, in this book a 'theory' is defined as a well developed explanation (sometimes supported by diagrammatic models) relating to a substantial phenomenon. A theory is generally wider-ranging in its scope than a model, is better developed (based on a more substantial body of evidence), and relates to a more substantial area of knowledge than a model. However, theories can also differ in the extent to which they provide a detailed explanation of some phenomenon.

Models and theories help us understand, and may enable us to make predictions in relation to, the phenomenon forming their focus. A number of selected models and theories have been introduced in other chapters of this book. The purpose of the present chapter is not exhaustively to list such models and theories, but rather to consider what they actually are, and to consider how they may differ in scope and depth.

Models of information behaviour

A model is a representation of how its creator thinks of a phenomenon at a particular point in time and from a particular perspective. Generally, models published in peer-reviewed sources such as books and journal articles are based on empirical research findings and/or an analysis by their creators of previous empirical and theoretical work in the area.

Often, work is cumulative, in that later models can build on previous ones. A model may be developed which elaborates an aspect of, or addresses a perceived gap in, an earlier one. Models may also be developed independently which address different aspects of a common, more general phenomenon. The following example shows how different models have developed to complement one another in addressing key aspects of information behaviour. The models of Ellis, Wilson and Erdelez have already been presented in more detail in Chapter 4. They are used again here to show the complementary nature of diverse models in gradually expanding our understanding increasingly to address a wide range of aspects of information behaviour.

Ellis (1989) developed his widely acknowledged model of information seeking (previously described in Chapter 4), as shown in Table 7.1.
Wilson went on (Wilson, 1999) to incorporate Ellis' model of information seeking behaviour within his earlier broader model (Wilson, 1981) which also included contextual factors that influence information needs and factors which act as barriers to information seeking (Figure 7.1).

Table 7.1 Ellis' (1989) model of information seeking	
Starting	Identifying information sources that are potentially starting points for seeking information.
Chaining	Following up leads from sources identified in information sources consulted. Backward chaining entails following up references cited in an information source you are consulting. Forward chaining involves finding citations to an information source you are consulting in new information sources.
Browsing	Browsing is scanning documents in the hope of finding useful information. This may entail flipping through a journal, scanning indexes or tables of contents, scanning library shelves, etc.
Differentiating	Differentiating entails selecting those sources, from all those of which you have become aware, that seem potentially most useful. Criteria for selection may include not only relevance, but approach and quality as judged, for example, from reviews or the opinions of colleagues.
Monitoring	Monitoring consists of keeping watch on sources identified as likely to contain relevant information relating to an identified area of interest. Core journals may be scanned regularly for new articles, or a particular database search may be repeated regularly in order to become aware of new information.
Extracting	Extracting entails working through information sources already identified as potentially containing useful information in order to identify useful information actually contained within them.
Verifying	Checking the accuracy of information.
Ending	Conducting a final search for information at the end of the project.

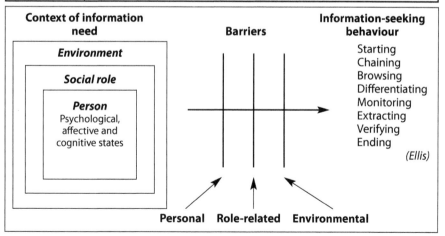

Figure 7.1 Wilson's model of information seeking incorporating Ellis' model

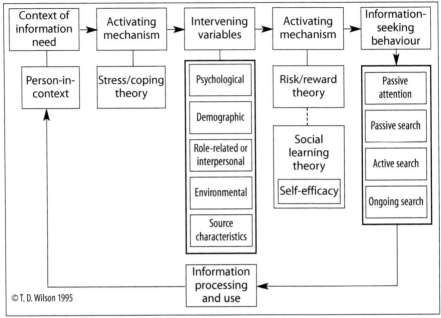

Figure 7.2 Wilson's 'revised general model of information behaviour' (Wilson and Walsh, 1996)

Wilson went on (Wilson, 1997) to broaden the focus of his model in a further version (Figure 7.2). In this version, Ellis' model is implicit in the 'Information-seeking behaviour' box shown at the top right. Information-seeking behaviour is expanded to show different modes such as passive attention and active search. Although not explicitly embracing the serendipitous information encountering that forms the focus of Erdelez's model (see below), 'passive attention' is moving in this direction. As described in the previous chapter, the model elaborates the mechanisms and variables that can affect information-seeking behaviour.

Other researchers have produced broader models that include consideration of elements not included in earlier ones. That of Godbold (2006) shown in Figure 7.3, for example, puts information seeking – which defined the scope of Wilson's model – in its broader context of information behaviour, adding the concepts *spreading, disputing, taking mental note of, disbelieving, avoiding, creating* and *destroying* information.

Although Godbold's model broadened the focus from information seeking to information behaviour, it did not directly address serendipitous information encountering, which forms the focus of Erdelez's (1999) model,

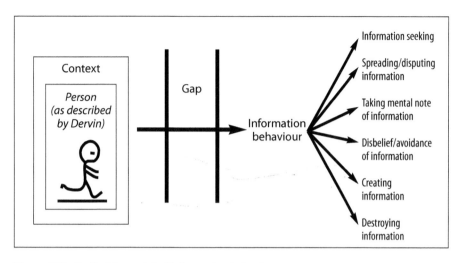

Figure 7.3 Godbold's model of information behaviour

which was described in Chapter 4.

Another feature of information behaviour not directly addressed by the models of Ellis, Wilson, Godbold or Erdelez became the focus of a model by Mansourian (Ford and Mansourian, 2006). He was interested in how people *fail* to find information, and produced a model of information 'invisibility' shown in Figure 7.4.

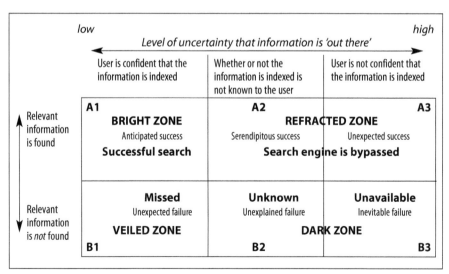

Figure 7.4 Mansourian's model of information invisibility

The model is based on interviews with researchers relating to recent searches for information. Whether or not a particular information source was indexed and potentially findable was thus a subjective perception on the part of each searcher. Information which they considered not indexed and therefore not out there to be found may or may not correspond with the reality of a search engine's index. Information the interviewees could not find may have been retrievable by a more expert searcher. For this reason, Mansourian uses the term 'cognitive invisibility', as opposed to a more technical objective invisibility. 'Search failure' is similarly a cognitive construction, indicating searchers' perception of the success or failure of a search – however they define success.

- In the **bright zone**, information was successfully searched for and found with no problems, as expected by the searcher.
- The **refracted zone** includes experiences in which the searcher finds relevant information not via a search engine, but by other means, such as bookmarked websites or URLs given by friends and colleagues. In sub-zone A2 the searcher does not know whether or not the information would have been retrievable via a search engine. In sub-zone A3, the searcher does not feel confident that it would.
- In the **veiled zone**, although searchers failed to find relevant information, they felt sure that there was information out there waiting to be retrieved, but that they had simply failed to find it.
- The **dark zone** includes cases where searchers failed to find relevant information but (a) were unsure whether it might be 'out there' and retrievable with greater effort or skill on their part (sub-zone B2), or (b) felt confident that it was not there waiting to be found (B3).

This is just one series of examples showing how emerging models may complement one another. Sometimes a new model may be developed which addresses a gap or extends the focus of previous ones, as Wilson's model of information seeking incorporated that of Ellis but extended its focus to factors that influence information needs and hinder information seeking, and as that of Godbold extended the focus to include not only information seeking but wider types of information behaviour. Such development is not necessarily sequential, however, and researchers may be working in parallel on models which address complementary aspects of the same broader phenomenon.

Researchers may also incorporate information behaviour as an element within models with a wider focus. A number of researchers have included the producers and communicators of information, and communications between providers and users in their models. As noted by Robson and Robinson (2013), whilst most models of information behaviour focus on information seeking and the information user, models of communication tend to emphasize the communicator and the communication process.

An example which seeks to integrate information behaviour with communication is that of Ingwersen and Järvelin (2005). As well as information seekers, their model includes a range of other 'cognitive actors' – including authors, database designers, human indexers – and selectors, who act in a gate-keeping role affecting the availability of information, such as reviewers, editors and conference organizers. Ingwersen and Järvelin acknowledge the influence on information and communication behaviour of the perceptions of the actors involved which in turn are affected by their organizational, cultural and social contexts.

A more recent example which adopts a relatively holistic focus, integrating information behaviour with communication-related activities, is the model of Robson and Robinson (2013). Based on a review of both types of model, they went on to propose a new model that includes consideration of both information seeker and the communicator or information provider (Figure 7.5).

In the model, dashed arrows indicate activities relating to communication, whilst unbroken arrows show those relating to information seeking. Information users include not only people with recognized and expressed information needs but also those with needs that remain unrecognized and/or unpursued, and those who receive information whether or not they act upon it. Information providers include not only individuals, groups and organizations who produce and communicate information (such as authors, publishers and opinion leaders) but also those who facilitate or control access to it (such as librarians). The model depicts several types of interactive activity (Table 7.2).

Theories of information behaviour

At one level, a theory may be considered as a formal explanation of some substantial phenomenon, based on a strong body of evidence that has been repeatedly confirmed on the basis of observations or experiments. A more relaxed definition allows inclusion of explanatory frameworks which, although not yet supported by numerous repeated observations, nevertheless attempt to provide a detailed explanation of a relatively complex phenomenon. What constitutes a *complex* phenomenon – and indeed a *detailed* explanation – can be relatively subjective and a matter of judgement.

The more relaxed definition of theory is used throughout this book. It

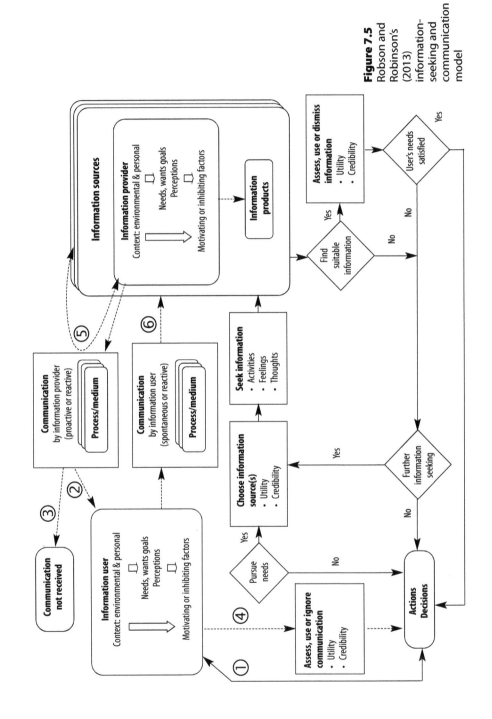

Figure 7.5
Robson and Robinson's (2013) information-seeking and communication model

Table 7.2 Types of activity in Robson and Robinson's (2013) information-seeking and communication model

Arrow	Activity
1	Information received may be assessed for usefulness and credibility, and may result in actions or decisions. These may be modified in the light of changes in the user's environmental and personal contexts
2	Information providers may communicate with users either proactively (e.g. by publishing and advertising information products) or reactively (e.g. by responding to a user query)
3	Communications may not necessarily be received by their target users
4	An information user who has received information may choose to evaluate, use or ignore it
5	Information providers may communicate with one another (e.g. librarians communicate with book suppliers in order to facilitate their own role as information providers to their users
6	Information users may communicate with information providers (e.g. a user may approach a librarian with an information request)

includes well substantiated large-scale theories based on numerous individual studies over an extended period of time, and relating to forces and mechanisms which drive and affect human behaviour across a wide range of activities. However, the definition adopted here also includes smaller-scale explanatory frameworks based on less substantial empirical evidence and relating to narrower aspects of human behaviour. These encompass many of the more advanced explanatory models of information seeking and other aspects of information behaviour. Thus, it should be borne in mind that the division between a model and a theory may not always be clear-cut, particularly in the case of advanced and explanatory models.

Thus the definition of a theory as used throughout this book and relating specifically to information behaviour is:

> An explanation of some observed information behaviour supported by a
> systematically obtained body of evidence.

The key defining feature of a substantive theory is that it seeks to *explain* rather than just *describe* some phenomenon. If we can understand the 'why' and 'how' of behaviour we have a greater chance of making accurate predictions relating to that behaviour. Such predictions, often in the form of testable hypotheses, enable us for example to build and test new systems and procedures, and to draw up research programmes designed further to increase our understanding of the behaviour. The nature of the evidence that is required to support explanations – and what are effective ways of gathering and interpreting it – are open to question and the subject of much debate.

Theories vary in terms of their generality and level of abstraction. A number attempt to apply theories developed outside the field of information to explain aspects of observed information behaviour. This may be done with a relatively narrow focus – for example, the application of a specific theory (such as 'satisficing theory', see pp 55, 91 and 125) to aspects of information behaviour. Alternatively a broader approach may be adopted in which a number of theoretical perspectives are integrated to form a more holistic explanatory model, usually of several aspects of information behaviour (for example, Wilson's work reported below).

Some theories which operate at a very high level of abstraction, and may constitute 'metatheory' rather than theory, to the extent that that they theorize about possible theories – about how behaviour might most effectively be conceptualized, researched and explained. Vakkari defines metatheories as consisting of:

> . . . ontological, epistemological, and conceptual pre-suppositions of a very general nature, they are not so much about processes like information seeking occurring in the social world as they are about the ways of thinking and speaking about these processes. . . . their cognitive function is to offer guidelines and directives for actual theory construction.
>
> Vakkari, 1996, 452

An example is Dervin's Sense-making Theory, which is described in detail below. This definition is used in this book. However, it is worth noting that, as Vakkari goes on to remark, Wagner, Berger and Zeldith (1989) consider metatheories also to include theories that are so abstract and general that they can apply to any type of social system. Thus, broad theories of information behaviour that transcend particular contexts and cases – such as Wilson's general model presented in Figure 7.2 (p. 144) – would be considered metatheories. Such a broad definition of metatheory is not used in this book.

There are numerous theories relevant to aspects of information behaviour. Indeed, in their classic text *Theories of Information Behavior*, Fisher, Erdelez and McKechnie (2005) provide an excellent overview of what they term 'conceptual frameworks that one may use to study different aspects of information behavior', including 72 metatheories, theories and models (Fisher, Erdelez and McKechnie, 2005, xx). Jamali (2013) notes that Houston (2009) lists 108 theories and models related to information behaviour. Jamali went on to conduct a study of the citation relationships between 51 of these theories (though he does not distinguish between models and theories).

The study emphasized the interdisciplinary nature of information behaviour, in that it found that information behaviour theories have drawn on 'resources from at least 29 other fields such as sociology, psychology, communication, education, computer science, medical science, behavioural science, business and management and so on'. The analysis also showed how some theories have had a particularly big impact on other researchers in the field of information behaviour in terms of being cited, for example work by Taylor (see p. 30), Ellis (see p. 50), Kuhlthau (see p. 52) and Bates (see p. 62). Approximately 80% of the theories studied were linked to each other in the citation network.

As noted above, rather than listing the wide range of existing theories, the present chapter seeks to consider essentially what theories are, and how they can differ in scope and depth. Some theories have been developed from research that is directly or closely related to information behaviour. Others, however, have been developed outside the area of information science but have been applied to aspects of information behaviour in view of their potential to illuminate this behaviour and approaches to studying it.

This chapter focuses on two influential but very different theories, selected to illustrate very different approaches and affordances. Activity Theory is an example of a theory developed outside the field but which is increasingly being used in information behaviour research. Sense-making is an example of a theory which from the start included key concepts of particular concern to information behaviour researchers – the notion of information needs, information seeking and making sense of information.

Activity Theory and information behaviour

Wilson (2006) provides an excellent overview of Activity Theory (sometimes referred to as Cultural-Historical Activity Theory) in terms of its origins in psychology and education and applications to research into information behaviour. Activity Theory is potentially useful in drawing to the attention important facets of human behaviour and its influences which may not necessarily be taken into account by researchers adopting other perspectives. In particular, Activity Theory emphasizes viewing human behaviour in its cultural, organizational and historical context to generate a more ecologically valid picture. This means paying attention to contextual elements of behaviour such as the division of labour that may apply in group activity, the cultural rules and norms in which activity takes place, and conflicts and disconnects between people interacting to achieve some goal. Such a relatively holistic perspective also implies that the study of behaviour must be

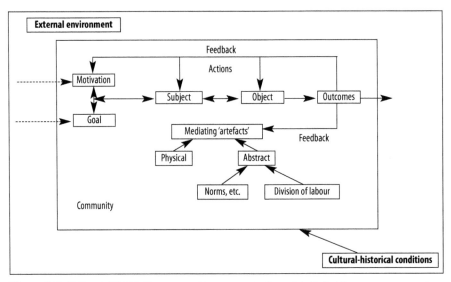

Figure 7.6 Wilson's (2006) diagrammatic representation of Activity Theory components and processes

conducted over a sufficiently long time scale to allow these aspects to be adequately explored.

Activity Theory posits that in order to achieve goals, subjects (a person or group of people) act on (with a view to transforming) objects (which may be physical, intellectual or social, and may be shared by a community) with tools (which may be physical or abstract intellectual), which leads to some result (which is not necessarily the achievement of the original goal). The result provides feedback to the subject(s) which may cause behaviour and goals to be modified. Activity may entail a division of labour amongst subjects working together to achieve the goal. This all takes place in the context of cultural and social rules and norms, and contradictions and tensions existing between subjects. Figure 7.6 shows Wilson's (2006) representation of the key components and processes of Activity Theory.

Activities are distinguished from the *actions* of which they are composed. In turn, actions are composed of operations. Activities are determined by motives; actions are achieved by operations.

Wilson takes the case of research conducted by the AIMTech Research Group at Leeds University to illustrate the benefits of adopting Activity Theory. This group has studied the use of mobile information systems by the emergency services (police, ambulance, fire and rescue). He notes that:

After a number of studies it was felt that the existing framework within which work was being pursued left some things unexplored and activity theory presented itself as potentially useful. . . . A review of this work suggested that, if activity theory had been adopted as the conceptual framework at the outset, certain aspects of the studies would have been either developed further or would have been included instead of being omitted.

Wilson, 2006

Activity Theory was deemed so useful that it was subsequently adopted by the group for its research and consultancy work. Wilson notes that its adoption means that the team will now ask about:

- the history of an innovation in the organization, to uncover previous attempts to implement technological change;
- the cultural context of the innovation, for example, the extent to which the advocates of innovation are aware of tensions in the organization that may prevent success and the extent to which the end users of the system are committed to the innovation;
- the rules and conditions under which the technology is to be applied (particularly important in police forces, where legislation guides all activity);
- the informal norms of behaviour in the affected work team(s) and how this might affect the innovation;
- the motivation for the innovation: for example, mobile systems may be introduced into a police force to reduce the time officers must spend in the police station, thereby enabling them to be more visible on the street;
- how the total activity system affects other activity systems in the organization: for example, providing a police officer with information at the point of need has implications for supervision, for the activities of the control room and for the provision of the underlying communications technologies.

Wilson, 2006

This approach was thought to enable a richer approach to conceptualizing relevant issues, and inclusion within the research focus of important concepts and issues that might otherwise have been ignored. Wilson also notes that he (Wilson, 2006) has:

. . . explored the relevance of activity theory for research in information-seeking behavior by revisiting previous research and retrospectively applying the framework. He shows, for example, how information flows in the social welfare activity of taking a child into protective care involve multiple activity systems in different agencies and how information seeking can be a collaborative activity, involving division of labor.

Wilson, 2008, 146

Allen, Karanasios and Slavova (2011) summarize the advantages of Activity Theory, which, as noted above, was adopted by the AIMTech Research Group at Leeds University. They note that it is particularly helpful in enabling:

- exploration of both individual and collective information behaviour and the interaction between the two
- exploration of interaction between multiple activity systems
- taking into account the broad context in which activity takes place and that shapes activity, including cultural historical aspects such as rules and norms of communities, transcending individuals
- taking into account the role of artefacts (e.g. technological tools) in mediating human activity
- enabling the deconstruction of activity into actions and operations, and differentiation between long-term collective activity (linked to overall motives) and short-term individual or group action (actions performed in order to realize an activity).

A good example of Activity Theory in action is the study by von Thaden described in Chapter 5.

THINK!

Look back at the description of von Thaden's research in Chapter 5.

No mention was made in that chapter of its use of Activity Theory, but re-read it now and think which aspects of the research made the choice of Activity Theory particularly appropriate.

Von Thaden notes that an aircraft flight deck is a complex safety-critical situation in which:

Finding, sorting, and filtering information under stress conditions can prove overwhelming to an individual pilot. It becomes further complicated when pilots with different levels of experience and different backgrounds must partner to convey and consolidate information across a team – an issue of 'group cognition'.

von Thaden, 2008, 1557

Effective information behaviour is essentially distributed and collaborative:

Individuals contextualize their behavior as it relates to their current situation within a group; they place the meaning of actions and information in relation to the activities of others and in relation to motives, intentions, and knowledge they ascribe to others or infer that others have. The knowledge of what the team's work entails, the disposition of the team's members, and the action–interaction of the team's members all influence, and are influenced, by how information is processed individually and within the team.

von Thaden, 2008, 1557

Investigating such a situation, as did von Thaden with the purpose of discovering what might be key factors influencing relatively effective and ineffective pilot performance, entails studying far more than individual pilot behaviour.

The situation can be thought of in terms of interaction between multiple activity systems. Flight-deck crew have to process, interpret and share information – adhering to Standard Operating Procedures – coming from their own local information systems, and also receive information from and interact with Air Traffic Control. They must also contend with environmental conditions and with other aircraft in the vicinity.

In addition to the paper cited in Chapter 5 (von Thaden, 2008), the author published another paper (von Thaden, 2007) in which she explicitly discussed the role of Activity Theory in this research. In this paper she notes that:

[I]nformation processed collaboratively by multiple crew members may be more robust than information processed by each individual, yet it requires social, organizational and technological mediation for continued support of group information retrieval in increasingly complex situations.

von Thaden, 2007

Social and cultural historical factors are important here. These include knowledge and interpretation of rules and norms applying to aircrew and the organizations that support them, such as standard operational procedures, as well as shared understandings, experience and relationships between crew members. The effects of these factors can perhaps best be perceived when they break down. For example, when crews change from flight to flight, social organization on the flight deck must be renegotiated each time. As von Thaden notes:

Thus, it remains difficult to quickly negotiate common ground and lay a framework for joint activity . . . Interpreting shared information is hampered by

> this lack of cultural and experiential common ground among flight crews.
>
> von Thaden, 2007

Errors may result in situations where there is some disconnect in shared experience or a lack of well oiled and established shared procedures and protocols for distributed collaborative activity. The emphasis that Activity Theory places on:

- the impacts of social and historical factors as well as immediate activity
- interactions between individual and group activity
- interactions of people with mediating artefacts such as flight-deck instruments
- 'activity' as the unit of analysis, rather than individuals or instruments

makes it particularly appropriate for the study of distributed information behaviour on the flight deck.

Dervin's Sense-making theory

THINK!

How far do you agree or disagree with the following statements?

1. Information behaviour research is all about trying to find *consistent repeated patterns* in the way people behave
   Strongly agree ☐ Agree ☐ Not sure ☐ Disagree ☐ Strongly disagree ☐
2. People's subjective *fantasies* and *intuitions* are not really a legitimate focus for serious systematic information behaviour research
   Strongly agree ☐ Agree ☐ Not sure ☐ Disagree ☐ Strongly disagree ☐

If you agreed with either or both of these statements, many researchers would agree with you. However, we now turn to a very influential theory which proposes that the search for consistent repeated patterns in behaviour is not the only way – and not necessarily the most effective way – to discover useful knowledge of information behaviour. The theory also proposes that whims and intuitions – along with a range of other difficult-to-measure ways of thinking – are a legitimate and potentially very useful focus for research.

Dervin's Sense-making theory is extremely broad in scope, in that it seeks to explain the fundamental processes underlying not only learning and problem solving, but also more generally coping with life and making sense of the world. Whilst using and building on a number of concepts and ideas that have been proposed and studied over many years in relation to information behaviour, the theory also breaks new ground in introducing a number of ideas and perspectives that are novel to researchers and practitioners in library and information science. It is a metatheory insofar as it includes within its focus issues relating to the relative usefulness (and limitations) of different approaches to generating knowledge of people's information behaviour.

Dervin's theory is predicated on a set of very detailed and specific premises about the nature of the human condition and of information, and about how people make sense of the world at a fundamental level. It is also a metatheory insofar as it addresses issues relating to the nature of theory, and of how we might effectively conceptualize human thought and behaviour and go about researching them.

Dervin argues that since not everything is connected, and things are constantly changing, reality is characterized by pervasive discontinuities or gaps. We constantly need to try to bridge such gaps in order to make sense of the world around us. Information seeking and use are central to this process. Humans are constantly moving through time and space. As they do so, they are frequently confronted by gaps which generate the need for information.

Sense-making is essentially mental and physical behaviour that enables a person to design their movement through time and space. It is predicated on a number of explicit premises. Dervin notes that:

> . . . knowledge is the sense made at a particular point in time-space by someone. Sometimes, it gets shared and codified; sometimes a number of people agree upon it; sometimes it enters into a formalized discourse and gets published; sometimes it gets tested in other times and spaces and takes on the status of facts. Sometimes, it is fleeting and unexpressed. Sometimes it is hidden and suppressed. Sometimes, it gets imprimatured and becomes unjust law; sometimes it takes on the status of dogma. Sometimes it requires reconceptualizing a world. Sometimes it involves contest and resistance. Sometimes it involves danger and death.
>
> Dervin, 1998, 36

It presents a series of metatheoretical premises about the nature of people and of information, and how people make sense of the world.

Information does not exist independently of humans. Rather, it is the product of our observing the world. We decide what to observe and how to observe, and we generate the interpretation of what we observe.

Knowledge and information are thus ultimately subjective. Even though shared and agreed interpretations may be labelled 'facts', these will not necessarily remain true over time and different circumstances. As Dervin notes:

> Some 'information' becomes agreed upon and is termed 'fact' for a given time-frame at least. Others are controversial and are called 'opinion' or 'delusion' depending on the socio-political context and/or the charity of the observer.
>
> Dervin, 1983, 5

What we can observe at a given moment is constrained by where we are. Also, we bring to bear our past experiences when interpreting the present. This has advantages and potential limitations. It enables us to consolidate interpretations to a certain extent, and sharing past interpretations with others facilitates a degree of triangulation to provide a potentially richer picture of the world around us. However, at the same time, we should not overlook the dangers associated with allowing our past to rigidify and limit our view of the present and to treat the present on the assumption that it will conform to the past.

Information should not be viewed just as embodied answers to problems waiting for transmission. There is a shift to an increasing realization that:

> While once knowledge was valued for providing answers, homogeneity and centrality, now we need to think of potentials for empowering and releasing creativity and diversity. While once we thought we could bask in the certainty of answers and solutions, now need to learn to appreciate the courage and creativity it takes to step into the unknown only partially instructed by information/knowledge. In this view, every next moment is unknown; and the step into it can never be more than partially informed.
>
> Dervin, 1998, 37

Information seeking and use are not, as is often assumed in more positivistic perspectives, essentially about the transmission of facts, views and opinions from a transmitter (a source of information) to a receiver (a person who seeks and finds an information source). Rather, they are concerned with constructing and reconstructing internal pictures of the world sense. Much traditional information behaviour research has focused on the finding and transmission of information rather than on the processes whereby individuals make use of their own and the observations of others to generate their views of reality.

Every individual is 'potentially static across time-space (as manifested in inflexibility, habit, rigidity, stability) or fluid across time-space (as manifested in flexibility, randomness, innovation, creativity)' (Dervin, 1999, 731). Much positivistic research has also tended to focus on behaviour that is relatively stable across time and space, which Dervin considers rigidified or habitualized. This is at the expense of focusing on dynamic processes that change over time or from situation to situation, on flexibilities and responsiveness to change. She notes:

> Such an approach ignores the mandate of the human condition – to make sense in a discontinuous, constantly changing universe when complete sense is not available as 'complete information'.
>
> Dervin, 1983, 6

Human thought and behaviour is characterized by uncertainties, ambiguities and contradictions as well as relatively stable aspects.

Dervin argues that sense-making (including information) behaviour can best be understood by focusing not on stable factors that may be observed and measured consistently across time and space (such as personality traits or demographic features like age and gender), but on how people respond to changing situations. Rather than basing predictions on the identification of consistent, repeating patterns of behaviour observed across different times and contexts, we can still aim to develop knowledge that will allow us to predict – but based on identifying patterns of how we respond to changing situations.

Dervin asserts that it is vital that we also focus on relatively fluid and unstable aspects of human behaviour as it changes over time and in different contexts, even though what might be thought of as a moving target presents difficulties in terms of research methodology. We should take as the unit of analysis not the individual, but rather the individual as they are experiencing the particular situation they are in.

Central to the process of making sense of the world and finding solutions to problems is the notion of sense-unmaking. If our current knowledge is likely to be insufficient for tomorrow's needs and answers, then being able to free ourselves from existing ideas and facilitating new directions and creative approaches becomes all the more important. However, Dervin argues that sense-unmaking is rendered more difficult because of a long Western tradition of assuming that there must exist 'right answers' to all our problems. It is also made more difficult by:

... the forces of power in society and in organizations, forces that prescribe
acceptable answers and make disagreeing with them, even in the face of the
evidence of one's own experience, a scary and risky thing to do. Even more
difficult is when the forces of power flow through an organization or system
hidden and undisclosed.

Dervin, 1998, 41

Attention is moved away from the primacy of formal information sources to
whatever informs sense-making. This may include not only ideas but also
feelings and emotions, hunches, dreams, wishes, confusions and anxiety. The
whole person is constantly evolving in terms of intertwined body, heart, mind
and soul. Sense-making thus pulls into prominence aspects of human
behaviour often overlooked or rejected as legitimate research constructs from
a more positivist perspective.

The processes involved in sense-making and sense-unmaking do not only
relate to the generation of factual knowledge (what Dervin calls 'factizing').
There are many others, including emoting, hunching, muddling,
consensusing, power-brokering and suppressing (Dervin, 1999, 732). Research
should focus on 'processes and verbs rather than descriptors and nouns'
(what what she calls 'verbings') (Naumer, Fisher and Dervin, 2008, 3). As
Naumer, Fisher and Dervin note:

> The Sense-Making Methodology focuses on process and the ways people
> communicate internally and externally to make and unmake sense. This
> approach leads toward studies concerned with how people define situations,
> how they integrate their contextual understandings into sense-makings, how
> they define their information needs, how they communicate with others. In
> exploring these research questions, the Methodology assumes it is important to
> focus on processes and verbs rather than descriptors and nouns.

Naumer, Fisher and Dervin, 2008, 3

Sense-making accepts that humans make sense of the world by identifying
all sorts of patterns and connectivities:

> not just causalities but spontaneities, simultaneities, temporalities, collaboralities,
> and so on. This includes not just connectivities that imply anchorings in the real
> (factizings, experiencings, structurings) but those that imply soarings beyond
> (narratings, fantasyings, imaginings) . . .

In essence, Sense-Making mandates that the connectings between entities and events that have been traditionally called theorizing and traditionally relegated to the researcher's superior tools and training become themselves a focus of study. A causal assumption would, for example, become an interpretive focus not merely an outcome of statistical testing or researcher extrapolating. By positioning ordinary persons as theorists, Sense-Making mandates that ordinary persons be asked and that the patterns – the connectivities – not be imposed by assumption. Where there are different 'readings' (and Sense-Making assumes there always will be) these must themselves be put into dialogue rather than making one reading central by caveat and homogenizing or marginalizing the rest.

Naumer, Fisher and Dervin, 2008, 735

Sense-making assumes that ordinary people – not just researchers – are theory makers in the sense that in order to plan and act in a world full of discontinuities (or gaps) with incomplete information, we must to an extent generate theories to design our 'next moves' at any point in time. Although such theorizing may be unconscious and unarticulated, Sense-making assumes that people can and will talk about 'how they make and unmake their worlds, how they see and struggle with the forces of power in their worlds, how they sometimes stumble about innocent of these forces, and how they sometimes collide with them' (Dervin, 1999, 733).

Power issues are a key feature of the theory:

Sense-Making assumes that issues of force and power pervade all human conditions; that humans are impacted by the constraining forces of structural power (both natural and societal) and that as individuals in specific situations they are themselves sites of power, to resist, reinvent, challenge, deny, and ignore.

Naumer, Fisher and Dervin, 2008, 732

Researchers must expose their own sense-making processes, including their interpretations, to scrutiny and not privilege them over those of the people they study. Rather than suppressing their own interpretations, researchers should test these in dialog with those they are studying, avoiding 'the potential tyrannies of interpreting the worlds for others' (Naumer, Fisher and Dervin, 2008. 734).

To summarize, Sense-making theory brings together in an integrated framework many concepts and ideas that are already familiar to professionals and researchers in information behaviour, for example: the notion of a gap or anomaly as the basis of an information need; the view that we should not restrict the focus of research and practice to cognitive aspects; and appreciation of the importance of 'non-logical' aspects of human thought and behaviour.

At the same time it introduces a number of newer ideas and foci for research and practice. It recognizes that it is important to include 'sense-unmaking' as well as 'sense-making'. Sense-making Theory proposes a relatively disruptive rather than purely cumulative view of how we need to research information behaviour. It does so by means of its extremely holistic view of the individual to include chaotic and non-logical as well as cognitive and ordered, its inclusion of a wide range of 'fodder' that feeds sense-making and sense-unmaking, including hunches, emotions, muddles, etc., as well as formal information sources. As Dervin notes:

> By definition, Sense-Making focuses on movement and fluidity, even when that movement and fluidity involves repetitions and habits. This web of connections is elusive and inherently paradoxical because it mandates theorizing (which has been traditional [sic] thought as freezing) something which is inherently fluid – process. At the same time, Sense-Making, in line with a variety of chaos theories, sees a new kind of understanding made possible by attending to seemingly disorderly processes.
>
> Dervin, 1999, 736

Sense-making also calls for a focus from nouns and descriptions to processes and 'verbings'. The unit of analysis should not be factors observed to be consistent over time, but should rather be ways in which people respond to changes. A major emphasis in practice and research should be on how to empower individuals to resist forces impeding change and to generate creative new ideas and approaches.

According to Case:

> Metatheory is theory about theory. It addresses the underlying philosophical assumptions about the nature of reality, and of knowledge, that stand behind a particular theory and the other theories and concepts most closely related to it.
>
> Case, 2013, 164

Sense-making is a metatheory in that it requires that researchers must consider different possible ways of theorizing, freeing themselves from a priori assumptions about how this should be done. Rather than suggesting possible research questions, sense-making requires researchers to think about how they think about, and derive and frame, their research questions in relation to different contexts. Dervin and Clark (1999) distinguish between theorizing which is focused on the phenomenon to be described and explained, and metatheorizing, which 'aims to guide our presumings, and lookings, and collectings, and analyzing'.

Sense-making also seeks to free the researcher from limiting assumptions about how research should be conducted:

> . . . allows the researcher to be freed of the riddle of understanding one noun-based interpretation through the lens of another noun-based interpretation. When noun-based theorizing . . . is used as the sole basis for extracting understandings what happens is that the standard for analyzing is inherently bound into the phenomenon. The conclusions become too readily tautological. It is as if we were mandated to describe an orange by calling it not-apple, or second-class fruit. Instead, Sense-Making mandates that the nouns be compared to each other outside a noun framework. This is what is meant when Sense-Making is described as a verbing methodology.
>
> Dervin and Clark, 1999, 735–6

The 'meta' nature of the theory is further reinforced by the fact that sense-making entails four levels of interpretation (or as Dervin puts it, 'quadruple hermeneutic'):

- all research entails interpretations (hermeneutic 1)
- in research into humans the focus is on interpretations (hermeneutic 1) of interpretations made by the people studied (hermeneutic 2)
- however, sense-making focuses not on interpretations per se (hermeneutics 1 and 2) but on the processes of interpreting – i.e. how interpretations are made. The focus is therefore not on interpretations (the end product) made by researchers, but on the interpreting (the processes) of researchers interpreting (hermeneutic 3) not the (hermeneutic 2) interpretations of others, but rather
- the interpreting of humans – i.e. how humans interpret interpretations (hermeneutic 4).

Summary

This chapter has discussed the notion of theories and models in information behaviour, exploring what they are before going on to describe two very different types of theory. Activity Theory was developed outside the field of information science, and has come to be applied to information behaviour relatively recently. It offers a set of analytic concepts and tools that emphasize the need to adopt a relatively holistic perspective and take into account the cultural, organizational and historical context in which information behaviour takes place. It foregrounds activity as the unit of analysis as opposed to individuals, and emphasizes the importance of studying distributed aspects of activity.

Dervin's Sense-making theory was from the start more directly related to individual information behaviour. It was originally developed in the area of communication studies, although drawing from a wide range of other disciplines. The concept of information behaviour was always central to the theory, which sought to develop a more sophisticated view of communication than the transmission theory prevalent at the time, in which information was viewed as an object to be passed from source to receiver. Strengths of Sense-making Theory include its foregrounding and emphasizing the importance of aspects of behaviour that are not restricted to rational cognitive thought.

So how are such theories and models useful to us as information practitioners? Models and theories are generated in order to enhance our understanding of some phenomenon – our present focus being on information behaviour. However, if our understanding of information behaviour is such that a given new model or theory will not lead to more effective practice, then it is arguably of no value to practice. As information professionals, we need to know about our own information behaviour and that of our clients, our potential clients and those whom we can affect in some way even though they are not likely to consult us or use our services.

Awareness of some highfalutin model or theory developed from esoteric laboratory-controlled experiments is unlikely to add much to the effectiveness of a librarian in a relatively simple and straightforward case of helping a client find and utilize information. The problem is that in more complex cases the sufficiency of our knowledge of information behaviour to enable us to act in optimally effective ways is less likely to be complete.

In real-life situations (as opposed to experimentally controlled conditions) detailed predictions, derived from some model or theory, of how a client is likely to react or behave given specific actions or particular approaches by an information professional are unlikely to lead to performance superior to that to be expected from a thinking and reactive practitioner based on their existing professional knowledge and experience. Indeed, the gap between much research and the concerns of practice is a well exercised theme.

However, models and theories may be useful to practitioners to the extent that they may suggest concepts, relationships and approaches that might be worth considering. Just as being aware of a particular model or theory can lead a researcher to ask particular types of questions that might otherwise have been ignored (insofar as they might diverge from current orthodoxy or from their habitual approach), so it can sensitize a practitioner to novel aspects of interaction with clients.

Thus, for example, awareness of Activity Theory may prompt researcher and practitioner alike to think more actively about the wider cultural and historical context in which an interaction is taking place, and about what other stakeholders might be involved with the client who is presenting. Thinking of the nature of provision of information about HIV/AIDS, for example, the practitioner may be prompted to reflect on what might be the perceived social and cultural pressures experienced by a person suffering from the disease in attempting to inform themselves about it. What other people or agencies are likely to be involved, and how does the information provided by the practitioner's organization enmesh with that provided by others? How might all concerned work together to provide the best possible information to the client? Awareness of Sense-making Theory might sensitize both researcher and practitioner to pay more attention to and take more account of the importance of the affective, and not strictly rational and logical, aspects of a client's perceptions, needs and interactions with information professionals and the services they provide.

Theories and models also form the basis for further research studies, some of which will result in implications for professional practice. Over time, as more and more work makes use of, and gradually refines, models and theories, implications for practice will sometimes become clearer, and ultimately become infused into received professional wisdom. For example, the now commonly accepted notion that the expressed needs that people initially present to information professionals are not necessarily an accurate reflection of what they might actually need was at one stage a model proposed by early researchers.

For further exploration of the role of models and theories, as well as key examples of information behaviour models and theories, the reader is referred to Parts 2 and 3 in Case (2012), to Fisher, Erdelez and McKechnie (2005) and to Spink and Heinström (2013).

References

Allen, D., Karanasios, S. and Slavova, M. (2011) Working with Activity Theory: context, technology, and information behaviour, *Journal of the American Society for Information Science and Technology*, **62** (4), 776–88.

Case, D. (2012) *Looking for Information: a survey of research on information seeking, needs and behaviour*, 3rd edn, Bingley, Emerald.

Case, D. (2013) Metatheories, Paradigms, and Theories. In *Looking for Information: a survey of research on information seeking, needs, and behaviour*, 3rd edn, Bingley, Emerald, 163–98.

Dervin, B. (1983) An Overview of Sense-making Research: concepts, methods and results, paper presented at the annual meeting of the International Communication Association, Dallas, TX, May, http://faculty.washington.edu/wpratt/MEBI598/Methods/An%20Overview%20of%20 Sense-Making%20Research%201983a.htm.

Dervin, B. (1998) Sense-making Theory and Practice: an overview of user interests in knowledge seeking and use, *Journal of Knowledge Management*, **2** (2), 36–46.

Dervin, B. (1999) On Studying Information Seeking Methodologically: the implications of connecting metatheory to method, *Information Processing & Management*, **35** (6), 727–50.

Dervin, B. and Clark, K. D. (1999) Exemplars of the Use of the Sense-making Methodology (Meta-theory and Method): in-depth introduction to the sense-making issues of the Electronic Journal of Communication, *Electronic Journal of Communication*, **9** (2, 3, 4).

Ellis, D. (1989) A Behavioural Model for Information Retrieval System Design, *Journal of Information Science*, **15** (4/5), 237–47.

Erdelez, S. (1999) Information Encountering: it's more than just bumping into information, *Bulletin of the American Society for Information Science*, **25** (3), www.asis.org/Bulletin/Feb-99/erdelez.html.

Fisher, K. E., Erdelez, S. and McKechnie, L. E. F. (eds) (2005) *Theories of Information Behavior*, Medford, NJ, Information Today.

Ford, N. and Mansourian, Y. (2006) The Invisible Web: an empirical study of 'cognitive invisibility', *Journal of Documentation* **62** (5), 584–96.

Godbold, N. (2006) Beyond Information Seeking: towards a general model of information behaviour, *Information Research*, **11** (4), paper 269, http://InformationR.net/ir/11-4/paper269.html.

Houston, R. D. (2009) *A Model of Compelled Nonuser of Information*, (unpublished doctoral dissertation), Austin, TX, University of Texas at Austin.

Ingwersen, P. and Järvelin, K. (2005) *The Turn: integration of information seeking and retrieval in context*, Dordrecht, Springer.

Jamali, H. R. (2013) Citation Relations of Theories of Human Information Behaviour, *Webology*, **10** (1), Article 106, www.webology.org/2013/v10n1/a106.html.

Naumer, C., Fisher, K. and Dervin, B. (2008) Sense-Making: a methodological perspective, paper presented at Sensemaking Workshop, CHI 2008, Florence, Italy, http://dmrussell.googlepages.com/Naumer-final.pdf.

Robson, A. and Robinson, L. (2013) Building on Models of Information Behaviour: linking information seeking and communication, *Journal of Documentation*, **69**(2), 169–93.

Spink, A. and Heinström, J. (eds) (2013) *New Directions in Information Behaviour*, Bingley, Emerald.

Vakkari, P. (1996) Information Seeking in Context: a challenging metatheory. In *ISIC '96: proceedings of an international conference on information seeking in context*, London, Taylor Graham, 451–464, www.informationr.net/isic/ISIC1996/96_Vakkari.pdf.

von Thaden, T. L. (2007) Building a Foundation to Study Distributed Information Behaviour, *Information Research*, **12** (3), paper 312, http://InformationR.net/ir/12-3/paper312.html.

von Thaden, T. L. (2008) Distributed Information Behavior: a study of dynamic practice in a safety critical environment, *Journal of the American Society for Information Science and Technology*, **59** (10), 1555–69.

Wagner, D., Berger, J. and Zeldith, M. (1989) Theory Growth, Social Processes, and Metatheory. In Turner, J. (ed.), *Theory Building in Sociology*, London, Sage, 19–42.

Wilson, T. D. (1981) On User Studies and Information Needs, *Journal of Documentation*, **37** (1), 3–15.

Wilson, T. D. (1997) Information Behaviour: an interdisciplinary perspective, *Information Processing & Management*, **33** (4), 551–72.

Wilson, T. D. (1999) Models in Information Behaviour Research, *Journal of Documentation*, **55** (3), 249–70, http://informationr.net/tdw/publ/papers/1999JDoc.html.

Wilson, T. D. (2006) A Re-examination of Information Seeking Behaviour in the Context of Activity Theory, *Information Research*, **11** (4), paper 260, http://InformationR.net/ir/11-4/paper260.html.

Wilson, T. D. (2008) Activity Theory and Information Seeking, *Annual Review of Information Science Technology*, **42**, 119–61, doi: 10.1002/aris.2008.1440420111.

Wilson, T. D. and Walsh, C. (1996) *Information Behaviour: an interdisciplinary perspective*, Sheffield, University of Sheffield Department of Information Studies (British Library Research and Innovation Report No. 10), http://informationr.net/tdw/publ/infbehav/index.html.

PART 3

Discovering and using knowledge of information behaviour

8

Research approaches

Introduction

In the previous chapter, we explored the notions of models and theories, which essentially derive from research. As information professionals, students or enthusiasts, we derive new understanding from research that may help us improve connections and interactions between people (ourselves as well as others). We all read the results of the research conducted by others, and many of us will engage in research ourselves, whether as part of educational courses to achieve a qualification, or as an aspect of our professional activity as we strive to improve the services we offer. This chapter is designed to provide an overview of key issues that it is important to know about, whether we are reading or conducting research.

Research is basically an attempt to generate new understanding of something. High-quality research adheres to certain procedures and standards so that the understanding that is generated is based on evidence rather than prejudice, bias or whim. However, what constitutes 'evidence' – indeed, what constitutes 'understanding' – may be subject to differing interpretations – and the associated procedures and standards may differ accordingly.

As a reader of research, you may consider the findings of some investigations more relevant and useful than those of others. For example, if your view of what constitutes acceptable evidence emphasizes the need for research findings to be based on large samples of people and strong statistical analysis, you may consider the findings of a small-scale qualitative study based on interviews with 20 people, with no statistics to back them up, to be inconsequential in terms of influencing what you think about the topic, or in terms of influencing your behaviour or professional activity. You may, on the other hand, find that a large-scale statistical survey you have read about – whilst providing a very convincing and apparently watertight statistical analysis – nevertheless lacks an appreciation of real-life complexities to the extent that it lacks relevance and potential application to your own situation. Similar differences in conceptions of what is and is not convincing and potentially useful evidence may influence researchers in their choice of methodological approach to a particular project – and even in the nature of their research questions.

Different types of research – and different types of knowledge

Research is all about creating new understanding. But we can go about this using very different approaches, and there may be differences in our very conceptions of what constitutes 'understanding' of a phenomenon, and what constitutes 'evidence' to support it. To illustrate these differences, consider the question in the **THINK!** box.

THINK!

What is it that you find interesting about information behaviour? (I presume that you are interested, since you are reading this book).

Two common but different approaches that could be taken by a researcher to learning about people's interest in information behaviour include the following:

(a)   The researcher might devise a questionnaire, asking respondents to indicate their level of agreement or disagreement with a number of statements such   as:

I am interested in information behaviour because I personally find it fascinating.
Strongly agree ☐ Agree ☐ Neutral ☐ Disagree ☐ Strongly disagree ☐

I am interested in information behaviour because knowledge of it may help me   in   my   work.
Strongly agree ☐ Agree ☐ Neutral ☐ Disagree ☐ Strongly disagree ☐

I am not personally deeply interested in information behaviour, but need to know about it in order to gain a qualification.
Strongly agree ☐ Agree ☐ Neutral ☐ Disagree ☐ Strongly disagree ☐

(b) Or the researcher could interview people using a direct open-ended question such as:

Why are you reading about information behaviour?

This question might be followed by more probing questions designed to illuminate and expand upon a person's previous answers, such as:

You just said that you think it's important to know something about information behaviour. Can you say more about this? Why is it important?

These two very different approaches will generate very different-looking data. They will both tell the researcher something about people's interest in information behaviour, but the nature of the 'understanding' generated, and of the 'evidence' supporting this understanding, will be very different.

Responses from a questionnaire using multiple-choice questions like the ones in part (a) are typically converted to numbers (e.g. strongly agree = 1; agree = 2; neutral = 3; disagree = 4; strongly disagree = 5). Data may also be collected on other factors such as the respondents' age, gender, education, etc., which again will be coded as numbers. The researcher will then perform statistical analysis on the numbers – for example, to find whether there is a significant relationship between, say, gender or age and different types of interest in information behaviour.

It may be, for example, that older people may display greater levels of intrinsic interest (indicated by positive responses to questions including 'I am interested in information behaviour because I personally find it fascinating') than extrinsic interest ('I am not personally deeply interested in information behaviour, but need to know about it in order to gain a qualification'). Normally, concepts such as intrinsic and extrinsic interest would be assessed by a number of questions rather than just one each as in the simplified example here.

The *understanding* generated by the questionnaire analysis would be the proposition that there is some link between the variables 'age' and 'type of interest' (intrinsic or extrinsic). These variables will be clearly defined and unambiguously measured (as numbers). The *evidence* for the existence of these relationships is statistical. The science of statistics tells us that, on the basis of an analysis of patterns in the numbers, the relationship between age and type of interest probably did not occur by chance. Furthermore, we can put a number on this probability. We can say, for example, that the probability of this pattern being due to pure chance (rather than a real relationship) is smaller than 1 in 20. We would write this as: $p<0.05$.

The interview data, however, will look very different. Typically interview data is transcribed word for word, and the data will consist of paragraphs of text – transcriptions of what the interviewer asked and what each interviewee said in response. There are various ways of analysing such data. A widely used method is to use some form of thematic analysis. This consists basically of repeatedly reading the transcripts (and/or listening to the audio recordings if the researcher has recorded the interviews), thinking about what the interviewees meant, and what the interviews therefore reveal, and coding different parts of the text as illustrating particular concepts. In this way, concepts, relationships between concepts, and broader themes may be identified.

The *understanding* generated from interview data can typically be rich and complex. It may reflect how relationships between concepts may vary in different contexts, and how elements of a phenomenon may affect each other in subtle and complex ways. The *evidence* supporting the picture painted by the analysis consists of the researcher's explanation of his or her analysis – the nature of the concepts and relationships between them – typically supported by illustrative quotations from the interviews.

THINK!

I have outlined potential strengths of each of these different approaches. Can you immediately think of limitations or criticisms of each?

One criticism of the questionnaire approach (as it is described above) is that typically the researchers start with a model that they are going to test. They have decided in advance (maybe from reading previous research, and/or based on their experience) that there are different types of interest that people may have in learning about information behaviour ('pure interest', 'to help them obtain a qualification', etc.) and that gender and age are possible related factors. The researchers list these concepts and include them in the questionnaire. But what about other factors that may affect people's interests? Unexpected factors that the researcher has not anticipated will not emerge from the study. This is *deductive* (as opposed to *inductive*) research. Using a deductive approach, the researcher defines some hypothesis or theory in advance, then sets out to test it to see if it is true or false. (We will explore inductive research shortly.)

Another criticism is that this approach typically assumes that concepts – and relationships between them – can be objectively measured and usefully reduced to numbers. The criticism is that in doing so, the researcher cannot reflect the complexity, ambiguity and context-dependent variability of real life.

The approach does, however, have the benefit of allowing the researcher to specify on the basis of statistical science precisely how likely it is that the relationships found are real and not the result of chance. This enables the results to be generalized to other populations of which the sample used in the research was a randomly selected representation.

By contrast, the open-ended qualitative interview approach (as described above) has the advantage of enabling unexpected concepts and relationships to emerge from the data, and also of allowing a complex and holistic picture to be painted of the phenomenon under investigation, without the need for everything to be measured as isolated variables. Research which allows concepts and relationships to emerge from the data – as opposed to using concepts which the researchers have already defined and testing relationships that they have hypothesized – is inductive research. However, a disadvantage of this approach is that it cannot draw on the strength of statistics as evidence of the extent to which results are real and generalizable. Indeed, advocates of this approach argue that they are not seeking statistical generalization. Rather, they talk of 'transferability'. The findings of a study may achieve a depth of understanding which, when coupled with a rich description of the situation and circumstances in which the interview data was collected, enables others to transfer the findings to other contexts on the basis of the extent to which there is a 'resonance' between the two. Someone reading the results of the study may find a depth and richness of understanding which rings true in, and contains understandings that can be used in, their situation.

The two hypothetical studies described above are simple examples of how research approaches can differ. They are symptomatic of a number of relatively fundamental dimensions by which we can think about research – about the nature of understanding that we can seek, the nature of evidence that is required to support it, and the ways we can and should go about seeking it. Such broad fundamental differences are often referred to as research 'paradigms'.

The next section introduces key paradigms which underlie much research, including that concerned with information behaviour. It is a somewhat theoretical issue, but worth spending a little time and effort on, since the differences portrayed are really fundamental to the enterprise of doing – and reading – research.

Research paradigms

A research paradigm is a broad approach to research which embraces a person's beliefs in relation to three key issues. The differences we have just been exploring are included in these issues, which are:

- **Ontology:** what is the nature of reality? Is there a single reality 'out there', common to us all and independent of people who observe it – or are there multiple 'realities' constructed by different people in different contexts?
- **Epistemology:** what is the relationship between the researcher and what is being researched? Can the researcher find out about the phenomenon as an independent observer who is separate from it – or is any new knowledge inevitably the product of the researcher interacting with, rather than simply observing, the phenomenon?
- **Methodology:** how can we find out about the phenomenon to be researched?
    — Should we adopt a deductive (top-down) approach in which we define our variables and establish a hypothesis to be tested at the start of the research, or adopt a more open-ended inductive (bottom-up) approach in which we minimize assumptions about what will turn out to be important factors and what we might discover about the phenomenon?
    — Should we adopt a quantitative approach, in which we treat data as numbers, and generate understanding on the basis of statistical analysis of these numbers – or a qualitative approach, in which data can include what people say or do, and we analyse this data by interpreting their underlying meanings?

Within social science research, including information behaviour research, there are a number of well recognized research paradigms, each characterized by a particular cluster of positions relating to ontology, epistemology and methodology. Two that are particularly opposed to each other are:

- **Positivism:** which is characterized by beliefs that
    — there is one reality 'out there', which exists independent of any observer
    — the researcher can investigate this reality as an independent detached observer
    — phenomena can be most effectively investigated using a deductive and quantitative methodological approach.

- **Interpretivism:** which is characterized by beliefs that
  — there are multiple realities, constructed in the minds of people, that are different for different people and different contexts
  — the researcher inevitably interacts with the phenomenon being investigated, and any knowledge generated by the researcher will be the product of this inevitable interaction
  — a phenomenon can most effectively be researched using an inductive and qualitative approach.

A third paradigm falls to some extent between positivism and interpretivism:

- **Post-positivism:**
  — as in positivism, reality is 'out there' and exists independent of any observer
  — although in principle the researcher could investigate reality as an independent detached observer, as in positivism, in reality this is not possible due to the frailties and imperfections of being human. Researchers should strive to minimize the effects of such imperfections and make their research as objective as possible and try to obtain the most accurate picture possible of the reality they are observing.
  — as in positivism, phenomena can be most effectively investigated using a deductive and quantitative methodological approach – but there is more recognition of the importance and role of context. The context surrounding the people being researched should be taken account of and far as possible controlled for. Interaction between the observer and the observed should be minimized, and controlled (acknowledged and allowed for) in the analysis and interpretation of data.

THINK!

Can you use both (a) positivist/post-positivist and (b) interpretivist approaches in the same research study – or are they ultimately incompatible?

For example, if you want to use a *questionnaire* designed to produce *quantitative* data for statistical analysis, does this mean you cannot in the same study also *interview* people and analyse the data *qualitatively*?

What would happen if you did?

There is much debate concerning the compatibility, or lack of compatibility, between different research paradigms. Some argue that the ontological and epistemological assumptions characterizing positivist/post-positivist and interpretivist paradigms are mutually incompatible. You cannot at the same time believe that there is one reality and that there are multiple realities.

Others argue that there are different levels and foci in social research, which may be better suited to one or other approach. A given phenomenon has different aspects. It seems perfectly reasonable to accept that some aspects of our social make-up and experiences are relatively common to us all, and may be illuminated by quantitative analysis. For example, many useful social and psychological models and theories have been derived from the statistical analysis of quantified data from observations and psychometric measures. Other aspects of social life are inherently 'messy', variable and context-dependent, and can best be understood using interpretive qualitative approaches.

It may be argued that viewing a phenomenon through only one lens can be unhelpfully restrictive in a complex, often ambiguous and incompletely understood world. Investigating a phenomenon from differing perspectives, and comparing what is discovered using different approaches may bring fresh understanding.

Post-positivist approaches may seem particularly suited to non-social areas of research, for example engineering or technology. Increasingly, however, the foci of social research studies (including those of information behaviour) are embracing elements which, whilst having important social and psychological dimensions, are also characterized by non-social features much more conducive to investigation via post-positivist approaches. Many modern phenomena of interest to information behaviour researchers have both human and technological aspects.

Take, for example, the design of a mobile phone. There are aspects of its design which we might think would be most appropriately tackled via the gathering of quantitative data, statistical analysis and a hypothesis-testing approach. Such aspects might include investigating the strength and properties of the materials required for its construction, and the need constantly to improve speed of performance. But issues such as the aesthetics of the phone's design, and the extent to which it successfully meets user requirements, might be most appropriately investigated via interviews and interpretive inductive analysis.

Mixed-methods research (Fidel, 2008) is becoming increasingly popular in information behaviour-related studies. This approach seeks to take advantage of the strengths of different methods whilst attempting to minimize their weaknesses by combining the perspectives they afford. Quantitative and qualitative, inductive and deductive approaches can be used in various combinations. A quantitative study using, for example, a questionnaire distributed to a large sample of people and analysed statistically may be based on findings that were previously inductively derived from a qualitative interpretive study based on in-depth interviews with a relatively small but carefully selected set of individuals. Or a qualitative interview-based study may be used to illuminate the results of a large scale quantitative study – to discover 'why?' and 'how?' aspects of the findings.

According to Hall (2012) a mixed-methods approach does not neatly map onto a paradigm in the same way as the approaches described above map onto positivism/post-positivism and onto interpretivism. Mixed-methods approaches are often associated with a 'pragmatist' paradigm, which is characterized by a practical orientation towards 'what works' rather than assumptions about the nature of knowledge. Pragmatism:

• rejects the argument of incompatibility between positivism/post-positivism and interpretivism
• supports the use of both qualitative and quantitative methods in the same study
• holds the position that the research question and the stage of the research cycle are more important than the methods used or the paradigm adopted.

However, some have argued that what does or does not work can only be determined at the end of a study, so cannot logically be used to select a particular approach. Another candidate is the 'realist' paradigm. According to Flowers (2009), realism arose from criticisms that positivism is too deterministic (leaving humans with little control over a reality controlled by universal laws) and that in constructivism (associated with interpretivist approaches) is too relative (multiple context-dependent realities being constructed in people's minds). Realism takes elements from both these paradigms, proposing that on the one hand . . .

• science should be rational, objective and empirically based
• real structures exist independently of our powers to perceive and study them, and
• social objects and structures may be studied scientifically

whilst on the other . . .

• rather than being explainable by universal laws of cause and effect, what we observe is the result of complex interactions between many factors, including tendencies and circumstances

- reality can exist on multiple levels
- knowledge is socially created.

Realism supports both inductive and deductive research approaches, emphasizing that coming at things at different levels and from different angles can enrich our understanding.

Research methodologies and methods

So far we have considered a number of approaches to improving our understanding of information behaviour via systematic research. These approaches have been characterized in broad terms of the underlying assumptions they implied concerning ontology (the nature of 'reality'), epistemology (the relationship between the researcher and the researched), and methodology. However, these broad approaches may be served by a rich variety of research methodologies and methods.

Methodology relates to views on how we can best go about discovering new knowledge – about choosing which methods and combinations of them will be most effective in helping us discover what we set out to discover. *Methods* are the specific things we do – like conducting a questionnaire-based survey, setting up an experiment, or interviewing people. A set of coherent views on what methods we should deploy, and how we should deploy them, is a methodology. There are many well developed methodologies and methods available to researchers.

In her review of recent trends in information behaviour research, Greifeneder (2014) notes that although mixed-methods research has increased, qualitative research approaches are still dominant – popular methods still being interviews, focus groups, surveys and observations. The use of content analysis and participatory research designs is increasing. In the period covered by the review (2012–14) the most frequently used methods were interviews, surveys and content analyses. Content analysis studies in Greifeneder's review included analyses of social networks such as YouTube and Twitter. For a detailed treatment of the range of research methodologies and methods available to the information behaviour researcher, the reader is referred to Pickard (2013).

Assessing quality in research

As a student of information behaviour – indeed, of anything! – you need to be able critically to evaluate information sources. Whether you are reading about a piece of research with a view to making use of the new knowledge it has generated, or considering conducting a piece of research yourself, you need to know what makes *good* research. You do not want to apply research findings only to find that the quality of the research is poor. And if you are engaged in research, you want to ensure that it is of high quality.

Indirect evaluation entails assessing the credibility and authority of the information based on factors external to the information itself, such as: 'Who is the author, and how well placed is s/he to talk about this topic? Has s/he any vested interests which might result in any bias? Is the information published in a source that is peer-reviewed?' Indirect evaluation can tell you how likely it is that the information is high quality – but does not guarantee this quality. For example, information published by an author in a high-quality peer-reviewed journal is more likely to be authoritative than information published in a journal that is not peer-reviewed. However, this is not to say that the second paper *is* of lesser quality – just that it might be, and that it would be a good idea to subject it to direct evaluation (discussed below) in order to assess its quality.

Direct critical evaluation consists of weighing up for yourself the strengths and weaknesses of what an author is saying – examining the evidence put forward to support and justify what they are claiming. Whether or not there is sufficient evidence to support a claim or argument is rarely a case of simply 'yes' or 'no'. Evidence needs weighing up in terms of its strengths and weaknesses. However, there are a number of generally accepted criteria whereby we can assess the quality of evidence put forward to substantiate particular claims. You can apply these criteria whether you are reading research produced by someone else – or conducting research yourself.

It is widely agreed that acceptable evidence should possess certain qualities. *Validity, reliability, objectivity* and *generalizability* are terms associated with positivist/post-positivist quantitative research. There are broadly similar concepts associated with interpretive qualitative research. In the list below, the interpretive/qualitative alternative concept is listed in brackets.

Internal validity (truth value)

This relates to the extent to which the evidence put forward actually relates to what is being claimed or argued. A lack of internal validity can happen when what the researcher thinks s/he is measuring or investigating is not what s/he is actually measuring or investigating. The researcher may claim that the data is telling him/her one thing when in fact it is telling him/her another.

For example, a researcher investigates information seeking amongst a sample of undergraduate students, and finds that women perform more Google Scholar searches than men. The researcher concludes that these is a link between gender and search frequency, and goes on to make a number of recommendations relating to how male students can be encouraged to make more use of Google Scholar. However, the researcher has failed to realize that in his sample a much greater proportion of the older students were female, and that older students in their later undergraduate years are required more to engage in independent research-based study. They are therefore much more likely to need to engage in information seeking using scholarly search tools like Google Scholar.

This type of error is far less likely to appear in a research paper that appears in a good-quality peer-reviewed journal or book, since expert reviewers should have examined it before it was accepted for publication. This is particularly the case with statistical research. In the case of qualitative research, based for example on interviews, it is common for authors to provide short quotations from the interviews to illustrate different points, or categories they have used to classify the data. You should look critically at any such quotations to judge whether they really *do* support what's being said. Again, one would expect a referee to have examined such issues when dealing with a good-quality peer-reviewed source. Nevertheless, it is desirable to be alert to possible errors of this type.

Reliability (consistency)

This quality relates to the extent to which the evidence is stable, and is likely to be the same if gathered at different times and/or by different observers. An example of evidence lacking reliability includes the following.

A series of experiments are conducted in which groups of people are asked to search the web for information. But some of the groups were conducted by different researchers, and the instructions given to the groups were not quite the same. This lack of control means that the data was not collected using a consistent measure. A lack of reliability can also affect validity since any differences found in the behaviour of the different groups may not relate to what the researchers think they do (i.e. the differences may be due to the different instructions rather than to differences in the groups).

Another example would be of researchers classifying interview statements into different categories – for example, those indicating frustration on the part of the interviewee, and others indicating boredom. If the criteria precisely defining these categories are not made clear, it may be that different people would classify a given statement differently. It may be classified as indicating boredom by one person, and frustration by another. If this were the case, then the codes used in the classification are not reliable.

Objectivity (neutrality)
This relates to the extent to which the evidence avoids bias. Bias may affect a study without the researcher necessarily being aware of it. For example, questions in a questionnaire might not be phrased completely neutrally, and may lead the respondent to answer in a particular way. Or an interviewer may ask a 'leading question' which gives a subtle indication to the interviewee of what the interviewer expects, or would ideally like, to hear.

Generalizability (transferability)
Generalizability (transferability) or external validity is the extent to which claims can be generalized from the specific context in which they were generated to other contexts. In statistical research, there are ways of assessing the extent to which findings are generalizable. These include ensuring that the sample used is big enough and randomly selected, and that the specific requirements for using the particular statistical tests used are not violated.

In the case of qualitative research, the extent to which findings may be transferable depends on the researcher providing rich information about the context and circumstances of the research. This information must be sufficiently rich for the reader to be able to assess the extent to which the research context and circumstances are sufficiently similar to their own context and circumstances to enable the findings to be applied to them.

An example of inappropriate generalization would be claiming that your findings relate to 'university students' when your sample consisted only of undergraduates – or that your results relate to 'how people search the internet' when your data relate only to the use of Google.

THINK!
Have you recently needed to read some research – whether for your job or for study?

If so, to what extent did you question its quality? Did you consider separately (a) how valid, (b) how reliable and (c) how generalizable (or transferable) it was?

Did the paper or book in which it was presented provide you with enough information about the research to be able to satisfy yourself of its quality?

Generally speaking, research reported in a good peer-reviewed journal should have already been checked in relation to these issues by expert reviewers – at least to ensure that there are no gross or obvious errors. But this is not to suggest that you do not also need to think carefully about how valid and applicable you consider it to be.

Sometimes information sources that you are reading simply do not tell you some of the things you need to know in relation to some of the criteria discussed above. If a paper lacks them, it does not necessarily mean that the research was badly conducted – particularly if it is peer-reviewed. Within the space constraints of a journal article, for example, it may not always be possible to provide convincing reassurance. In this case, you may have to combine extrinsic with intrinsic criteria to assess the work – i.e. make sure it is from a peer-reviewed, high-quality publication. The fact that a source is peer-reviewed provides an element of extrinsic evaluation of the quality of a piece of reported work. If it is not, and the key information is not contained in the information source, it may be a case of accepting the findings with appropriate caution and caveats, rather than rejecting them out of hand. It may also be possible to search for and find other sources that corroborate the points made in the original source. But this can be time-consuming.

Much depends on what you need the information for. If you are studying at more basic undergraduate levels the most reasonable and practical strategy may be generally to accept peer-reviewed sources and use their findings – but make any criticisms that you feel are appropriate based on a good critical reading of it. At more advanced levels – or if as a practitioner you are intending to implement change or practice based on research findings – it may be more appropriate to examine in greater detail, using intrinsic criteria, the quality of the research and its applicability to your situation of its findings.

The 'darkness to light' ratio

For many years the predominance of relatively post-positivist research approaches in information science meant that arguably our models and theories were limited by the fragmentary nature of much of our relatively narrow quantitatively derived knowledge. However, although acceptance and application of interpretive research has burgeoned more recently, the objectively untested nature of much of our more holistic qualitatively derived knowledge leaves gaps of a different nature. Indeed, Ford has drawn attention to the dilemma posed by these differences:

> Overly-analytic states of knowledge are characterized by fragmentation – at worst, isolated facts lacking integration into any coherent wider conceptual

picture. . . . As a result, much research in information science has arguably provided highly reliable answers to highly meaningless questions. The take-up of qualitative research approaches is now widespread in user oriented research. But without critical interaction with complementary perspectives the increasing use of subjective analysis of introspections using small samples of information users threatens to supply highly meaningful questions with highly unreliable answers. Some balance and integration must be achieved between the two extremes.

Ford, 1999, 1151

The limitations associated with research may be thought of as curtains preventing us from viewing the 'reality' beyond (whether we consider this to be one objective reality or multiple subjectively constructed realities, depending on our perspective).

Our existing knowledge ranges between two extremes, which to some extent mirror the different research approaches discussed above. One is like scattered pinpricks in the curtain, allowing clear and deep, but narrow and relatively unconnected views through to the reality beyond. The other may be characterized as more extensive areas where the curtain is thinned, allowing complex, interconnected but hazy shapes to show through. Typically, we tend to trace them onto the curtain, elaborating their detail to represent what we imagine to be their reality.

It is arguably all too easy to ignore the extent of curtain and our consequent lack of clear knowledge about important issues. For example, we may sometimes falsely equate over-simplified research contexts with more complex reality, or we may confuse internal coherence and plausibility with robustness and generalizability. Our wish to develop practically applicable yet robustly evidence-based knowledge may encourage us to be over-optimistic in relation to assessing the extent of our secure knowledge, and to mask the extent of the 'darkness to light' ratio.

Within such context, it is all the more important critically to evaluate what we read – to question its validity, credibility and generalizability. When you are reading or conducting research, try constantly to imagine alternative contrary interpretations and see if they sound equally reasonable. Generalizations are often made in the discussion and conclusions sections of articles. It is a good idea to check back to the evidence presented in the earlier parts to see if the claims are reasonably supported by this evidence. Think whether the evidence (data, analysis and interpretation) fully support the claims being put forward. The golden rule is – always think critically.

Research and practice

Research into information behaviour, like any science in which people are central, has many limitations and research findings that are inevitably subject to ambiguities, hidden complexities and uncertainties. It is all too easy unwittingly to allow bias, errors and unaccounted-for confounding variables to play their part in generating research findings, rendering them less valid, reliable and applicable than the researcher might – in all good faith – believe them to be.

As we have seen in the section above on research methodologies, we can try at least to minimize if not eradicate some of these effects via the application of rigorous quality criteria designed to address issues of validity, reliability and generalizabilty. However, in the case of statistical research, the very procedures designed to avoid bias and maximize clarity, precision and accurate measurement can have the effect of removing whatever phenomenon is being researched from its 'real-world' context. Although the extent to which the research findings are statistically generalizable to the wider population from which a sample was taken, the artificiality of the way variables are isolated and narrowly defined in order more accurately to measure them can result in a loss of 'ecological validity'. Results obtained in tightly controlled experimental conditions might be generalizable in that the same results might also be found in a repeat of the experiment using a different sample from the same population. But what is discovered about human thought and behaviour may be far from applicable to the real world of professional practice.

Other approaches to research enable investigations to take place in naturalistic 'real-world' contexts, and are more accepting of the messiness and complexity of real life. They make available to the researcher procedures, approaches and quality criteria which avoid the need to define, isolate, measure and recombine variables in such a way that ecological validity is lost. However, what they gain in potential real world applicability they arguably lose in terms of other limitations. In attempting to maximize depth and subtlety of understanding, qualitative research studies are often based on much smaller samples of people than are their quantitative counterparts. Nor can they benefit from the apparent greater certainty of relatively objective measures of reliability and generalization characterizing quantitative work.

THINK!

Do you have any view of the value (or otherwise) of 'theory' – especially if you are a library/information practitioner?

Do you, for example, consider it to be largely unrelated to – or even the opposite of – 'practice'?

Or do you think theory actually informs practice in useful ways?

At least partly due to the limitations inherent in research described above, there is arguably a considerable 'research/practice gap' between practitioners and researchers within librarianship and information science, which has been the focus of a number of studies. Dervin and Reinhard (2006), for example, investigated the perceptions of a sample of mainly USA-based researchers and practitioners concerning 'user studies' research and the research/practice divide. The interviewees came from the fields of library and information science, human–computer interaction and communication/ media studies. They included academics and practitioners. The sample had a greater proportion of academics, though most also had experience as practitioners. 'Users' were interpreted broadly to include:

> . . . persons who have been conceptualized in one way or another as the voluntary or intended users of information, media or communication systems: citizens, employees, patients, patrons, audiences, students, clients, customers, constituencies, recipients and so on.
>
> Dervin and Reinhard, 2006

They found that most interviewees struggled with the research/practice divide. Most also thought that there were difficulties with research in that:

- our knowledge of users is insufficient
- user research is shallow and fragmented rather than integrated and cumulative
- we may not even be aware of what are the important questions to be asked.

Most agreed that there are problems with the research/practice divide – more specifically that:

- researchers and practitioners have different priorities, and often ignore each other
- there is a lack of incentive and of structures to support interaction and collaboration between researchers and practitioners.

Both researchers and practitioners were amongst those who commented on problems associated with research, attributing problems to both researchers and practitioners in considering that:

- researchers are often remote from everyday real life and are concerned

with toy problems
- researchers are often motivated by self-interest and money
- the research they produce is not useful in terms of practical system design
- many practitioners are hyper-critical and anti-intellectual, and often research-illiterate
- many practitioners are institution-focused, and the deadlines and pressures faced by practitioners can prevent rigorous research.

Koufogiannakis (2011, 1) also discussed the relationship between research and practice, drawing a distinction between science and art. Art is defined as 'professional knowledge of your craft, intuition, experience, tacit knowledge, reflection, creativity, values, people-skills', whilst science is 'systematized knowledge, explicit research, methodological examination, investigation, data'. In her judgement as a library and information practitioner, she estimated that professional practice is in most cases around 30% science and 70% art.

Practitioners' professional knowledge, entailing experience and intuition is rich and applicable to real life situations, but is often not formally tested and validated using academically rigorous procedures and quality standards. Formal research, however, whilst benefitting from the application of such procedures and standards, is often criticized as lacking 'ecological validity' – real-world usefulness.

Koufogiannakis insists that practitioners need both art and science:

> We need to embrace both the science and the art of evidence based practice – otherwise, we will overlook important elements of the whole situation that practitioners work within. Doing so is not neat and tidy, but does that really matter? LIS is a social science, and the 'social' implies 'messy' because people and real-life situations are not easily controlled. The art of our craft allows us to embrace the messy situation, find ways to be creative, put our professional judgements to use and find the best solutions to meet the needs of individual users by applying the best of what we find in the research literature together with the best of what we know is likely to help this person.
>
> Koufogiannakis, 2011, 2

Ideally we need more evidence-based practice and practice-based evidence. This will entail generating more research that is useful (applicable) yet scientifically robust. This ambition might be furthered by a number of measures, including:

- more involvement in work-relevant research by practitioners
- research agendas becoming more sensitive to the real-life needs of practice
- research findings being more effectively communicated to practitioners
- practice-relevant needs being communicated more effectively by practitioners to researchers
- more two-way interaction between practitioners and researchers at informal, as well as formal levels.

The needs of practice would be well served by an evidence base that is as wide-ranging yet coherently integrated as possible. Much past and current research has been criticized as being shallow and fragmented when evaluated in terms of what it tells us about people and information that is practically useful. Arguably, as well as smaller individual studies we need more large-scale co-ordinated research efforts, and greater integration of studies in order to develop cumulative understanding rather than a disconnected series of snapshots. Efforts are being made in relation to such ambitions in that:

- There is increasing pressure on academics, particularly in UK universities, to engage in research that has – and to provide quantifiable evidence of – real-world impact. This should inevitably entail greater interaction between researchers and practitioners.
- There is increasing acceptance and use by academics of research methodologies that recognize and attempt to take account of real-world complexity and 'messiness'.
- There are an increasing number of journals aiming to contribute to evidence-based practice by communicating research findings to practitioners.
- There is increasing interest in evidence-based librarianship, not least in the form of the open-access peer reviewed journal Evidence Based Library and Information Practice (http://ejournals.library.ualberta.ca/index.php/EBLIP/index).

Types of evidence that the practitioner can bring to bear on a given problem are wide-ranging, and may include theoretical, empirical and experiential. Such evidence may emanate from expert practitioners, published research, one's own professional knowledge and experience, and/or one's own systematically collected data and observations. As Koufogiannakis notes:

> Practitioners bring evidence to the table through the very action of their practice.

> The local context of the practitioner is the key, and research cannot just be simply handed over for a practitioner to implement. . . . All forms of evidence need to be respected and the LIS professional, with his or her underlying knowledge (a part of soft evidence), is at the centre of the decision making process. Different types of evidence need to be weighed within the context in which they are found, and only the practitioners dealing with that decision can appropriately assign value and importance within that context.
>
> Koufogiannakis, 2013

She calls for more research mapping the best evidential sources for particular types of question, and providing guidance to practitioners on how critically to interpret and evaluate such sources. The relationship between research and practice is receiving increasing research attention.

A recent example is a study by MacDonald, Bath and Booth (2014). As part of a wider study, the authors explored the way in which busy health service managers in a publicly funded district health authority in Nova Scotia used information, including research, to inform their critical decisions relating to matters such as developing practice-based guidelines, planning disease prevention strategies and complying with safety standards. Initial interviews suggested that the managers did not tend to search for primary research to inform their critical decision-making, and therefore the researchers set about answering the question: 'If these health service managers informed decisions with research, how did they acquire it?'

Further investigation revealed that decisions were often made in a context of the need to meet tight deadlines and a lack of time to seek and interpret primary research. There was a need for information from multiple sources and to blend this with local contextual knowledge. The primary source of information was often other people brought together specially to share relevant knowledge. Decision making tended to entail a satisficing strategy (see the section on the relationship between 'internal' and 'external' factors in Chapter 6), based on a blend of administrative efficiency and a 'good enough' solution rather than an optimal one selected from multiple considered alternatives.

Different decisions required different types of information. Where research-based information was required to inform decisions, it reached the managers via one or more of eight routes:

1 Managers tended to prefer sources in which it had already been digested and blended, as integrated into professional guidelines, standards, regulation and legislation.

2 They also consulted gatekeepers who engaged in seeking, filtering and synthesizing research-based information.
3 Although generally preferring other approaches, they did when necessary search for information directly themselves, or indirectly via a librarian or other staff member.
4 They also set up working groups to address issues, identifying gaps in their knowledge and distributing the task of seeking relevant information between members of the group.
5 Sometimes colleagues in other organizations were contacted to consult them in relation to what information and processes they used in similar situations.
6 Information was also gathered from attendance at conferences and workshops relevant to issues being faced.
7 Advice could be specifically requested in relation to an issue from academics, provincial government representatives and external consultants.
8 When seeking approval for decisions, they would sometimes be communicating using Situation-Background-Analysis/Alternative-Recommendation briefing notes, which may be supported by relevant research.

The authors conclude that although health service managers tend not to seek, evaluate and synthesize research information for themselves:

> Typically research reaches them through more indirect routes, in the form of standards or after being filtered by colleagues or by research summaries. Health services managers thus find research blended with experience and expertise, already appraised for credibility and filtered for value and relevance, to be more easily applied within their intense work environments.
>
> MacDonald, Bath and Booth, 2014

It is possible that the future relationship between practitioners and the research literature will become more rather than less complex. Finlay et al. (2013) for example, published an interesting review of 4827 peer-reviewed papers from 20 library and information science journals published between 1956 and 2011. They sought to establish the percentage written by library practitioners. They found that overall there had been a steady increase in librarians' authorship of papers, with a sharp increase from 1997 to 2006. However, after 2006 there had been a sharp decline, whilst papers authored by non-practitioners had shown a sharp increase.

Although this may be a blip that will change over time, the authors suggest that it is also possible that this may be due to the rise in librarians' use of blogging and social media to publish practitioner-based literature. These provide a more immediate channel to publish ideas, and may allow a length and style of article more suited to practical professional needs. In the academic library context such a shift in choice of publishing outlet may also be coupled with a move away from the requirement for librarians to publish in peer-reviewed journals in order to gain tenure, and a move in some universities in the USA to strip librarians of faculty status.

Finlay et al. suggest that, if present trends continue, librarian-authored papers could decline to represent less than 20% of the scholarly literature by the end of the decade. Such a decline is likely to impact the subject matter of scholarly communication, in that papers published by librarians tend to address topics associated with library services more than do papers authored by non-librarians.

Disengagement from the scholarly literature on the part of practising librarians may affect their familiarity with current research, and particularly in an academic library context may affect interactions with staff and students who are engaged in research. There are also likely to be implications for students wishing to enter the library profession if they are being taught by academics whose research and publishing interests rarely extend to issues directly relevant to professional practice and services. Finlay et al. also note a decline in library and information science students' dissertations focusing on libraries.

Summary

This chapter has discussed different approaches to conducting research. It is important to be aware of such differences, whether you are a consumer or generator of research. There are well established criteria by which the quality of research can be judged, and it is important to ensure that these are met before considering whether or not research findings can be applied. Without such checks, biased, invalid and unreliable assertions may pass for bona fide research findings.

However, research has many limitations, and the need for practitioners as well as academics to contribute to our growing research base cannot be overestimated. Rarely can research findings offer a ready solution to complex professional problems. But they can often stimulate new thinking and suggest new approaches worth trying. We need a vibrant culture of new ideas and experimentation, with two-way collaboration between academics and practitioners. However, we must balance the twin needs of moving forward but at the same time experimenting ethically. We must avoid inadvertently disadvantaging clients as we try new things.

For a more detailed examination of approaches to research in information behaviour, the reader is referred to Part 4 in Case (2012).

References

Case, D. (2012) *Looking for Information: a survey of research on information seeking, needs and behaviour*, 3rd edn, Bingley, Emerald.

Dervin, B. and Reinhard, C. (2006) Researchers and Practitioners Talk About Users and Each Other: making user and audience studies matter – paper 1, *Information Research*, **12** (1), paper 286, http://InformationR.net/ir/12-1/paper286.html.

Fidel, R. (2008) Are We There Yet?: mixed methods research in library and information science, *Library & Information Science Research*, **30** (4), 265–72.

Finlay, S. C., Ni, C., Tsou, A. and Sugimoto, C. R. (2013) Publish or Practice?: an examination of librarians' contributions to research, *portal: Libraries and the Academy*, **13** (4), 403–21.

Flowers, P. (2009) Research Philosophies – Importance and Relevance, MSc by research, Cranfield School of Management, www.scribd.com/doc/39607668/Research-Philosophies-Imp-and-Relevance.

Ford, N. (1999) The Growth of Understanding in Information Science: towards a developmental model, *Journal of the American Society for Information Science*, **50** (12) 1141–52.

Greifeneder, E. (2014) Trends in Information Behaviour Research. In *Proceedings of ISIC, the Information Behaviour Conference, Leeds, 2–5 September, 2014: Part 1*, (paper isic13), http://InformationR.net/ir/19-4/isic/isic13.html.

Hall, R. (2012) Mixed Methods: in search of a paradigm. In Le, T. and Le, Q. (eds) *Conducting Research in a Changing and Challenging World*, Hauppauge, NY, Nova Science Publishers, 71–8.

Koufogiannakis, D. (2011) Evidence Based Practice: science? or art?, *Evidence Based Library and Information Practice*, **6** (1), https://ejournals.library.ualberta.ca/index.php/EBLIP/article/viewFile/9862/7847.

Koufogiannakis, D. (2013) What We Talk About When We Talk About Evidence, keynote address at EBLIP 7, *Evidence Based Library And Information Practice*, **8** (4), 6–17, http://ejournals.library.ualberta.ca/index.php/EBLIP/article/view/20486/15965.

MacDonald, J., Bath, P. A. and Booth, A. (2014) Reaching Health Service Managers with Research, *Information Research*, **19** (4), paper 649, http://InformationR.net/ir/19-4/paper649.html.

Pickard, A. J. (2013) *Research Methods in Information*, 2nd edn, London, Facet Publishing.

9

Research methodologies in action

Introduction

The purpose of this chapter is not to list and discuss the range of methodologies and associated methods available, but rather to present three case studies which illustrate fundamental dimensions of difference in approach, giving a flavour of what they can offer and what might be their limitations. The first is a hypothesis-testing approach in which numerical data is *quantitatively* analysed in order *deductively* to test a predefined hypothesis. The second entails a *qualitative* analysis of textual data in order *inductively* to explore a phenomenon in a more open-ended way.

Hypothesis testing: a deductive quantitative study

Anand and Gomez-Mejia (2014) report a study that sought to test a number of specific hypotheses that had been developed based on a review of relevant theory and previous research. The study focused on the information-seeking behaviour of the members of top management teams in a selection of small American entrepreneurial firms. In particular, they sought to investigate the effects of types of reward structure on the seeking of information from outside 'affiliate' organizations (customers and vendors). The researchers hypothesized that:

- The higher the proportion of income that is made up of cash incentive payments (relative to base pay) the more top managers will engage in information seeking from external affiliate sources. This effect will be more pronounced in higher-technology-intensive firms.
- Base rates of pay will have a moderating effect. This moderating effect

will be stronger in the case of higher-technology-intensive firms.
• Information seeking from external affiliate sources will decrease when
  cash incentives are linked to aggregate performance.

The reasoning behind these hypotheses was built on risk-bearing theory, and
was as follows:

• The larger the proportion of cash incentives relative to base pay, the
  greater the risk for executives in that they are more dependent on
  immediate and short-term performance for their payment. They are
  therefore more likely to 'play it safe' and focus on 'harvest' strategies
  which emphasize maximizing income from existing popular products (as
  opposed to engaging in more fundamental or revolutionary but risky
  developments).
• Information from affiliate sources is most likely to be helpful in supporting
  harvest strategies and maximizing short-term performance rather than
  leading to more fundamental longer-term changes. This is because
  affiliates such as customers and vendors are 'intimately cued into the
  firm's products, processes, markets and competitors – hence information
  obtained from them is highly relevant for identifying immediate threats
  and opportunities' (Anand and Gomez-Mejia, 2014, 71).
• Maintaining good relationships with customers and vendors is
  particularly important in avoiding potential problems in the immediate
  and short term. This is because these affiliates are potentially able
  unilaterally to end their relationship if they are discontented. They are
  also influential and likely to be listened to by the chief executive officer
  and shareholders. Executives may thus feel vulnerable and consequently
  maintain greater contact with and seek information and advice from
  affiliates to keep them 'on board'.
• These effects are more likely to be felt by technology-intensive firms,
  since the environment in which they operate is highly complex and
  dynamic. Trends, markets and what is likely to be successful are difficult
  to predict. Information changes rapidly and product life cycles are short.
  Knowledge requires constant updating. This type of firm is particularly
  needful of high levels of knowledge and information. Finally, because of
  their size, most smaller firms do not have many specialized staff and
  have to rely more on information from outside for new information.

The research was designed to test the hypotheses described above. To do this
the researchers established independent, dependent and control variables.

An independent variable is a measure of something that the researcher thinks might have an effect – in this case, differences in the type of reward structure used in different firms. A dependent variable is a measure of what the researcher thinks will be affected by the independent variable – in this case, information behaviour. Control variables relate to some other phenomena which the researcher thinks might also affect the dependent variable (in this case, the size of the firm and the length of time an executive has been with the firm). These are kept the same across all the sample so that the effects of the independent variable on the dependent variable can be isolated from (and are thus not confounded by) the possible effects of the control variables. The independent variables in this study related to:

- whether base salary was higher or lower than immediate competitor firms
- the percentage of salary made up of cash incentives
- the percentage of cash incentives that were linked to aggregate performance.

The dependent variables were related to information seeking from external sources – specifically:

- the extent to which information was sought from affiliate and other external sources
- the extent to which they sought the information via face-to-face contact, e-mail, letter, fax, etc.

Control variables were:

- the size of the firm
- the number of years the respondent had been with the firm.

The hypotheses were tested using two randomly selected samples of small US entrepreneurial firms. The first set consisted of technology-intensive firms, the second set of firms defined as low-technology in terms of having a less than 5% ratio of research/development to sales. For both samples, a two-stage survey was conducted in which first data from each company relating to top management reward structures was gathered, and second key executives from the top management team (identified to the researchers by the chief executive officer of the firm) were surveyed about their information seeking. Chief executive officers identified 436 top executives from 177 high-technology and 259 low-technology firms, who were then invited to participate in a mail-based survey. Of the 436 sample, 249 top executives responded – 95 from high-technology and 154 from low-technology firms.

The data was analysed using regression – a technique designed to establish whether there is a statistically significant relationship between variables. This technique does more than establishing simply whether variables are correlated. Correlation is limited, in that, if variable A correlates with variable B, it tells us nothing about whether A is likely to have caused B, or vice versa. In other words, correlation analysis tells us nothing about the *direction* of any influence. However, although regression still cannot tell us about *causality* (whether B is caused by A), it can indicate a *direction* in the relationship. It can tell us whether A can *predict* B. Put another way, for every increase or decrease in scores for A, there is a corresponding increase or decrease in scores for B (but not necessarily vice versa). So A can be considered to predict B, whilst B cannot necessarily predict A.

The results of the regression analysis supported the hypotheses, suggesting that the use of cash incentives in top executives' pay structures is indeed linked to more information seeking from affiliate sources, and that this effect is more pronounced in the case of technology-intensive firms. The greater the extent to which cash incentives were linked to aggregate performance, the less information was sought from affiliate sources. Also, in the case of technology-intensive firms, the link between cash incentives and information seeking from affiliate sources was much stronger when the executives' base pay was lower. The use of cash incentives had no significant effect on information seeking from 'sources outside the core value chain (such as colleagues, consultants, and universities)' (Anand and Gomez-Mejia, 2014, 78).

This research took a very specific and detailed hypothesis, and set about testing it using statistical analysis. All the variables were tightly defined, as were the precise relationships between them. Even so, a good deal of inference was needed to bridge the gap between the numbers and what might be more generally applicable knowledge. Such a research approach is less well suited to a more open-ended exploratory study in which the key variables and relationships may not be known in advance. The next example shows the application of a research approach that is more amenable to this type of research question.

Situational Analysis: an inductive qualitative study

Sen and Spring (2013) used Situational Analysis to study young people's information behaviour in relation to coping with long-term illnesses. They analysed a series of interviews with 30 young people which had previously been collected and made available on the Youth Health Talk website of the DIPEx charity.

The research was inductive (as opposed to deductive), in that the researchers did not have a preconceived notion of what might be the concepts, or any hypothesis concerning the likely relationships between them that they wished to test. Rather, they wanted openly to discover what were the key concepts and relationships characterizing the situations they were investigating, allowing these to emerge from the data. The study was qualitative in that the data consisted of the transcripts of interviews rather than numbers, and these were analysed semantically in order to identify concepts and themes rather than counted and analysed statistically.

Situational Analysis is a development of Grounded Theory, which is an inductive methodology in which theory is developed from data. It is inductive in that data gathering and analysis precedes the development of theory. Rather than starting with ready-made concepts and relationships derived from existing theory, relatively open-ended data is first collected and analysed in order to establish tentative initial categories and underlying themes. These categories and themes are refined and developed through further iterative data collection and analysis. The resultant theory is thus thoroughly grounded in data. As Lazar, Feng and Hochheiser (2010) note:

> [W]hen conducting experimental research, we normally start from a pre-formed theory, typically in the form of one or hypotheses, we then conduct experiments to collect data and use the data to prove the theory. In contrast, grounded theory starts from a set of empirical observations or data and we aim to develop a well-grounded theory from the data. During the process of theory development, multiple rounds of data collection and analysis may be conducted to allow the underlying theory to fully emerge from the data (Corbin and Strauss, 2008; Myers, 1997). Therefore, some researchers refer to the theory generated using this method as the 'reverse-engineered' hypothesis.
>
> Lazar, Feng and Hochheiser, 2010, 283

Situational Analysis is a development of Grounded Theory pioneered by Clarke (2005). As Mills, Chapman, Bonner and Francis (2007) note, the original Grounded Theory is rooted in a post-positivist perspective, and Clarke (2005, 72) was keen to move it on 'around the postmodern turn'. Recall from the section on research paradigms in Chapter 8 that post-positivism posits that there is one objective reality 'out there' waiting to be discovered – even though our measurements are fallible. This is perfectly compatible with constructivism, which posits that we each construct our own version of reality based on our perceptions and observations, but since these are inherently fallible, our view of reality is inevitably flawed.

A postmodern perspective is also constructivist, but goes a step further in positing that '[a]ll reasoning and judging takes place from within some local context shaped by a narrative about reality and carried forward within a community of tradition created by that narrative' (Olson, 2007, 127).

Hoffman (2008) notes that postmodernism

> brought with it a questioning of the previous approaches to knowing. Instead of relying on one approach to knowing, [postmodernists] advocate for an epistemological pluralism which utilizes multiple ways of knowing. This can include the premodern ways (revelation) and modern ways (science and reason), along with many other ways of knowing such as intuition, relational, and spiritual.

Post-modernism is characterized by scepticism relating to reason and rationality, an emphasis on differences rather than similarities and the rejection of the idea of social laws governing behaviour. It acknowledges irregularities, contradictions and instabilities, and places an emphasis on acknowledging power balances and imbalances (not least between researchers and research participants) and the role of ideology in establishing and maintaining relationships. 'Truth' is viewed as plural, context-bound and historically generated through discourses. A principal focus is on studying how truths are generated and maintained, particularly using discourse analysis. Harder, more extreme, forms of postmodernism are deconstructive in that they seek to expose oppressive power structures hidden in and maintained by what are put forward as generally accepted truth, knowledge and 'meta-narratives'. Their goal is to expose, question and deconstruct prevailing authority sources and structures.

Essentially, the original (Glaserian) version of Grounded Theory as espoused by Glaser (who, with Strauss, developed the approach) was based on the positivist assumption that there is an objective truth 'out there' that can be uncovered through the gathering and analysis of data. A post-positivist perspective still maintains that there is a truth to be discovered, but acknowledges the difficulties and complexities introduced by the fallibilities of measurement and the inherent bias of humans including the researcher. Strauss later diverged from Glaser, developing a new (Straussian) version of Grounded Theory based on his constructivist perspective, entailing relativist and symbolic interactionist assumptions that there is no one true picture 'out there' waiting to be uncovered. Rather, there are multiple 'realities', since the external world is essentially a symbolic representation which each of us constructs. The researcher is a 'facilitator of multi-voice reconstruction' (Lincoln and Guba, 2005, 196) and collects and analyses data in interaction with participants. Although it took account of the notion that each of us essentially constructs our own reality, this approach stopped short of a more postmodern perspective. The reader interested in exploring Grounded Theory in more depth is referred to Pickard (2013) and Charmaz (2014).

Situational Analysis is a version of Grounded Theory developed by Clarke to be compatible with a post-modern perspective. It can be an appropriate and useful approach even if a more extreme postmodern perspective is not adopted. It offers an approach that enables an emphasis to be placed on:

- the holistic 'whole situation' in which people think and act
- the social worlds and arenas in which they operate and which may affect their thoughts and actions
- contradictions and instabilities and confusions in people's experiences
- the multiple perspectives that different actors may have on given issues and situations
- the situation (rather than the individual person) as the unit of analysis.

It also offers a useful set of mapping techniques, appropriate to teasing out what are key issues and factors in a situation, how people relate to their social worlds and arenas, and the positions they take (and do not take) in relation to these factors.

Sen and Spring (2013) took advantage of the features of Situational Analysis in a study of the relationship between information behaviour and young people's coping with long-term illness. They argue that the focus of Situational Analysis on identifying complexities and instabilities in social life is particularly suited to studying health-related issues, since these can often entail instabilities caused by illness. The suitability of the approach for integrating the notions of arenas and social worlds was also deemed useful for the study. They note that:

> Situational Analysis is an expansion of the Arena/Social Worlds framework which explores social worlds as different arenas where multiple worldviews exist with processes of negotiated interaction (Strauss et al., 1981; Clarke, 2005). . . . Social worlds are groups with shared commitments to activities (Clarke, 1991). They come together in arenas where they focus on a given issue, and are prepared to act in some way (Strauss et al., 1981).
>
> Sen and Spring, 2013, 643–4

They aimed to achieve a holistic picture of young people's experiences within the context of the social worlds they inhabited, focusing on:

> . . . information and knowledge exchanges, the young persons' social context, communication issues, relationships, and tensions experienced when learning to cope with their conditions.
>
> Sen and Spring, 2013, 642–3

As the interview data was analysed, emerging concepts and themes were mapped visually using three interrelated cartographic techniques offered by the Situational Analysis approach: situational maps, social worlds/arenas maps and positional maps.

In situational maps, an initial conception of the overall situation is mapped, including what seem to be the main actors, elements and relationships between them. This mapping is iterative, and the researchers move from 'messy' versions to an 'ordered' version of the maps. Social worlds/arenas maps enable the depiction of the social worlds inhabited by the actors and the arenas in which they negotiate and interpret their situations. Figure 9.1 shows the social worlds/arenas map from the study.

Positional maps enable the plotting of key positions adopted (and not adopted) by the young people, with due regard to complexities, controversies and differences. On the basis of the data, Sen and Spring developed an 'information coping trajectory' for which they created the positional map shown in Figure 9.2, entailing movement across five key positions. Essentially, as young people became aware of their condition-related information needs, and successfully came into contact with and processed appropriate information, their levels of confidence and ability to cope increased to a state of what Sen and Spring term 'information health'. A further stage entails the sharing of information with others to enable them in turn to achieve information health. The positions are as follows:

1 **Information deficiency**. A person at pre-diagnosis or diagnosis stage may simply lack the information needed to enable them to understand the situation they are in. This may, when accompanied by a lack of maturity lead to them being unable to cope.
2 **Feeling ill-informed**. After diagnosis, a person may be in receipt of basic information, but for various reasons this may be insufficient to address their real needs. The person may not possess the knowledge or skills to be able to interpret and use the information effectively, or the information itself may not be sufficient to address their needs. This may

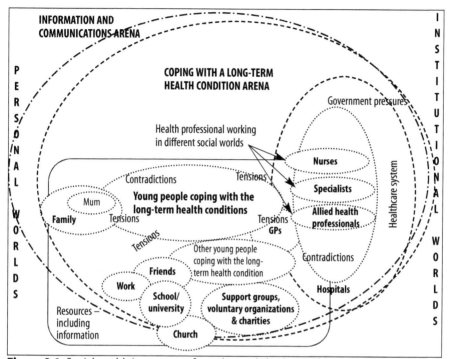

Figure 9.1   Social worlds/arenas map from the study by Sen and Spring (2013, 648)

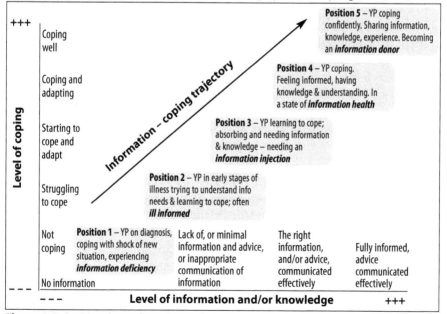

Figure 9.2   Positional map from the study by Sen and Spring (2013, 649)

lead to confusion or misunderstanding, which in turn may lead them to experience fear, anger, denial or rebellion.

3 **Having an information injection**. The young person may receive an 'injection' of information which is useful in helping them understand their situation, and to develop ways of coping with it. They may come into contact with such information independently, or if they do not have the capability to do so, with the help of others.

4 **Having information health**. Sen and Spring (2013, 652) define a person who has 'information health' as one who has the information they need and 'feels informed, has gained knowledge and understanding, and feels confident in using that information to make decisions'. In relation to their own situation, this enables them to start to negotiate their own healthcare, and develop greater levels of understanding of their situation.

5 **Being an information donor**. This may occur when a person possesses information and knowledge that is potentially useful to others in enabling them to achieve information health, and feels motivated to share it.

The research used the affordances of Situational Analysis, which were particularly helpful in enabling the researchers to identify a number of 'silent voices', variations in people's experience, different constructions of phenomena by different actors, change in situations and people's responses to them over time, conflicting experiences and discourses, movement from instability and mixed emotions to more stable coping, communication disconnects between different actors coming together from different social and professional worlds to engage in health discourses in various arenas, and power struggles and conflicts being played out in the institutional healthcare arena where healthcare decisions were negotiated.

Mixed-methods research: a mixed-methods study

Recall from Chapter 8 that mixed-methods research entails the blending of quantitative and qualitative and/or deductive and inductive approaches. Researchers adopting this approach reject the argument that these approaches are incompatible and explicitly seek to take advantage of the complementary affordances of each. An example of a mixed-methods study is that of Pluye, Grad, Repchinsky et al. (2013).

These researchers investigated the information seeking behaviour of three types of clinician in Canada – 10 nurse practitioners, 10 pharmacists, and 10 medical residents – searching for information using the e-Therapeutics+ electronic resource. The research questions they sought to address related to four levels of outcome:

1 situational relevance
2 cognitive impact
3 information use, and
4 patient health outcome.

Their research questions were:

> What is the impact of the first three levels of outcomes of information-seeking (situational relevance, cognitive impact, and information use) on the fourth level (patient health outcomes)?'

and

> For how many patients does a clinician need to retrieve clinical information from electronic resources to report health benefits for one . . .?
>
> Pluye et al., 2013, 109

They termed the latter concept the NNBI – the 'number needed to benefit from information', considering it important in that it could be helpful:

- in future research designed to measure the relative usefulness of electronic information resources in different contexts
- to librarians, in helping them select the most effective information resources in terms of which have the highest benefit/cost ratio
- to patients, in having the confidence to ask librarians to seek more information in relation to issues that have high stakes for them (such as a treatment with serious potential side effects)
- to motivate clinicians to seek information, insofar as a low NNBI for a particular source of information would indicate the likelihood of finding useful information
- to policy makers, in providing justification for providing incentives for searching on the grounds that existing information is likely to be found and to have an impact on healthcare.

The researchers adopted a mixed-methods approach, blending (a) a quantitative longitudinal study with a qualitative multiple case study, and

(b) deductive analysis in which data was classified into predefined categories of information use and health outcomes, with inductive data analysis in which the data was analysed to discover new emergent themes.

Quantitative data was gathered relating to the clinicians' searches and their ratings for each search in terms of categories of information use and health outcome. Qualitative data consisted of interview transcripts and think-aloud protocols, field notes, screen captures and videos, search logs and the retrieved hits. Data were also gathered on the participants' perceptions of the context and objectives of each search, the relevance and cognitive impact of information retrieved, the use to which the information was put in relation to a specific patient, and patient health outcomes.

This quantitative and qualitative data was blended into 'clinical vignettes' (narratives describing the searches across multiple dimensions). These were intended to allow the description and testing of the four levels of outcome. In all 130 vignettes were produced, in which cases related to the following patient health outcomes: an increase in patient knowledge; avoiding an unnecessary or inappropriate intervention; preventing disease or deterioration in health; an improvement in health; and an increase in patient satisfaction.

The numerical NNBI score was calculated by dividing the total searches for a specific patient by the total cases with a minimum of one beneficial patient health outcome as described in the vignettes. A statistical multiple logistic regression analysis was also carried out in order to measure the impact of situational relevance, cognitive impact and information use on patient outcomes. The researchers conclude that their investigation:

- provided empirical support for their proposed four-outcome model of information seeking
- generated a potentially useful new concept – the number needed to benefit from information (NNBI)
- found links between perceived patient health and two of the information-seeking outcomes (situational relevance and information use)
- found infrequent but novel links between information seeking and transitory negative patient health outcomes, and between beneficial patient health outcomes and browsing as opposed to direct searching.

The qualitative vignettes provided rich narratives describing how information impacted the four different outcomes proposed by the model. However, the logical regression analysis produced only sparse results.

Finding information relevant to sharing with a patient or home/family caregiver – an example of a level 1 outcome (situational relevance) – was linked to perceived health benefits. However, the statistical strength of this link fell just below the level of statistical significance. It was nevertheless felt to be a trend worth reporting. Using retrieved information to persuade the patient or other health professionals to make changes – an example of a level 3 outcome (information use) – was linked with perceived health benefits at a statistically significant level.

The researchers report other findings, which, although only encountered in a small number of cases, they considered worth reporting due to their novelty, in the sense of not having been reported at the time in existing literature. There was one case of transitory negative impact of information on patient health (not previously reported except in laboratory conditions):

> . . . a nurse mentioned to P23 that the current dose of domperidone was higher than the maximum recommended dose. As a result of their search for information, P23 decreased the dose, which was followed by a return of symptoms, and led P23 to reincrease the drug dose.
>
> Pluye et al., 2013, 118

After the dose was re-increased the patient recovered. There were also three cases in which patient health was beneficially affected due to browsing rather than direct searching, leading the researchers to claim that browsing-related outcomes, although rare, are not negligible. They note that browsing is not usually linked with such an outcome.

In this case, the use of a mixed methodology allowed the potential of triangulated evidence to support findings. The qualitative vignettes produced rich descriptions of how information seeking impacted perceived health outcomes, and arguably validated and illustrated the researchers' hypothesized model of information-seeking outcomes. They also allowed for the inductive identification of new unanticipated relationships, which appeared in only a small number of cases but which the researchers nevertheless considered to be interesting and worthy of reporting.

Had the statistical regression analysis produced significant results, the combination of qualitative and quantitative evidence to support common themes would have been very powerful. In fact, the quantitative analysis produced only very limited results. However, a quantitative measure of the usefulness of an information source (the NNBI) potentially useful to clinicians, librarians and patients was generated.

Comparing approaches

The first two studies described above were very different, and arguably illustrate the essence of two very common but drastically varying approaches. The first was deductive and quantitative. It was deductive in that the researchers started by developing specific hypotheses based on previous research, and set out to discover whether these hypotheses were supported by data. The research was quantitative in that:

- the data was numerical: questions either asked directly for a numerical response (e.g. the percentage of total salary represented by cash incentives), or as choices on a Likert scale (e.g. 'not at all, a few times a year, several times a month, several times a week, and several times a day'), which were converted to numbers for the analysis
- and the analysis comprised testing to see whether there were statistically significant relationships between the numbers.

The second piece of research was inductive and qualitative. It was inductive in that key factors and relationships between them emerged from the analysis of the data, as opposed to being predefined as hypotheses to be tested. To this extent the research was open-ended, since unexpected findings could result. The research was qualitative in that the data (textual accounts given by young people in interviews) was not coded and reduced to numbers for statistical analysis. Rather, the data was analysed to identify what were the key concepts, relationships and themes concerning the young people.

THINK!

The first two studies described above adopted very different approaches. Take a few minutes to list what you consider to be the main *strengths* of:

(i) a deductive hypothesis-testing approach (as used in the first study), as opposed to a more open-ended inductive approach (as used in the second).
(ii) quantitative data collection and analysis (as used in the first study), as opposed to qualitative data collection and analysis (as used in the second).

Now reverse the process and list what you consider to be the main weaknesses of each relative to the other.

The first study is a good example of how statistics can provide robust evidence of relationships based on well established mathematical principles. In this case a regression analysis established that the predictive relationship between the dependent and independent variables was highly unlikely to have occurred by chance. Indeed, it could tell us exactly how unlikely this was in terms of a precise level of probability. This is indicated by the expression 'p =' or 'p<' followed by a number.

In relation to the first hypothesis, the relationship between (a) the effects of cash incentives on information seeking and (b) the extent to which a firm was technology-intensive or low technology (the subject of the first hypothesis) was significant at the level of p<.01. What this means is that the probability of this relationship being due to pure chance is 1 in 100. A level of p<.05 is widely accepted in social science research as a minimum acceptable probability level. It represents a 1 in 20 chance of the result having occurred by chance.

The relationship proposed in the second hypothesis proposed that the interactive effect of base-pay and cash incentives on information seeking would be observed more strongly in high-technology firms was found to be significant at p<.001. This indicates a 1 in 1000 chance that the result occurred by chance. Hypothesis 3 predicted that the greater the extent to which cash incentives are linked to aggregate performance criteria, the less likely TMT members would seek information from affiliate sources. This relationship was significant at p<.01.

However, although the numbers are extremely precise – for example, that the chances of the results having occurred by chance only being 1 in 100 – it is important to be aware of the limitations of such approaches. In the study by Anand and Gomez-Mejia (2014) described above, the statistics cannot tell us that changes in the way in which top executives are rewarded *result in* changes in their information behaviour. Other variables not known about by the researchers and omitted from the study could be the real cause of the observed links between the dependent and independent variables. The attribution of cause and effect must be inferred from circumstantial evidence. Logic tells us that it is not possible for it to be differences in executives' information behaviour that is influencing differences in their reward structures. But this still cannot confirm that other factors are not at play. A probability level of .01 indicates that there is a 1 in 100 chance of the results having occurred by chance. There is no guarantee that this case is not that 100th case. Also, there is nothing magic about the number 100. The results could be pure chance in 10 cases out of 1000. A probability of p<.05 is generally accepted in social science research to be worthy of reporting. This represents only a 1 in 20 chance of the results having occurred by chance.

Thus, research results like this cannot be 'canned' as established fact, enabling researchers to move on and build upon these facts quickly to accumulate knowledge. It is often the case that research boasting significance levels of p<.05 or p<.01 when replicated in other studies produces conflicting results and even counter-evidence. Even in 'harder' sciences such as biology and medicine, writers have noted a 'decline effect', in which what are at one point in time are considered well established 'facts' gradually become obsolete or contradicted. Schooler (2011) for example notes that:

> Many scientifically discovered effects published in the literature seem to diminish with time. . . . It has since been reported in a string of fields . . . and in meta-analyses of findings in biology and medicine.
>
> Schooler, 2011

Ioannidis reinforces this point:

> There is increasing concern that most current published research findings are false. [...] Moreover, for many current scientific fields, claimed research findings may often be simply accurate measures of the prevailing bias.
>
> Ioannidis, 2005

The effect has been likened to a 'half-life' after which findings become outdated or proved to be incorrect. There have been empirical studies of this phenomenon. An example is a study by Poynard, Munteanu, Ratziu et al. (2002). They explored the 'half-life' of medical facts, taking studies on cirrhosis and hepatitis published from 1945 to 1999 as their focus. They hypothesized that facts derived from medical studies which exhibited what is generally accepted as good methodology would have a longer half-life than those exhibiting poorer methodology. They found that in 2000, when their research was conducted, only 60% of the conclusions of the studies were still considered by a panel of experts to be correct; 21% were considered to be false, and 19% obsolete. There was no significant difference in the half-life of conclusions resulting from studies that had used as good methodology and those deriving from lower quality studies.

It is important to bear in mind that although results based on statistics look extremely precise, there is still a chance that they have been obtained by chance. Often the interest of a piece of research lies in findings that seem to identify factors that cause or affect phenomenon. However, as previously noted, statistics cannot *per se* tell us about cause and effect. They *can* tell us that as one measure increases or decreases, so does another. But it is the researcher and/or the reader who must *infer* that this relationship suggests that something is caused or influenced by particular factors. Such an inference may seem logical – especially if what appears to be the causal or influencing factor precedes the phenomenon that is deemed to be caused or influenced by it. But there is always the possibility that both have been affected by some other unidentified confounding variable(s).

Another limitation in typical quantitative studies relates to what may at first sight be seen as one of their advantages, namely the precise definition, isolation and measurement of variables. According to classic scientific method, a complex phenomenon is decomposed into its constituent elements each of which is isolated and measured. This enables the relationships between variables to be studied cleanly, the statistical contribution of each variable being clearly visible in the analysis. However, there is some truth in the adage that 'real life' is much messier than this. It can often be the case that when reduced to isolated and precisely measurable variables, a complex human phenomenon loses some of its reality. This is the case when the essence of the phenomenon is holistic interaction and complexity. To take a simple example: observing and measuring aspects of the behaviour of an insect in the laboratory can tell us many interesting things about that insect, but would not necessarily be the most appropriate way of developing a more holistic ecological understanding of the complex ways in which it interacts with other creatures and its environment.

Indeed, being better able to cope with the holistic complexity and messiness of real life is an advantage often associated with qualitative interpretive research approaches such as that deployed in the study of young people's information behaviour conducted by Sen and Spring described above. Rather than using numerical measures of isolated variables (which inevitably simplifies the phenomenon) a qualitative interpretive approach, relatively speaking, preserves complexity and messiness where these characterize the phenomenon being studied. Such approaches are not limited to looking for statistical patterns in numbers – numbers to which observations of human thoughts and/or behaviours are reduced. Rather, they seek to identify and preserve deeper meanings expressed in words and behaviour which are not necessarily reducible to such numbers and statistical patterns. Complex holistic interactions can be expressed and become data sources.

The very subjectivity which must be avoided in the interests of objective statistical analysis can offer richness in the analysis of complex qualitative data. Researchers can bring to bear human qualities of empathy and deep subjective perceptions to understand at a deep level the 'what', 'how' and 'why' of people's experiences, thoughts and behaviours. Qualitative research is often inductive, and the emergence of concepts and themes from the data (of course, via the interpretation of the researcher) can result in avoidance of the limitations associated with the researcher's preconceptions and ability to foresee the variables that are important in understanding the phenomenon being studied.

Such research is also often naturalistic, in that an attempt is made to study people in their natural environment – as opposed to controlled experimental conditions. Although data may often be collected in the form of interviews in which people are asked to reflect after the event rather than being directly observed in what they say and do in their natural environment, some qualitative (e.g. ethnographic) approaches do entail observing people and sharing their experiences more directly in their natural environment.

Qualitative interpretive research will often make use of 'theoretical sampling', in which participants are selected on the basis of how richly they might be able to illuminate the emerging understanding of phenomenon under investigation. They may be selected, for example, because they have particularly deep relevant experience, or because they provide very different perspectives. Because researchers are seeking deep understanding rather than statistical generalization, they are not limited by the requirement to use a randomly selected sample representative of the population to which they wish to generalize. Being freed from this requirement can enable qualitative researchers to maximize the richness of the data they gather.

However, what some see as the strengths of this type of research may be considered its Achilles' heel by others. The rich but relatively small samples typical of many qualitative studies, coupled with the freedom to eschew random selection as a way of choosing them, mean that statistical generalization is not possible. Qualitative researchers' counter-claim is that they are not seeking statistical generalization, but rather deep understanding which will be 'transferable' (as opposed to 'generalizable') to other similar contexts. Transferability is based on resonances between the research context and some other context(s) in which the findings may provide useful insights. The extent to which resonance may be established by someone wanting to apply findings depends on the richness and detail with which the researcher describes the context and circumstances of the research – often referred to as 'thick description'.

The same applies to subjectivity. The very subjectivity that enhances the sensitivity with which we can interpret, empathize with and understand our research participants' interview statements and observed behaviours may be considered a weakness from more post-positivist quantitative perspectives. Such perspectives emphasize the need to maintain objectivity in order to maximize the accuracy and reliability of our measurements of variables and their analysis. With subjectivity comes the possibility of variability in perceptions and interpretation. In comparison, statistical studies offer objectivity in defining and measuring and analysing data. This objectivity allows us to estimate precise levels of statistical significance and confidence with which they can be generalized to the wider population. Credibility in qualitative interpretive studies must be established in a less objective way, essentially by convincing the reader that what was done was systematic and consistent, and that the researchers have taken due account of their own potential biases and the subjectivities involved in the research.

THINK!

Some researchers are of the opinion that a positivist or post-positivist paradigm (often characterized by a deductive quantitative approach) and an interpretivist paradigm (often characterized by an inductive qualitative approach) are fundamentally incompatible, since they represent fundamentally different views of the nature of 'reality' and how we can find out about it. Obviously, mixed-methods researchers disagree with this view, arguing that both approaches can be used within a single study – the strengths of each approach to an extent mitigating the limitations of the other to shed light on a common phenomenon from different angles.

Take a few minutes to consider – what is your position in relation to this issue? Is there a fundamental clash between the basic assumptions of the two approaches? And if so, would it make a nonsense out of trying to combine them both within a single study?

Clearly, different research approaches are characterized by different sets of advantages and limitations. To an extent they can be viewed as fundamentally incompatible, and to an extent as complementary – a view espoused by researchers engaging in mixed-methods approaches. Deeper aspects of methodology, such as one's position relating to ontology (the nature of reality) and epistemology (how we can know about reality), would seem to be less amenable to allowing a mixed approach utilizing a blend of approaches than more procedural aspects such as particular methods of data collection and analysis. For example, if one takes the position that 'reality' is socially constructed, subjective and relative, it is difficult to consider as merely complementary the position that there is one objective reality 'out there' waiting to be accurately measured.

However, my own position in relation to the complementary or otherwise nature of different approaches is that when it comes to studying human behaviour, real life is so complex that multiple views can all be useful, and that different studies conducted from post-positivist, constructivist and post-modern perspectives all have the potential to illuminate different aspects of the same phenomenon. Increasingly, researchers are going further in that they mix different approaches within the same study, adopting a pragmatic paradigm which rejects such a notion of incompatibility.

As humans, we have physical and mental aspects. Some appear relatively objective in the sense that we all seem to share similar anatomy and processes. But we also display subjectivity and variance, which may be inter-mixed with those considered to be more objectively established. Outcomes of the same medical procedures, for example, may vary greatly depending on the patient's mental outlook.

Summary

This chapter has provided three examples of studies that are illustrative of very different approaches to research. For many years, in information science as well as other disciplines, using a deductive quantitative approach was the standard scientific method, characterizing high-quality research. However, researchers in the social sciences became increasingly aware of the limitations and inappropriateness of such approaches in failing to address key characteristics of research involving people and society, and began using more open-ended exploratory inductive qualitative approaches.

In the field of information behaviour, an influential proponent of adopting qualitative research for studies of information-seeking behaviour was Wilson. He commented that:

> The vast majority of studies of 'information needs' has been conducted under a relatively crude conception of the 'scientific method', using self-completed questionnaires as the main data-collection instrument. Social researchers of many kinds have become disenchanted with this model of research and are turning increasingly to a consideration of 'qualitative research' either as a complete alternative to quantitative research or, at least, as a preliminary.
>
> Wilson, 1981, 11

Wilson noted that qualitative research was about developing new concepts rather than applying pre-existing ones, and 'given the state of theory in information science (that is, its undeveloped state) it can well be argued that "developing concepts" is what is needed' (Wilson, 1981, 11). Since then qualitative approaches have become widespread in information behaviour research (Wilson, 2010).

The third example given in this chapter was of a mixed-methods study. As noted in Chapter 8, there has been increasing recent interest in the use of mixed-methods research entailing a blend of qualitative and quantitative approaches. Whilst some regard these as un-combinable, to the extent that they are based on fundamentally incompatible ontological and epistemological assumptions, researchers are increasingly adopting a mixed-methods approach as a way to triangulate different types of evidence to illuminate and understand the same and related phenomena.

The reader is referred to Chapter 9 in Case (2012) for further examples of studies illustrating different research approaches.

References

Anand, V. and Gomez-Mejia, L. R. (2014) The Impact of Cash Incentives on TMT Information Seeking Behavior in Entrepreneurial Firms, *Journal of High Technology Management Research*, **25** (1), 68–82.

Case, D. (2012) *Looking for Information: a survey of research on information seeking, needs and behaviour*, 3rd edn, Bingley, Emerald.

Charmaz, K. (2014) *Constructing Grounded Theory*, London, Sage.

Clarke, A. (1991) Social Worlds/Arenas Theory as Organisational Theory. In Maines, D. (ed.), *Social Organization and Social Process: essays in honor of Anselm Strauss*, New York, NY, Aldine de Gruyter, 119–58.

Clarke, A. (2005) *Situational Analysis: Grounded Theory after the postmodern turn*, Thousand Oaks, CA, Sage.

Corbin, J. and Strauss, A. (2008) *Basics of Qualitative Research: techniques and procedures for developing Grounded Theory*, 3rd edn, London, Sage.

Hoffman, L. (2008) *Premodernism, Modernism, and Postmodernism: an overview*, www.postmodernpsychology.com/Philosophical_Systems/Overview.htm.

Ioannidis, J. P. A. (2005) Why Most Published Research Findings are False, *PLOS Medicine*, **2** (8), e124, doi: 10.1371/journal.pmed.0020124.

Lazar, J., Feng, J. H. and Hochheiser, H. (2010) *Research Methods in Human–Computer Interaction*, Wiley.

Lincoln, Y. and Guba, E. (2005) Paradigmatic Controversies, Contradictions, and Emerging Confluences. In Denzin, N. and Lincoln, Y. (eds), *Handbook of Qualitative Research*, Thousand Oaks, CA, Sage, 191–215.

Mills, J., Chapman, Y., Bonner, A. and Francis, K. (2007) Grounded Theory: a methodological spiral from positivism to postmodernism, *Journal of Advanced Nursing*, **58** (1), 72–9.

Myers, M. (1997) Interpretive Research in Information Systems. In Mingers, J. and Stowell, F. (eds), *Information Systems: an emerging discipline?*, London, McGraw-Hill, 239–66.

Olson, R. E. (2007) *Reformed and Always Reforming: the postconservative approach to evangelical theology*, Grand Rapids, MI, Baker Academic.

Pickard, A. J. (2013) *Research Methods in Information*, 2nd edn, London, Facet Publishing.

Pluye, P., Grad, R., Repchinsky, C., Jovaisas, B., Johnson-Lafleur, J., Carrier, M-E., Granikov, V., Farrell, B., Rodriguez, C., Bartlett, G., Loiselle, C. and Légaré, F. (2013) Four Levels of Outcomes of Information-Seeking: a mixed methods study in primary healthcare, *Journal of the American Society for Information Science and Technology*, **64** (1), 108–25.

Poynard, T., Munteanu, M., Ratziu, V., Benhamou, Y., Martino, V., Taieb, J. and Opolon, P. (2002) Truth Survival in Clinical Research: an evidence-based requiem?, *Annals of Internal Medicine*, **136** (12), 888–95.

Schooler, J. (2011) Unpublished Results Hide the Decline Effect, *Nature*, 24 February, 470(7335):437, doi:10.1038/470437a.

Sen, B. A. and Spring, H. (2013) Mapping the Information-coping Trajectory of Young People with Long Term Illness, *Journal of Documentation*, **69** (5), 638–66.

Strauss, A., Schatzman, L., Bucher, R., Ehrlich, D. and Sabshin, M. (1981) *Psychiatric Ideologies and Institutions*, New Brunswick, NJ, Transaction Books.

Wilson, T. D. (1981) On User Studies and Information Needs, *Journal of Documentation*, **37** (1), 3–15.

Wilson, T. D. (2010) Fifty Years of Information Behavior Research, *Bulletin of the American Society for Information Science and Technology*, **36** (3), 27–34.

10

Using knowledge of information behaviour to design information systems

Introduction

Knowledge of people's information behaviour is potentially useful for:

- helping *people* to become smarter – helping them to develop knowledge and skill in relation to finding, evaluating and using information in pursuit of fulfilling their information-related needs
- helping us design and develop smarter *tools* – tools which can incorporate and make use of knowledge of information behaviour in order to behave more intelligently and provide more effective support for the people who use them, in pursuit of fulfilling their information-related needs.

Helping people develop and improve their own information behaviour skills is the prime concern of information literacy activity. Part of this entails developing awareness of the limitations of information systems and working to compensate for these via human ability.

THINK!

Clearly, we can use knowledge derived from research into information behaviour to help people become smarter – to teach them to avoid strategies and habits that research suggests are ineffective, and to adopt those that research suggest are more productive.

But can you think of ways in which we might be able to incorporate such knowledge into search tools and other information systems themselves – in order to develop smarter systems?

The design of effective information systems entails enabling them to compensate as far as possible for the frailties of human abilities. At the simplest level, a computer-based search system is able to store, sort and retrieve volumes of information simply impossible for a human to even begin to handle. But human input is obviously necessary in terms of telling the system what to search for, and evaluating the results.

However, in recent years information system designers have been able to leverage much more subtle knowledge of people's information behaviour in order to provide more sensitive forms of support. Such information behaviour knowledge includes awareness of the importance of allowing users to choose between different ways of exploring an information space – for example broad-based exploratory browsing or specific topic search, and of the importance of recognizing different levels of uncertainty relating to information needs at different stages of exploration.

A bridge between the development of smarter retrieval mechanisms and efforts to help users consciously become smarter is the use of 'search interventions' designed to maximize the quality of their input to the system.

A search intervention is the provision of some prompt or information processing mechanism, relevant to executing a search, that is external to the searcher and separate from the retrieval mechanisms of the search tool. It may be implicit, supplanting certain information processes – i.e. performing them on behalf of the searcher – or explicit, stimulating conscious information processing by the searcher.

Interventions may be implicit and not necessarily require conscious reflection. They may entail inducing information processing to take place without the searcher necessarily being conscious of the process. An example of this type of intervention is work suggesting that simply providing more space for users to enter search queries (without explicitly drawing their attention to the change) encourages longer queries (e.g. Franzén and Karlgren, 2000; Belkin, Cool, Jeng et al., 2002), which is likely to result in more effective queries. Whilst it may be that searchers do consciously notice a longer search box, it would also seem reasonable to think that many users would not necessarily have to do so for it to have an effect.

However, interventions may also be relatively explicit, in that users' attention is specifically directed to them in order to stimulate a conscious response. An example of an intervention that would seem to rely on conscious searcher response is reported by Belkin, Cool, Kelly et al. (2003). They conducted an experiment in which the effects of different query elicitation methods were explored. Users of an interactive information retrieval system were presented with a five-line scrollable search query box labelled: 'Information problem description (the more you say, the better the results are likely to be)'. They were told that queries could be entered as multiple full sentences or questions. A control group were given an identical search query box. However, this was labelled: 'Query terms', and the users were told that they should enter their queries as a list of keywords or phrases. Longer initial queries resulted in increased satisfaction with searches, and fewer query iterations being required to achieve equivalent retrieval performance. Belkin et al. concluded that:

> . . . our quite simple interface-based query elicitation technique results in significantly longer, and more useful searcher queries in a Web searching task than typical query elicitation, for a best-match information retrieval system.
>
> Belkin et al., 2003, 209

Some experimental systems even attempt to provide 'scaffolding' support to users, designed to enable them to maximize the impact of the knowledge and skills that they already possess. Such systems may, for example, prompt the user to think deeply about the nature of their information needs, and to maximize the suitability and usefulness of the information they give as input to the system. Such systems may be referred to as 'metacognitive', to the extent that they attempt to provide support for users in thinking about their own cognitive processes, thereby opening the possibility of these processes becoming more accessible to them and subject to improvement via this consciousness.

Metacognition is closely associated with self-awareness (Fisher, 1998; Silvén, 1992). It is essentially 'thinking about thinking', entailing an awareness of one's own mental processes. This includes not only knowing what one is thinking, but also evaluating one's thought processes and possibly choosing to change them. Researchers have attempted to build systems which in various ways attempt to provide support for the use of metacognitive skills – particularly in learning contexts – by prompting users to engage in metacognitive activity. Researchers such as Hill (1995) and Land and Hannafin (1996) have suggested that deficiencies in people's metacognitive skills may be mitigated using 'scaffolds' (support structures for people engaged in activities that are just at or beyond their independent abilities).

Researchers have only relatively recently attempted to build metacognitive scaffolding into information systems. Quintana, Zhang and Krajcik (2005), for example, have developed scaffolding to support online information seeking, relating to task understanding and planning, monitoring and regulation, and reflection. Their system provides training in online enquiry task structures and tools for reflection in the form of an ongoing summary of activities.

Because of the increasing complexity of the internet, there has been a growing interest in metacognition in the context of web search and online enquiry, and various studies have attempted to investigate the impact of interventions designed to promote metacognitive behaviours amongst online searchers (e.g. Stadtler and Bromme, 2007); Wiley, Goldman, Graesser et al., 2009). An example of interventions designed to help people reflect on their own intellectual activity is the work of Cole, described below.

Cole's 'enabling' information retrieval system interface

Interesting work is reported by Cole, Cantero and Ungar (2000), who developed an information-seeking support system for university students to help them with their academic work. This system used an 'uncertainty expansion device', which encouraged students, when engaged in information seeking, to consider the task from a variety of possible angles. A complementary 'uncertainty reduction device' helped them to move towards the later stages of preparing their academic task. Cole et al. found that the students making use of the system received better marks for their assignments on average.

Cole's work recognizes the inherently imprecise nature of 'information needs', and builds on theoretical perspectives, including those of Kuhlthau, Taylor, Belkin and Oddy (reference to these elsewhere in book). Recall, from the section on information needs in Chapter 3, Taylor's (1968) proposition that awareness of one's information needs may vary from unconscious to explicitly known and clearly expressible. Cole argues that in the early stages of an academic assignment the overall problem or topic may be clear, but the associated information needs may be much less so, and not explicitly known or expressible by the learner.

Recall also from the same section the paradox expressed by Belkin, Oddy and Brooks (1982a; 1982b) whereby information systems generally require information seekers to express what they do not actually know. This applies particularly in the early exploratory stages of an academic assignment, corresponding to Kuhlthau's 'focus formulation' stage (referred to in the section 'Basic information-seeking processes and activities' in Chapter 4), when the student is likely to be seeking information for their assignment. Cole, Cantero and Ungar (2000) map the nature of the sub-tasks and associated information needs onto each of Kuhlthau's six stages:

1 At the **Initiation** stage, the task is to 'recognize a need for information' and the need is for '*background* information'.

2   At the **Selection** stage, the student must 'identify and select the general topic' and requires '*relevant* information'.

3   At the **Exploration** stage, the task is to 'investigate information on the general topic in order to extend personal understanding', and the associated need is again for '*relevant* information'.

4   At the **Formulation** stage, the student needs to 'form a focus from the information', requiring '*relevant/focused* information'.

5   At the **Collection** stage, the student must 'gather information related to the focused topic', again needing '*relevant/focused*' information.

6   Finally, at the **Presentation** stage, the task is to 'complete search and prepare to present findings', the associated need again being for '*relevant/focused*' information.

As Cole and colleagues note:

> We can envisage Kuhlthau's six stage ISP as a series of visits to the academic library where on each visit the undergraduate reads something that shifts his or her information need, abstract space or cognitive state as he or she progresses from stage 1 to stage 6 of the essay writing process.
>
> Cole, Cantero and Ungar, 2000, 484

Cole argues that the information needs students have at these stages are very different. The expressed information need which forms a query to an information retrieval system may not correspond well with what may subsequently turn out to be the information need as more fully understood at a more advanced stage of learning. The learner's information need may be refined and awareness of the need may increase during, and as a result of, interaction with the devices offered by the system. Cole argues that a different intervention device would be appropriate for each of Kuhlthau's six stages. A key function of these devices is that they should stimulate the learner to expand and reduce their levels of uncertainty depending on their current stage. The examples that follow relate to an information system designed to support a common form of academic essay – the 'argument' type essay typical of the social sciences and humanities:

> . . . which requires the undergraduate to create relations between two or more situations, phenomena, time periods etc. in the term paper. The student can then argue a point of view.
>
> Cole, Cantero and Ungar, 2000

For example, uncertainty *expansion* is appropriate at the Exploration stage, when the learner's task is to find relevant information to extend his or her personal understanding of the broad topic. The intervention for this stage asks the student to expand his or her uncertainty by thinking of four alternative statements of what the focus or thesis of the essay could be – and for each, to assess how likely it is to end up being the one selected for the final version of the essay and why.

Uncertainty *reduction* rather than expansion is appropriate at the Formulation stage, when the student needs to decide on a clear focus for the essay. At this stage, the student needs to integrate data that they have gathered from various sources to form a coherent whole. In the case of a 'compare and contrast' type of essay this might entail, for example, assessing the relationships between different accounts of some historical event, and taking a particular position which would form the main thesis or argument of the essay. Rather than expanding the range of alternative possible positions, this state requires the student to converge on a selected point of view – thus reducing rather than expanding uncertainty. An intervention device to support this type of activity asks the student to consider how to bring together different elements. It asks the student to list the linkable elements and the bridging element that will link them.

The idea behind these devices is that by encouraging students to think in particular ways they will more effectively be able to formulate their information needs at different stages of the essay writing process. Cole (2001), in a study of 60 Concordia University students, reports statistically significant improvements in their grades when using these devices compared to a control group.

The overall aim of the research was to:

> . . . design an 'enabling' diagnostic–prescriptive tool to be added on to the front-end of an information retrieval (IR) system; this tool is specifically designed for undergraduates seeking information for a course term paper/research paper. The tool will eventually (i) diagnose the undergraduate's information need by assessing what stage he or she is at in the information search process, (ii) prescribe information that will satisfy that need and (iii) 'enable' the undergraduate to better perform the task that brought the student to the IR system looking for information.
>
> Cole, Cantero and Ungar, 2000, 499

Cole (2014) has further developed his ideas, based on his research into information behaviour, into a proposal for a search engine that would provide better support for exploratory search than is provided for currently by the main search engines, providing an example of such a system for students who need to do research for an assignment.

Interaction with the system entails five stages, as shown in the figure. In stage 1, the searcher is asked to make a list of four questions for which they would like the search engine to provide an answer. In stage 2, they are asked to rate each of the four questions in terms of the probability that it will form the main final information need. Stage 3 entails the searcher being asked to try themselves to answer the question identified in stage 2, based on their existing knowledge. They are then asked in stage 4 to state *why* they believe this to be a good answer, being prompted to give three reasons for their belief assumptions based on their existing knowledge. In stage 5 the searcher is told that these three belief assumptions form their *real* information need, and that they must seek information to provide evidence to prove or justify them, thus providing evidence that the answer given in stage 3 is true. Cole notes that:

> The information need of the searcher, when it is fully actualized after using this exploratory search engine, is based on the searcher's real information need, not a compromised form of the information need, which is presently the case with current search engines.
>
> Cole, 2014, 54

Cole is using his research into the information needs and information-seeking behaviour of students to propose the design of a search engine that is more attuned to the searcher's real, as opposed to compromised, information needs. He goes on to note that:

> Exploratory search is not now adequately served by current search engines. The conception of the searcher's query to the search engine, after she has utilized the exploratory search engine . . . is an entirely different conception of the searcher's information need than the model of information need the Google search engine is based on now.
>
> Cole, 2014, 54

The PATHS project

PATHS is an interactive interface to large digital libraries, allowing users to explore their contents in innovative and personalized ways. PATHS is an acronym for Personalised Access to Cultural Heritage Spaces. It was developed as part of a European Commission-funded project completed in

2014, co-ordinated by Mark Stevenson and Paul Clough of the University of Sheffield.

PATHS has been applied to a range of cultural heritage collections, most notably Europeana, which is a portal offering unified access to collections of cultural heritage artefacts provided by a wide range of European institutions. These currently consist of more than 20 million items, including paintings, films, books, archival records and museum objects, provided by some 1500 institutions, including, for example, the British Library and the Louvre.

A key innovative feature of the interface is the fact that its design is based on knowledge of people's information behaviour. Knowledge of the different ways people go about searching for and using information drives the options presented to each user to provide a personalized searching and navigation experience.

The design is predicated on a number of observations derived from an analysis of the information behaviour literature (e.g. Goodale, Clough, Fernando et al., 2014):

- Different people may have different predominant navigational styles, linked to more fundamental 'cognitive styles'.
- These different styles may require different navigational patterns when exploring a large digital collection of information/resources.
- Following a navigational path that suits one's predominant style can enhance the effectiveness of the resultant learning, compared with following a path that does not match one's style.
- Although at the level of individual steps and resources selected in a given navigational session individual paths may be highly idiosyncratic and unique, at a more general structural level there are some clear features characterizing broad classes of approach.
- These features map well onto possible interface design features, resulting in the possibility of personalizing the interface to meet the unique requirements of each individual.

Recall that such stylistic differences in the way different people go about searching for and using information were introduced in the section on 'internal' factors in Chapter 6. PATHS focused particularly on the global/analytic dimension of difference. As noted in this section, relatively analytic individuals tend to experience the components of a complex structured field analytically, as separate from their background. They are good at imposing structure on a relatively unstructured field.

Relatively wholist individuals, however, tend to be less good at such structuring and analytic activity. They tend to perceive a complex stimulus globally as a gestalt. This means that they can often be particularly good at seeing the 'big picture' – gaining a broad conceptual overview and seeing relationships between concepts. However, they are more dependent than their more independent analytic counterparts on receiving help from others (e.g. teachers and guides) in relation to structuring and analytic activity. They also tend to be more socially oriented. Individuals also vary in the extent to which they thrive in navigational conditions characterized by guidance (external mediation) versus autonomy. This difference appears to be linked to fundamental cognitive style, and is linked to the wholist/analytic dimension.

The PATHS project aimed to build an experimental system and investigate the extent to which people with different cognitive styles explored and experienced an information system in different ways corresponding to what might be expected from a review of the cognitive style literature. The motivation to develop such a system derives from previous research, which found that the extent to which an information system does or does not support an individual's preferred navigational style can affect the effectiveness of their information seeking and use.

THINK!

The PATHS team were faced with the problem of designing an interface which could adapt its approach to the very different needs of people with different cognitive styles as described above.

Can you think of features that the designers could build into the interface to achieve this? What would you do?

What the PATHS team did was as follows. They built into the PATHS system different modes of exploration to cater for these very different styles. Two key features of the global/analytic difference are catered for in the PATHS interface: broad exploratory versus narrow specific navigation, and dependent versus independent exploration. Broad exploratory and narrow, more specific, approaches to navigation are offered by the choice between keyword 'Search' and 'Explore' mode:

- **Search** allows users to search using standard keyword-based methods. They can *search* for individual items in the collection and/or for paths – collections of items put together via some theme by someone else and made available to others in the system.
- **Explore** provides two functions. The first offers the user a slideshow showing a random collection of content from the collection. The second

offers a tag-cloud providing a visual overview of the collection. Items in the tag cloud can be clicked to enable exploration.

Paths allow the user to either (a) choose to follow a navigation path through the collection already created by someone else, or (b) create their own path. Paths are sets of items in the collection that are arranged in a sequence that people can follow. A narrative and descriptions of the items can be added. These can be published so that others can follow them. They might be created, for example, by a teacher or art enthusiast, a museum curator – or indeed any other user. Users may modify existing pathways or create new ones from scratch. They can put together their own sequences of items, adding descriptions, comments and tags if they wish. People can search for already available paths using the Search facility described above. Users can leave and come back to pathways if they wish to follow up information about one or more of the items. The items are displayed in the same way that they would be if they were accessed by another route (e.g. through the search interface). A choice of guided discovery versus independent exploration is offered by the ability either freely to search and explore autonomously, or to choose to receive guidance by following a path.

In the first published user study of the PATHS system (Goodale, Clough, Fernando et al., 2014), a number of experiments and questionnaires were used to generate data on how people used and reacted to the PATHS system. This first published study investigated the effects of the wholist/analytic cognitive style. It is planned to investigate the guided/autonomous dimension of cognitive style in later research.

The cognitive style of each person participating in the research was measured using Riding's Cognitive Style Analysis instrument (Riding, 1991). As noted above, the research focused on the wholist/analytic style and, based on the review of cognitive style research literature, it was hypothesized that wholist users would, relative to their more analytic counterparts, engage in more broad-based exploratory navigation compared to narrower, more specific, search-based activity. They would be keen to obtain a broad overview before committing energy to more detailed analysis.

The *questionnaire survey* of users' reactions to using the PATHS system provided some statistically significant results. The sample size for the *experiments*, however, was too small to provide statistically significant results, but the direction of differences found in behaviour relating to cognitive styles was consistent with that suggested in the hypotheses. This was interpreted as being indicative of a trend worthy of further systematic investigation. To summarize the findings: it was hypothesized that wholists would be more likely than analytics to want to establish a clear overview of the topic they are exploring early on, before drilling down to detail. This was supported by the data relating to users' observed navigation behaviour. Relative to analytic users, wholists:

- made greater use of the tag cloud feature (which is good at giving a visual overview of the collection)
- made fewer specific searches
- made more general rather than specific queries
- made less use of the faceting function (which supports focusing narrowly on the collection rather than exploring it more generally)
- added items to their workspace without examining them in detail more than analytic users – wholists added them more directly from a path or from search results as opposed to analytic users, who tended more to view them prior to adding them to their workspace
- browsed through more pages before selecting items to add to the workspace (again, suggesting that they were trying to get an overview before committing to detailed examination).

Users were asked to rate PATHS in terms of how good it was at supporting a range of activities. Significant correlations were found between cognitive style and attitudes towards a number of PATHS features. Analytic users felt significantly more than did wholist users that:

- PATHS was good at supporting serendipity/discovery
- PATHS provided good support for inventiveness and the development of new ideas
- PATHS was good at supporting the finding of items related to a topic
- the PATHS Explore function was high in inventiveness, usefulness and ease of use.

However, wholists rated PATHS more highly than did analytics in relation to providing good support for communicating with other people.

The links between cognitive style and observed *behaviour* supported the researchers' hypotheses. Wholists made greater use of the PATHS facilities that supported broad exploratory navigation, serendipity and the generation of relationships and new ideas. However, with the exception of features supporting being socially communicative (a characteristic of the wholist rather than the analytic), the findings of the *attitudes* survey were the inverse of the hypothesized relationships, providing an interesting paradox. People rated PATHS better at supporting the activities in which they were expected to be weaker, namely: exploring, engaging in relatively divergent thinking in the form of being inventive, developing new ideas, discovering things, experiencing serendipity, and relating ideas (finding items related to topics). The researchers suggest a tentative explanation of this apparent paradox (which they represented in diagrammatic form shown in Figure 10.1):

> In those activities in which they are strongest, they may have less need for, and accord less value to, those features of the PATHS system that support them. Conversely, they need and value features that support them in relation to activities in which they are naturally weaker.
>
> Goodale et al., 2014, 990

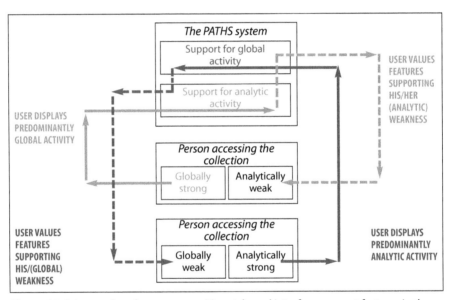

Figure 10.1 Interactions between cognitive style and interface support features in the PATHS system (Goodale et al., 2014)

This is a good example of how the testing of a model produces results which, whilst to an extent supporting the model, also reveal unanticipated findings that pose new questions and lead to a tentative refinement in the original model – the testing of which in turn becomes an agenda for further research.

The original theory proposed that users with a wholist cognitive style would navigate in a top-down way, first wanting to establish a good overview of what it is they are exploring before being concerned with finer detail. Analytic users would dive into detail much sooner. The findings do to an extent support this theory, but in relation to the observed *behaviour* of the people participating in the experiments. Results relating to the *attitudes* to the system, however, were the converse of what was expected. Trying to figure out the meaning of such apparently contradictory results led the researchers to propose a new refined version of the theory as shown in Figure 10.1 which differentiates between users' behaviour and their attitudes. Whilst they may behave in accordance with their cognitive style strengths, they seem to favour support in relation to their cognitive style weaknesses. With hindsight, this seems reasonable – but the proposition will require testing.

Supporting serendipitous knowledge discovery: the IF-SKD model

Workman et al. (2014) have developed the Interaction Flow in Serendipitous Knowledge Discovery (IF-SKD) model, based on knowledge of the nature of people's serendipitous information-discovery behaviour and incorporating details of requirements for a system to support such behaviour. Although it is theoretical at present, they also suggest a number of techniques and systems that could operationalize key system requirements. Based on a review of relevant research studies, the researchers identified the following key themes characterizing serendipitous information discovery:

- Serendipitous discovery is an iterative process.
- It often entails changing or clarifying one's initial information interests and integrating new topics. The researchers note a conceptual link with Bates' 'berrypicking' (see Chapter 4, section on information-seeking strategies) in which a person's perceived information need may change as new information is acquired.
- A person's existing knowledge is an important element in serendipitous discovery. Burkell, Quan-Haase and Rubin (2012), for example, identified having a prepared mind, and the act of noticing, as key components of serendipitous discovery within online environments, and noted that 'the meaning of serendipitously encountered information is expressed within its relationship with prior knowledge' (quoted in Workman et al., 2014, 504).
- Lessening the burden of the need for cognitively demanding information organization can facilitate serendipitous discovery (Leong et al., 2008).
- Visual cues can prompt serendipitous browsing in libraries (Spink, 2004).
- Short-term memory plays a crucial role. The researchers quote De Bruijn and Spence's (2008) work, which suggests that visual cues are interpreted and selected in less than a second either for discarding or retaining.

• The way information is organized and presented plays a key role.

Workman et al. here build on previous work relating to literature-based knowledge discovery. They also note that:

> Swanson (1986) was the first to demonstrate literature-based discovery through identifying fish oil's potential therapeutic role in Raynaud's syndrome. Swanson noted that, despite published research noting dietary fish oil's therapeutic effects on blood viscosity, platelet aggregability, and vascular reactivity, and observances of the negative involvement these issues have in Raynaud's syndrome, no one had publicly deduced that dietary fish oil may have therapeutic applications for Raynaud's syndrome.
>
> Workman et al., 2014, 501

Generalizing this work led to literature-based knowledge discovery strategies, including the following: find associations between topic A (in the above case, dietary fish oil) and another topic B (platelet aggregability, blood viscosity, and vascular reactivation), and between B and a further topic C (Raynaud's syndrome). In this case, the associations were that A reduces B, and that B consists of elements linked to C. Explore possible associations between A and C – in this case, that A may be useful in treating C.

This type of thinking has led to further literature-based discovery techniques. In 'open discovery', topics (B and C) linked to an initial topic (A) are discovered. In 'closed discovery', topics A and C have been identified as possibly having some link, and the task is to discover a topic B which illuminates this association.

However, Workman and colleagues intend their proposed system to go beyond such A-B-C open or closed strategies, and intend that their model may facilitate this. They consider 'information foraging' to be an appropriate procedural model to represent key aspects of how people go about information discovery. This is an information-seeking strategy in which a person progressively identifies and explores information 'patches' where the 'scent' of relevant information is strongest. As they have noted, Goodwin et al. (2012) proposed that this be used as a guiding principle in the development of literature-based discovery systems. Based on these various themes, they developed the Interaction Flow in Serendipitous Knowledge Discovery (IF-SKD) model, in which user interaction takes place with the system as follows.

• First, the user presents to the system an initial topic of interest. The envisaged system would provide support for the user in defining their initial topic by allowing them to engage in exploratory browsing of a range of general topics covered by the system, and/or using a search facility.

- The system would then present to the user a broad selection of topics that are either directly linked to, or have a looser association with, the initial topic. The presentation would be designed in such a way as to minimize the user's cognitive load, by using what the researchers term a 'conceptual short-term memory (CSTM)' display. This presents a semantic map showing concepts linked to the initial topic by arcs indicating relationships.
- The user can then if s/he wishes (i) clarify the topic (ii) integrate other topics to explore their inter-connections with the original topic or (iii) completely change the initial topic and input this afresh. Assuming (i) or (ii), the system would retrieve and present information associated with the clarified or augmented topic using the CTSM display. In order to minimize cognitive load it would aggregate duplicated information.
- The process would continue iteratively until the user decides to stop, at which point s/he can explore the information retrieved or save the output for later consideration – if desired, in the CSTM display format.

Clearly the extent to which such a system actually succeeds in facilitating serendipitous information discovery – as opposed to simply facilitating exploratory browsing and search facilities – depends on the appropriateness (for such discovery) of what is presented to the user in response to his or her initial and subsequently modified topics. This depends in turn on the quality of the algorithms that drive the identification of associations between topics. The researchers note that this algorithm:

> . . . should include a function that assesses semantic similarity (e.g., hypernymic, synonymous, associative) and relational similarity (e.g., treats, causes) between concepts and organizes them based on these factors. A shuffle feature could also alleviate the user's cognitive load. The data elements presented to the user could be randomized by the algorithm, according to user-preferred weights, such as semantic similarity, relational similarity, or general concept class (e.g., diseases, genomics).
>
> Workman et al., 2014, 509

They consider a range of systems and techniques that could be useful within their broader model to operationalize key requirements, including the identification and presentation of topics associated with the user's initial topic of interest. SemRep (Rindflesch and Fiszman, 2003) uses natural language processing techniques to analyse and represent text as succinct subject-predicate-object statements. Semantic MEDLINE (Rindflesch, Kilicoglu, Fiszman, and Rosemblat, 2011) is able to take such statements and summarize them visually in an interactive graph (Kilicoglu et al., 2008). The authors note that the IF-SKD model could be integrated into the Semantic MEDLINE system.

The model is at this stage purely theoretical, in that it is a design based on a review of research into serendipitous information discovery. However, whilst it incorporates elements found to be present in, and to characterize, serendipitous information encounters, these elements may be necessary but not sufficient for serendipity to occur. However, the authors do attempt to demonstrate the potential usefulness of the IF-SKD model by replicating a historical case of literature-based discovery. They based the demonstration on a particular study that discovered the mechanism that explained the link between testosterone and diminished sleep quality. A key factor in the original researchers' discovery was finding two key seminal papers by other researchers which led to the new knowledge. They replicated the literature search strategy of the original researchers – but within the IF-SKD model, to see what would have been different. They implemented this IF-SKD demonstration utilizing SemRep and dynamic summarization as used in Semantic MEDLINE. They concluded that:

> An application that implemented the model (with SemRep and Dynamic summarization providing data computation) would have retrieved the seminal papers . . . amid 30% less data.
>
> Workman et al., 2014, 507

Summary

Knowledge of human information behaviour can help us help people to become smarter – to be able better to know the true nature of their information needs; to become familiar with the best tools and techniques they can use to satisfy them; to be aware of their own limitations and those of the information systems they use; and to learn ways in which they can minimize the effects of these weaknesses and exploit these strengths.

It can also usefully inform the design of information systems better to support information seeking in other than direct search of the type supported in current search engines. A number of experimental systems have been developed which attempt to exploit knowledge of information behaviour in order to enhance the capabilities of information search and discovery tools better to enable people to satisfy their information-related needs. Many of these are at the research stage, since much of our knowledge of people's information behaviour is still tentative. We still lack robust, empirically supported, models and theories of information behaviour which can be applied directly to the design of information systems.

The results of the PATHS project are a good example. The PATHS discovery system was designed on the basis of many years' research into cognitive style theory. If this theory were 'true' then the results from experiments with users would conform perfectly with predictions based on theory. In reality, and for reasons outlined in the 'Research and practice' section of Chapter 8 (page 186), the findings were to an extent confirmatory, but to another extent surprising and unexpected, leading to further questions. So rather than mandating the immediate full development and deployment of the PATHS search and explore interface, as in most cases of information behaviour research the findings mandate further research in order to refine and modify where necessary the underlying theory on which the experiments were based.

The development of the IF-SKD serendipitous knowledge discovery model is also a good example of attempts to lay the groundwork for the development of future systems that may be able to support not only the more familiar tasks supported by current mainstream information systems, but tasks that are much less susceptible to control and empirical study, such as serendipity and knowledge discovery.

Much research is ongoing in universities. However, the scale and costs of experimental work that can be supported within the academic community is small compared to the resources that a company like Google can bring to bear. Indeed, the major search engine companies are active in research designed to improve their products – and a central component of such research relates to information behaviour. There is a good overview of the various types of academic research supported by Google at http://research.google.com/university. Search engine providers also can and do run frequent live experiments in which the effects on users' information behaviour of small changes and tweaks in their system can be viewed as the system is used by vast numbers of people. To read more about research into information retrieval systems in relation to information-seeking research, the reader is referred to Ingwersen and Järvelin (2005).

References

Belkin, N. J., Cool, C., Jeng, J., Keller, A., Kelly, D., Kim, J., Lee, H.-J., Tang, M.-C. and Yuan, X.-J. (2002) Rutgers' TREC 2001 Interactive Track Experience. In Voorhees,

E. M. and Harman, D. M. (eds), *The Tenth Text Retrieval Conference, TREC 2001*, Washington, DC, GPO, 465–72.

Belkin, N. J., Cool, C., Kelly, D., Kim, G., Kim, J-Y., Lee, H-J., Muresan, G., Tang, M-C. and Yuan, X-J. (2003) Query Length in Interactive Information Retrieval. In *SIGIR 2003: Proceedings of the 26th Annual International ACM SIGIR Conference on Research and Development in Information Retrieval, July 28 – August 1, 2003, Toronto, Canada*, ACM, 205–12.

Belkin, N. J., Oddy, R. N. and Brooks, H. M. (1982a) ASK for Information Retrieval: part I, background and theory, *Journal of Documentation*, **38** (2), 61–71.

Belkin, N. J., Oddy, R. N. and Brooks, H. M. (1982b) ASK for Information Retrieval: part II, results of a design study, *Journal of Documentation*, **38** (3), 145–64.

Burkell, J., Quan-Haase, A. and Rubin, V. L. (2012) Promoting Serendipity Online: recommendations for tool design, paper presented at the 2012 iConference: Culture, Design, Society, iConference 2012, 7–10 February, Toronto.

Cole, C. (2001) Intelligent Information Retrieval: Part IV: testing the timing of two information retrieval devices in a naturalistic setting, *Information Processing & Management*, **37** (1), 163–82.

Cole, C. (2014) Google, Tear Down this Wall to Exploratory Search!, *Bulletin of the Association for Information Science and Technology*, **40** (5), 50–4.

Cole, C., Cantero, P. and Ungar, A. (2000) The Development of a Diagnostic-prescriptive Tool for Undergraduates Seeking Information for a Social Science/Humanities Assignment: Part III: enabling devices, *Information Processing & Management*, **36** (3), 481–500.

De Bruijn, O. and Spence, R. (2008) A New Framework for Theory-based Interaction Design Applied to Serendipitous Information Retrieval, *ACM Transactions on Computer–Human Interaction (TOCHI)*, **15** (1), 5.

Fisher, R. (1998) Thinking about Thinking: developing metacognition in children, *Early Child Development and Care*, **141**, 1–13.

Franzén, K. and Karlgren, J. (2000) *Verbosity and Interface Design*, SICS Technical Report TR00-02, Stockholm, Swedish Institute of Computer Science (SICS).

Goodale, P., Clough, P. D., Fernando, S., Ford, N. and Stevenson, S. (2014) Cognitive Styles Within an Exploratory Search System for Digital Libraries, *Journal of Documentation*, **70** (6), 970–96.

Goodwin, J. C., Cohen, T. and Rindflesch, T. C. (2012) Discovery by Scent: discovery browsing system based on the Information Foraging Theory, paper presented at the IEEE International Conference on Bioinformatics and Biomedicine Workshops (BIBMW).

Hill, J. (1995) *Cognitive Strategies and the Use of a Hypermedia Information System: an exploratory study, unpublished dissertation*, Florida State University, Tallahasee, FL.

Ingwersen, P. and Järvelin, K. (2005) *The Turn: integration of information seeking and retrieval in context,* Dordrecht, Springer.

Kilicoglu, H., Fiszman, M., Rodriguez, A., Shin, D., Ripple, A. and Rindflesch, T. C. (2008) Semantic MEDLINE: a web application to manage the results of PubMed searches, paper presented at the Third International Symposium on Semantic Mining in Biomedicine.

Land, S. M. and Hannafin, M. J. (1996) A Conceptual Framework for the Development of Theories-in-Action with Open-Ended Learning Environments, *Educational Technology Research and Development,* **44** (3), 37–53.

Leong, T., Vetere, F. and Howard, S. (2008) Abdicating Choice: the rewards of letting go, *Digital Creativity,* **19** (4), 233–43.

Quintana, C., Zhang, M. and Krajcik, J. (2005) A Framework for Supporting Metacognitive Aspects of Online Inquiry Through Software-based Scaffolding, *Educational Psychologist,* **40** (4), 235–44.

Riding, R. (1991) *Cognitive Style Analysis,* Birmingham, Learning and Training Technology.

Rindflesch, T. C. and Fiszman, M. (2003) The Interaction of Domain Knowledge and Linguistic Structure in Natural Language Processing: interpreting hypernymic propositions in biomedical text, *Journal of Biomedical Informatics,* **36** (6), 462–77.

Rindflesch, T. C., Kilicoglu, H., Fiszman, M. and Rosemblat, G. (2011) Semantic MEDLINE: an advanced information management application for biomedicine, *Information Systems and Use,* **31** (1/2), 15–21.

Silvén, M. (1992) The Role of Meta-cognition in Reading Instruction, *Scandinavian Journal of Educational Research,* **36** (3), 211–21.

Spink, A. (2004) Multitasking Information Behavior and Information Task Switching: an exploratory study, *Journal of Documentation,* **60** (4), 336–51.

Stadtler, M. and Bromme, R. (2007) Dealing with Multiple Documents on the WWW: the role of meta-cognition in the formation of documents models, *International Journal of Computer-Supported Collaborative Learning,* **2**, 191–210.

Swanson, D. R. (1986) Fish Oil, Raynaud's Syndrome, and Undiscovered Public Knowledge, *Perspectives in Biology and Medicine,* **30** (1), 7–18.

Taylor, R. S. (1968) Question-negotiation and Information Seeking in Libraries, *College and Research Libraries,* **29** (3), 178–94.

Wiley, J., Goldman, S. R., Graesser, A. C., Sanchez, C. A., Ash, I. K. and Hemmerich, J. A. (2009) Source Evaluation, Comprehension, and Learning in Internet Science Inquiry Tasks, *American Educational Research Journal,* **46** (4), 1060–1106.

Workman, T. E., Fiszman, M., Rindflesch, T. C. and Nahl, D. (2014) Framing Serendipitous Information-seeking Behavior for Facilitating Literature-based Discovery: a proposed mode, *Journal of the Association for Information Science and Technology,* **65** (3), 501–12.

11
Conclusion

We are increasingly awash with information. Access to vast quantities is easier than ever, especially via the web, as is the ability of anyone and everyone to publish information to large audiences on social media. The information readily and instantly available to us is representative of a myriad of different views and perspectives and displays hugely varying levels of quality. Citizen journalism, for example, offers immediacy of access to news of events which is made available with unfettered scope in terms of the angles, interpretations or spin put on it by its authors. Social media continuously spouts forth well considered critical and creative thoughts alongside inconsequential chitchat.

However, there is a great difference between living in an *information*-rich world and a *knowledge*-rich world. We acquire knowledge by selecting and processing information. But a greater volume of information does not necessarily translate into a greater volume or depth of useful knowledge. Knowledge generated from poor-quality information is in most cases less valuable and effective than knowledge generated from high-quality information, the finding and effective processing of which is a central component of information behaviour. Just as the uncritical consumption of high volumes of junk food can lead to physical illness, so the uncritical consumption of high volumes of low-quality information can result in intellectual ill health. By intellectual ill health I mean an inability to function in an effective evidence-based way in making important decisions and solving problems in our lives. By low-quality information I mean information that is inaccurate, unreliable, biased or not relevant to the purpose for which it is being sought and used.

In relation to all aspects of our life, the ability to know what is needed, to find potentially relevant information, and to evaluate, select and use it is important. Information literacy – the ability to adopt appropriate and effective information behaviour – is crucial if information is to be critically evaluated and integrated (or chosen not to be) as useful knowledge. The need critically to evaluate information has always been present in relation to more traditional published sources from reputable and well established publishing sources. But our current access to such a volume and range of sources, displaying such variety and variability in quality and credibility, brings with it the constant possibility of our finding or encountering seriously inaccurate and biased information. This potential problem is likely only to increase.

We all need skills in mining high-quality information – 'panning for gold' as Edwards (2006) put it – to turn into valuable knowledge. We need to know what knowledge is needed at particular points in time and in different circumstances for effective decision making and problem solving, and what information is required to generate it. We need to know how to find the best-quality information for the task in hand, to critically evaluate it for quality and relevance, and effectively process and use it. We also need to know how to protect ourselves from (to know to ignore, avoid or reject) information that is, for example, biased, incorrect or hateful. We also need to understand, and help people counter, inappropriate and ineffective information behaviour.

There are tools, people, systems and organizations whose role it is to help us in doing this – in finding, accessing and critically processing information, and developing our skills in so doing. Well developed evidence-based understanding of people's information behaviour, both actual and potential, effective and ineffective, is vital if we are to improve the effectiveness of these agents, and insofar as our understanding is incomplete, we need to engage in research.

However, despite an increasing volume of information behaviour-related research, we still arguably lack robust applicable models and theories. Relevant to this issue is a criticism that has for some time been levelled at research into human aspects of information science, that much of it has been small-scale and fragmented, providing a snapshot view of phenomena – as opposed to more integrated findings that can be directly compared and contrasted in order to generate cumulative integrated understanding.

There is arguably a need for more co-ordinated, long-term, large-scale research programmes which focus on information behaviour with both breadth and depth. At present, there is little attempt to replicate results, and often ostensibly similar studies seem to result in conflicting findings, suggesting the existence of confounding variables that have not been taken into account. If more integration and collaboration between multiple researchers could be achieved, we may be able to focus on agreed priority areas and generate triangulated evidence that begins to paint a coherent picture. Having said this, smaller-scale efforts by motivated individuals with creative ideas must not be squeezed out in favour of the large-scale, co-ordinated project. This may be where interesting and productive new ideas emerge. We need both types of effort.

Another related criticism is that research in relation to information behaviour has not generated knowledge capable of being applied with confidence in specific practical instances – whether by librarians or by system developers. For this reason amongst others, there is still a considerable disconnect between much published research and the needs of practice. We arguably need to develop a much better knowledge base to support not only the development of theory but also the needs of evidence-based practice. Indeed, Case asks:

> And what of the *utility* of information behavior studies? The origins of today's investigations lie in earlier 'information needs and uses' research aimed at improving the performance of an institution's operations. . . . Yet to read some of today's information-seeking research it would seem that we have now reached the point where the scholarliness of the studies correlates with their degree of *uselessness* for institutional purposes.
>
> Case, 2012, 370–1

However, any science involving the cognitive, affective and social aspects of humans is limited in its scope to produce incontrovertible and predictive models and theories, due to the complexity of people and the contexts in which they operate. Thus, specific studies, and specific models and theories, rather than providing prescriptions to practitioners for actions – and accurately predicting the outcomes of those actions – are more likely to be useful in a rather more diffuse way. By this I mean sensitizing us to complexities and *possible* explanatory mechanisms underlying information behaviour, and suggesting what might be potentially useful actions in given circumstances. But such suggestions will remain tentative best guesses, and what happens in practice can be observed and used to refine and modify understanding of the limitations and value of a model or theory to inform its future use.

Students of librarianship and information management – whether taking an initial university course to prepare themselves for entry into the professions, or engaging in formal in-service education as existing professionals – are working in a research-informed environment. In relation to information behaviour, what they are likely to gain is arguably less specific knowledge to be directly applied in their work, but rather a more generalized appreciation of tendencies and complexities associated with human behaviour that may inform their practice, as well as knowledge of the potential and limitations of systematic research and how to go about engaging in evidence-based practice. They will be informed of models and theories that are suggestive of what factors and possible mechanisms might usefully be taken into account when making professional decisions and taking work-based actions. At best, these will be tentative hypothesized suggestions – subject always to testing and feedback based on experiencing the effects of any decisions or actions.

Nevertheless, there is surely scope for the generation of more directly applicable, practically useful research. One way of improving the situation will be by greater collaboration between practitioners and researchers – for information professionals to engage in their own work-based research as well as working with academics, and for academic researchers to work more closely with practitioners in terms of setting meaningful foci for their work, and where possible real-world contexts in which to conduct it. Research could also often be better communicated. There is scope for more journals explicitly to target practitioners, with instructions to authors to communicate clearly the findings of their research to practitioner members of their audience. Dedicated research-based professional journals such as the peer-reviewed open-access *Evidence Based Library and Information Practice* represent an encouraging trend in the effective communication of potentially useful research.

As noted by Koufogiannakis (2013), there is a need for greater levels of collaboration between academic and professional worlds in terms of:

- joint contributions to and attendance at the same conferences
- the communication to researchers of what are pressing evidential needs of information professionals
- engagement by practitioners in their own work-based research as well as research collaborations between practitioners and both academic researchers and system developers.

One way in which information behaviour research could potentially produce findings of greater relevance to practice is in focusing on information outcomes – defined here as whether and how information is used, and what impact it has on the user and others. These are central concerns of professional information practice. Such practice is geared to helping people and organizations achieve desirable effects and outcomes, and knowledge of the nature of effects of information, and the extent to which desired outcomes are achieved by acquiring and processing it, is essential for the evaluation and improvement of services.

Yet not many information-behaviour studies have focused on outcomes, as noted by Case and O'Connor (2015). From a survey of papers published in four key information science journals between 1950 and 2012 they found that outcome studies rose from none from the 1950s to 1981 to approximately 27% of information-behaviour studies in more recent years to 2012. Only some 8% of these were empirical studies. However, although the number of studies reviewed was considerable (1391), only four key information science journals were selected. It is possible that, particularly in more recent years, with the expansion in the number of journals providing potential publication outlets for researchers interested in information science and information behaviour, that this is a conservative estimate.

Nevertheless, information outcome studies would seem to be relatively rare compared to those in the areas of information needs and information seeking. The authors went on to outline a number of difficulties and complexities associated with attempting to investigate information outcomes:

> Dunn (1983) and Rich (1997) explain the many ways in which information use might be defined and why it is often difficult to measure. Rich (1997, pp. 15–16) notes that we may have initial difficulties in determining exactly what qualifies as 'information'; beyond that, there are a series of relevant stages: acquiring or receipt, which does not imply reading; reading, which does not guarantee understanding; understanding, which does not imply further action on that basis; and, finally, an influence, action, or other impact. Even in this final stage, the notion of 'influence' (meaning 'contributed to a decision, an action, or to a way of thinking about a problem') suggests delays in effects that may render the connection between receipt and effect unobservable.
>
> Case and O'Connor, 2015, 8

Case and O'Connor also note that there is a lack of reliable and ethical methods for observing and recording the way information is used, concluding that 'Clearly, measuring the outcomes of information is challenging, and that may be why many researchers have not attempted to do so.' (Case and O'Connor, 2015, 8).

However, as the use of digital media becomes increasingly pervasive in our information behaviour, records of our use – as well as our seeking – of information will become more extensive. Such records will provide an increasing volume and range of raw material for researchers wishing to include information use and outcomes in their studies. The types of information use and outcomes digitally recorded and (with the important caveat that legal and ethical issues surround the accessing of databases of electronic activity) available for analysis is rapidly increasing. Data relating to use and outcomes may result, for example, from people commenting on and sharing information on social media, through e-mail communications and text messaging. Commentary on papers appearing in electronic journals which encourage online comments and discussion is available digitally, as are details of the tracking of the way information from one information source becomes incorporated into new ones.

In the future an increasing volume and range of relatively new forms of data and information will be available for analysis, including so-called 'big data' and records of social media interactions. Such data will increasingly include records of how data and information is used. New forms of information behaviour are likely to become the focus of research which relate to ways in which people cope with, and fail to cope with, the torrent of data and information which can so easily engulf them.

Information behaviour is central to all aspects of our lives – intellectual, emotional and social. It is therefore unsurprising that a wide range of disciplines have developed an interest in it. This trend is likely to continue, offering the prospect of our developing a multifaceted understanding of the ways in which we go about acquiring information and transforming it into knowledge, the contexts in which we do this, the effects of a range of factors influencing this behaviour, and how we might be able to develop improved skills and systems to enhance the effectiveness with which we go about learning, decision making and problem solving.

With greater interest being paid to information behaviour by researchers across a range of disciplines we can expect new research questions to emerge, along with new research foci, methods and lenses. The future is also likely to throw up new research questions, as more and more information becomes readily available at any time and in any location; with the ubiquitous presence of mobile devices capable of accessing an increasing range of information systems, arguably previously discrete information accessing and processing contexts become blurred (Burnett and Erdelez, 2010).

Looking to the longer-term future, it may be possible to develop an appropriate common vocabulary and knowledge-representation scheme enabling the findings of each new study to be mapped onto a large-scale, dynamic and cumulating knowledge map. Such a virtual device might enable the mapping of concepts and relationships – relating to findings, perspectives and research methods – onto a common language and ontology. The contexts of each piece of research would be richly described, so that findings from different studies could be compared, contrasted and, to an extent, cumulated. In this way our current state of knowledge relating to different aspects of information behaviour could be interrogated from different perspectives by practitioners as well as researchers.

The armoury of intellectual tools with which we approach evidence-based practice is increasingly likely to embrace different conceptions of what constitutes 'good enough' evidence. Koufogiannakis (2013) notes that effective evidence-based practice relies on a range of evidence of which academic research is but one strand. It also relies on the blending of knowledge based on professional experience and intuition and knowledge derived from formal systematic study. Each must respect the value of the other. We will need increasingly to be able to harness the opposing forces of diversity (entailing a wide range of foci, lenses and methodologies) and integration (entailing the avoidance of fragmentation) if we are to develop wide-ranging yet deep understanding of information behaviour. Whilst continuing to develop theory, we also need to infuse both practice with research and research with practice. We need to harness the complementary strengths – and minimize the limitations – of professional expertise and formal research.

References

Burnett, G. and Erdelez, S. (2010) Forecasting the Next 10 Years in Information Behavior Research: a fish bowl dialogue, *Bulletin of the American Society for Information Science and Technology*, **36** (3), 44–8, www.asis.org/Bulletin/Feb-10/Bulletin_FebMar10_Final.pdf.

Case, D. (2012) *Looking for Information: a survey of research on information seeking, needs and behaviour*, 3rd edn, Bingley, Emerald.

Case, D. O. and O'Connor, L. G. (2015) What's the Use?: measuring the frequency of studies of information outcomes, *Journal of the Association for Information Science and Technology*, doi: 10.1002/asi.23411.

Dunn, W. (1983) Measuring Knowledge Use, *Knowledge: creation, diffusion, utilization*, **15** (1), 120–33.

Edwards, S. L. (2006) *Panning for Gold: information literacy and the net lenses model*, Adelaide, Auslib Press.

Koufogiannakis, D. (2013) EBLIP7 Keynote: What We Talk About When We Talk About Evidence, *Evidence Based Library And Information Practice*, **8**(4), 6-17, http://ejournals.library.ualberta.ca/index.php/EBLIP/article/view/20486/15965.

Rich, R. F. (1997) Measuring Knowledge Utilization: processes and outcomes, *Knowledge and Policy*, **10** (3), 11–24.

APPENDIX
Defining 'information' and 'information behaviour'

It was noted in Chapter 2 that many existing definitions in the literature of the key terms 'data', 'information', 'knowledge', 'behaviour' and 'information behaviour' leave room for uncertainty, in that there is sometimes variation between them, and often they do not provide sufficient elaboration to enable the reader to answer the sort of more probing questions necessary for a robust understanding of the precise extent and limits of each. Such questions include the following:

- Many definitions specify that 'information' is data that is structured and interpreted to render it meaningful. But when we gather and analyse 'interview data' this is surely not devoid of structure and meaning, so why do we not speak of 'interview *information*'? Why does what is a widely accepted definition of 'data' and 'information' seem to break down here?
- Cloud patterns and the sound of rain are data capable of being meaningfully interpreted – for example, to indicate current and future weather. As such they constitute *potential* information. But does 'information behaviour' include behaviour relating to *potential* information (i.e. data with *potential* to be meaningfully interpreted) as well as *actual* information (data that *has been* meaningfully interpreted)? If so, does this mean that information behaviour is concerned with processing all items of data that are potentially capable of being meaningfully interpreted which reach our senses? This would imply that information behaviour includes mental processes including seeing, hearing, touching, feeling, perceiving and thinking. How then does it differ from basic psychology?

- Many definitions contrast 'information' and 'knowledge', information being external to a person (often existing in recorded form such as text or pictures), which the person processes and internalizes as knowledge (i.e. integrates within their own knowledge structure). Yet many definitions include 'information use' as a component of information behaviour. To the extent that a person has to *understand* information (internalize it) before being able meaningfully to *use* it (as opposed simply to repeating it without understanding) it is surely knowledge rather than information. So does 'using information' imply only unthinking verbatim use? Surely we should rather talk of 'using *knowledge*'? But if we do, this can include almost any aspect of our thinking and acting, since anything we think entails using our knowledge. Should information behaviour thus embrace *any* field of intellectual activity? How is it different from, say, politics, history, psychology or engineering?
- If knowledge is defined as essentially residing in a person's brain (as opposed to information, which is relatively external to the individual), how does this square with the notion of distributed or collective knowledge – knowledge which is more than the sum of each individual person's knowledge? Collective *information* can be located, for example, in libraries. But where precisely could collective *knowledge* be stored?
- What precisely is 'behaviour'? Does it include *perception* and *thought* as well as action? For example, is 'having a need' *behaviour*? If not, then how does a study of information needs constitute an information behaviour study?
- Wilson defines information behaviour as:

> . . . the totality of human behavior in relation to sources and channels of information, including both active and passive information seeking, and information use. Thus, it includes face-to-face communication with others, as well as the passive reception of information as in, for example, watching TV advertisements, without any intention to act on the information given.
>
> Wilson, 2000, 49

whilst Ingwersen and Järvelin include the generation and management of information in their definition as the

> . . . generation, acquisition, management, use and communication of information, and information seeking'.
>
> Ingwersen and Järvelin, 2005, 259

- If passively receiving information (e.g. whilst watching television) with no intention to act on anything seen constitutes information behaviour, as Wilson argues, what does *not* constitute information behaviour, since we are constantly bombarded by information (potential and actual) in all aspects of our lives. Surely there must be some differentiation between simply existing in a torrent of informational stimuli (TV news, environmental noise, other people's conversations, etc.) and information behaviour?
- Does information behaviour include *organizing* or *managing* information? These would seem to fit within 'the totality of human behaviour relating to sources and channels of information' included in Wilson's definition. Also, *management* is directly referred to in Ingwersen and Järvelin's definition. But if so, how does information behaviour differ from cataloguing and indexing – and from librarianship and information management more generally? Are these or are they not examples of information behaviour?
- Do the definitions of the components of information behaviour include their negatives? For example is *not* having an information need, and *not* seeking information, information behaviour? Does *not noticing information* constitute information behaviour?

These are just some of the legitimate questions that need answers if we are to develop a robust understanding of what exactly should and should not be considered information behaviour. We need to be sure what it is, and is not, if we are to avoid (a) making over-extensive claims that our field encompasses other well established fields of study and practice (such as psychology, education and communication), or (b) restricting our field to its limited historical roots thus arguably excessively limiting its actual and potential importance.

References

Ingwersen, P. and Järvelin, K. (2005) *The Turn: integration of information seeking and retrieval in context*, Dordrecht, Springer.

Wilson, T. D. (2000) Human Information Behavior, *Informing Science*, **3** (2), 49–55.

Index

Activity Theory   82–4, 151–6
affective aspects   7–8 , 42–4, 50, 52,
      73, 84–5, 100, 103, 108–10, 111–
      19, 128–30, 143, 160, 162, 165,
      204
age   103–5
Agosto   102, 125–7
AIMTech Research Group   152–4
Anand and Gomez-Mejia   195–8
Anomalous State of Knowledge
      (ASK)   31
applying information *see* using
      (including applying)
      information
ASK *see* Anomalous State of
      Knowledge
attribution   105–6
avoiding information   1, 7, 14–18,
      22, 29, 41–4, 49, 81, 105, 113,
      115–19, 144–5, 238

Bates   33, 54–5, 62, 151, 229
Bawden and Robinson   78, 132
behaviour (definition of)   10–13
Belkin   31–3, 36, 218–20
berrypicking   33, 62–3, 229
bounded rationality   125–7
bright zone   145–6
broad scanners   58

browsing   14, 18–19, 51, 53–6, 60, 65,
      68–70, 92, 101, 206–7, 218, 227,
      229, 231

Chatman   124, 131
Choo, Detler and Turnbull   55–6, 71,
      91
CIBER Research Group   60–1, 64
Clarke   199, 201
Clough   224, 226
cognitive   29, 35, 41–3, 50, 52, 63, 73,
      82, 84–5, 100, 102, 104, 112–19,
      126, 128, 143, 147, 150, 161–2,
      164, 205–6, 221, 229, 231, 239
      (*see also* cognitive dissonance;
      cognitive invisibility; cognitive
      styles; metacognition)
cognitive dissonance   128
cognitive invisibility   145–6
cognitive styles   100–1, 106–9, 224–9,
      233
Cole   30–1, 33–4, 36, 63, 131, 220–3
collaborative information behaviour
      77–95, 102, 154–6
communication models   146–7
consistency *see* reliability
      (consistency) in research
consolidators   58

context   15, 42, 62–3, 78, 85, 100–1,
111, 113, 115, 119–30, 143–5,
147–9, 151–6, 158–61, 177, 190

dark zone   145–6
darkness to light ratio   184–6
data (definitions)   10–13
deductive research   174–6, 195–8,
208–14
deep divers   58
deependers   58
Dervin   36–7, 113, 150, 156–64, 187
destroying information   7, 14, 17, 22,
44, 115, 144–5
Detler *see* Choo, Detler and Turnbull
distributed information behaviour
9, 11–12, 90–4, 154–6, 164, 246
Distributed Information Behaviour
System model   91–4

easy win strategies *see* least effort
Ellis   50–3, 56, 71, 91, 108, 127–8,
142–6
emotions *see* affective aspects
encountering information *see*
information encountering
epistemology   150, 176, 178, 180,
200, 213, 215
Erdelez   65–6, 142–5
extensive searching   61
external and internal factors
(relationship between)   125–32
external validity   183

factors influencing information
behaviour   99, 132
fast surfers   58
Fisher (née Pettigrew)   13, 15, 120,
123–4
flight decks   15, 90–4, 154–6
Foster   62–3, 66–70

gender   100–3
generalizability   88, 123, 132, 175,
181, 183, 185–6, 212–13, 230 (*see*
also transferability)
Glaser   200–1

Godbold   144–6
Gomez-Mejia *see* Anand and Gomez-
Mejia
Google generation   60–1, 64
Grounded Theory   199–201

Heinström   58, 108–12
hiding information   7, 22, 43–4
HIV/AIDS   7–8, 14, 43–5, 115–16,
165
Hyldegård   84–5, 88

IF-SKD model *see* Interaction Flow in
Serendipitous Knowledge
Discovery model
ignoring information   7–8, 14–15,
17–18, 22, 43–4, 149, 238
inductive research   174–6, 198–204,
208–14
information (definitions)   10
information behaviour (definitions)
9–28
information encountering   14, 16–
19, 23, 43, 58, 64–70, 91–2, 99,
144, 229, 232, 238 (*see also*
serendipity)
information grounds   123–4
information horizons   95, 124–5, 132
information landscapes   34–5
information literacy   25–6, 34, 73,
94–5, 102, 217, 238
information management   22, 25, 94,
239, 247
information needs   8–9, 15–18, 20,
25, 29–45
information practice   35–6, 120
information retrieval   25–8, 31–2, 73,
79–81, 85, 122, 155, 218–23, 233
information seeking   1, 8–9, 11, 13–
18, 26, 29, 31, 33, 37, 39, 41,
42–4, 49–73, 77–81, 87, 89–92,
99, 101–3, 105–18, 120, 124–31,
143–51, 153–4, 157–8, 182, 191,
195–8, 204–7, 209, 214, 219–23,
225, 229–30, 232–3, 239, 241,
246–7

information use *see* using (including applying) information
Ingwersen and Järvelin 13, 147, 246–7
insiders 124
Interaction Flow in Serendipitous Knowledge Discovery (IF-SKD) model 229–32
internal and external factors (relationship between) 125–32
internal validity (truth value) 181–2
interpretivism 161, 177–9, 181, 184, 211–13
invisibility (cognitive) *see* cognitive invisibility

Jansen *see* Reddy and Jansen
Järvelin *see* Ingwersen and Järvelin
Johari Window 38
Johnston and Webber 25–6

Karunakaran, Reddy and Spence 77–9, 87–9
knowledge management 25–6, 28
Koufogiannakis 188–90, 240–1, 243
Kuhlthau 52–3, 56, 71, 84–5, 114, 121, 220–1

least effort principle 58, 61, 63–4, 125–7
life in the round theory 124
literacy 25–6
Lloyd 34–6

Mansourian 61, 105–6, 111, 125–7, 145–6
Marchionini 50, 54–5
metacognition 117, 219–20
metatheory 150, 157, 162–3
methodology *see* research approaches
midpoolers 58
minimalist searching 61
mixed methods research 178–80, 204–7, 213–15

models 2–3, 8–9, 14, 31, 33, 37–8, 49–55, 62–3, 67, 77, 84–8, 90–2, 101–2, 114, 125–32, 141–65, 174, 178, 184, 206–7, 214, 223, 228–33, 238–40
monitoring 14, 17–18, 51, 53–6, 65, 71, 91, 101, 128, 143, 219

Namuleme 43–5, 113–16
nervous searching 61
neutrality *see* objectivity (neutrality) in research
non-linear information seeking 62–3, 67, 108

objectivity (neutrality) in research 121–3, 174, 177, 179, 181, 183–5, 199–200, 211–14
ontology 150, 176–7, 180, 213, 215, 242
organizational factors and perspectives 9, 15, 26, 37, 55, 77, 87, 89, 94, 99, 115, 120–3, 147, 151, 153, 155, 160, 163
outsiders 124

Paisley 119–20
paradigms *see* research approaches
Pask 56–9
PATHS project 223–9
perfunctory searching 61
personality 101, 109–12, 131–2, 159
Pettigrew *see* Fisher (nee Pettigrew)
Pluye 204–7
positivism 158–60, 176–9, 181, 200, 213
post-modernism 200–1, 213
post-positivism 177–9, 181, 184, 199–201, 212–13
power browsing 60
practice and research *see* research and practice
practice–research divide *see* research and practice
pragmatism 179–80

qualitative research 176, 198–205, 208–14
quality in research 180–4
quantitative research 176, 195–8, 208–14

Reddy *see* Karunakaran, Reddy and Spence
Reddy and Jansen 85–6
refracted zone 145–6
reliability (consistency) in research 181–3, 186, 212
research and practice 2, 142, 164–5, 184, 186–92, 223, 239–43
research approaches 10, 159–63, 171–93, 195–215, 243
research methodologies *see* research approaches
research methods *see* research approaches
research paradigms *see* research approaches
research–practice divide *see* research and practice
Robinson *see* Bawden and Robinson
Robinson *see* Robson and Robinson
Robson and Robinson 147–9

safety critical information behaviour 90–4, 155–6
satisficing 125–6
Savolainen 35, 37–8, 112–13
scaffolding 219
self-efficacy 105–6
Sen and Spring 198–204
sense making 36–7, 156–63
serendipity 14, 16, 18, 55, 58, 64–70, 92, 99, 123, 145, 227–33 (*see also* information encountering)
Shah 82
shallowenders 58
Shenton 38–41
Situational Analysis 198–204
skimming 60, 71
small world theory 124, 131

social factors and perspectives 11, 16–17, 34–5, 38, 43, 62, 78, 83, 85, 88, 90, 100–2, 107, 113, 123–5, 128–302, 143–4, 147, 150, 152–3, 155–6, 165, 178–80, 188, 200–4, 213–14, 225, 227, 239, 242
Sonnenwald 124–5
Spence *see* Karunakaran, Reddy and Spence
Spring *see* Sen and Spring
Stevenson 224
stigma 7, 43, 45, 115, 129

task complexity 120–3
task difficulty 121–3
Taylor 30–1, 33, 39, 220
theory 2–3, 9, 13, 30, 33, 36–7, 56, 63, 102, 105, 124–5, 129–32, 141–65, 174, 178, 184, 186–7, 189
theory and practice *see* research and practice
transferability 88, 95, 175, 183, 212 (*see also* generalizability)
triggers 86–7
truth value *see* internal validity
Turnbull *see* Choo, Detler and Turnbull

using (including applying) information 16–17, 20–2, 81, 87, 239–43

validity 181–6, 188
validity (internal) *see* internal validity
veiled zone 145–6
von Thaden 90–4, 154–6

Webber *see* Johnston and Webber
Wilson 14–15, 41–2, 52–6, 71, 80, 86, 88, 101–2, 114–15, 123, 127–31, 141–6, 150–4, 214, 246–7
Workman 229–32